WRITING ACTIVITIES

For Every Month of the School Year

Ready-to-Use Writing Process
Activities for Grades 4-8

CAROL H. BEHRMAN

**THE CENTER FOR APPLIED
RESEARCH IN EDUCATION**
West Nyack, New York 10994

Library of Congress Cataloging-in-Publication Data

Behrman, Carol H.
    Writing activities for every month of the school year : ready-to
-use writing process activities for grades 4-8 / Carol H. Behrman.
        p. cm.
    ISBN 0-87628-974-X
    1. English language—Composition and exercises—Study and teaching
(Elementary)—United States. 2. Education, Elementary—Activity
programs—United States. 3. Interdisciplinary approach in
education—United States. I. Title.
    LB1576.B429 1997
    372.62'3'044—dc21   97-7551
                                                                CIP

10 9 8 7 6 5 4 3 2 1

ISBN 0-87628-974-X

ATTENTION: CORPORATIONS AND SCHOOLS

Prentice Hall books are available at quantity discounts with bulk purchase for educational, business, or sales promotional use. For information, please write to: Prentice Hall Career & Personal Development Special Sales, 240 Frisch Court, Paramus, New Jersey 07652. Please supply: title of book, ISBN number, quantity, how the book will be used, date needed.

**THE CENTER FOR APPLIED RESEARCH
IN EDUCATION**
West Nyack, NY 10994
A Simon & Schuster Company

On the World Wide Web at http://www.phdirect.com

Prentice Hall International (UK) Limited, *London*
Prentice Hall of Australia Pty. Limited, *Sydney*
Prentice Hall Canada, Inc., *Toronto*
Prentice Hall Hispanoamericana, S.A., *Mexico*
Prentice Hall of India Private Limited, *New Delhi*
Prentice Hall of Japan, Inc., *Tokyo*
Simon & Schuster Asia Pte. Ltd., *Singapore*
Editora Prentice Hall do Brasil, Ltda., *Rio de Janeiro*

Again for Edward, who makes it all possible

ACKNOWLEDGMENTS

To my husband, Edward, for his extraordinary
proofreading skills and everything else.
To my New Jersey writer's group for their love,
perceptiveness, and invaluable critiques.
To my editor, Connie Kallback, for her
encouragement, guidance, and unfailing upbeat attitude.

ABOUT THE AUTHOR

Carol H. Behrman was born in Brooklyn, New York, graduated from City College of New York, and attended Columbia University's Teachers' College, where she majored in education. She married Edward Behrman, an accountant, and moved to Fair Lawn, New Jersey, where they raised three children. They currently reside in Sarasota, Florida. For many years, Behrman taught grades five through eight at the Glen Ridge, New Jersey Middle School, where she created a program utilizing the writing process, that combined language arts with word-processing instruction. She has written nineteen books, fiction and nonfiction, for children and young adults, and has conducted numerous workshops on the writing process for students, teachers, and aspiring writers. She serves as writer-in-residence at Chautauqua Institution and has been an adjunct lecturer at Seton Hall and New York University's Writing Center.

Mrs. Behrman is also the author of *Write! Write! Write!* (The Center, 1995) and *Hooked on Writing!* (The Center, 1990).

ABOUT WRITING

- American students need more writing instruction.

- Writing assignments should be interesting and exciting for students rather than onerous and boring.

- Writing skills are acquired by guidance in correct writing techniques and by continuous writing experiences.

- The ability to write clearly and easily often leads to lucid and logical thinking.

Not many parents, teachers or educators at any level would disagree with these statements. Yet, although schools almost always offer multiple semesters of mathematics and reading where youngsters are constantly drilled in the skills necessary to acquire competence in these disciplines, it is rare to find courses in writing as part of the curricula at the K-12 level. Goals for writing competence are generally included as part of other courses, usually in the English department. Educators who are handed the responsibility of teaching writing must do so along with a variety of other subject matter they are obliged to stress. There is seldom enough time in the day or in the school year for even the most dedicated advocate of the importance of writing to include the amount of instruction that students need in order to become successful communicators.

Even widespread use of the writing process does not seem to have solved this problem. Most teachers who are involved with writing instruction are familiar with the writing process. It has been used extensively for quite a few years, and has proven to be an effective method of teaching writing skills. More and more schools throughout the country are incorporating it into their instruction. Yet, we still hear loud and regular complaints that the graduates of twelve years of elementary and secondary education cannot write.

Some of these complaints may be unjustified. Many young people *are* acquiring greater competency in writing. These successes are leading to greater expectations, and that is all to the good. But there is still much dissatisfaction, particularly in the academic and business communities. Seminars are sprouting around the country, held both within and outside of the workplace, that offer to transform the participants into effective written communicators. These workshops promise to impart the secrets of writing effectively and efficiently. Often, they even guarantee to **make writing fun!**

If seminars for adults can teach all these writing skills and make it fun, the question becomes, why hasn't this been done during the K–12 years?

The answer seems to be obvious. We have accomplished a lot, but much more still needs to be done.

Students need *more* writing experiences. Even classes where students have a good number of writing assignments may not be offering enough ongoing practice to those who need it the most.

Writing assignments must be *relevant* to the lives and interests of today's youngsters. There are many wonderful exercises available for the development of writing skills, but if these seem to the students like dull, "school-oriented" tasks, their interest and full participation will never be engaged and writing will continue to be an academic chore that has no meaning outside the classroom.

Writing should be *fun*. If both the approach of the teacher and the activity is one that stresses the pleasures of writing, students will come to look upon writing assignments as exciting challenges rather than dull tasks. Just look at the growing number of adults now pouring millions of words into computer communication programs such as the Internet. Many of these people who now cannot seem to find enough hours in the day for all the writing they want to do might well have been reluctant writers in school.

We want writing to be relevant, exciting, and fun, but those of us engaged in writing education must never forget that our ultimate aim is to transform our students into effective communicators. This means that sloppy, ungrammatical, disorganized material is never acceptable. Although it may sometimes seem as though combining fun with a literate product is like trying to perform a high-wire act, using the steps of the writing process can help both teacher and student to reach this goal.

This volume is offered as one tool in the ongoing attack on writing illiteracy. Although designed for the same grade levels (4–8) as the author's previous writing process activity books, *Hooked on Writing* and *Write! Write! Write!*, the format differs in several significant ways.

The previous resources were organized by skills. Each chapter consisted of a variety of activities designed to develop competence in a particular skill, such as paragraph writing, essay writing, letter writing, journalism, creative writing. The sections of this volume are arranged, like a calendar, according to month. Each month contains a variety of writing activities and skills linked to seasonal and monthly events. In any one month, you can find suggestions for essays, letters, creative writing, language development, etc.

Since these activities are based on calendar dates that celebrate social, historical, and cultural anniversaries and events, they lend themselves easily to interdisciplinary projects with other areas of the school curriculum. The table of contents for each chapter indicates where linkages can be made with Reading, Science, Social Studies, Art, Music, or Physical Education.

These carefully-planned, interesting activities can assist teachers and students:

1. by making writing relevant to what is going on in the students' lives and world at the time of the assignment by tying it into monthly and seasonal activities, holidays, and anniversaries.

2. by offering activities that are fun and challenging to students.

3. by incorporating in these activities strategies and goals for specific writing skills and techniques.

4. by using clear, easy-to-understand, student-friendly directions that make these activities useful for independent as well as teacher-directed lessons.

5. by suggesting activities that can be used for interdisciplinary purposes.

6. by using the steps of the writing process, wherever possible, to assist students to acquire more competent writing skills.

Carol H. Behrman

HOW TO USE THIS RESOURCE

The activities are arranged by month in accordance with the school year calendar, beginning with September and ending with June. There is a list of activities (the equivalent of a table of contents) at the beginning of each month's section, outlining the activities for that month.

Each month contains 12–14 activities. Each activity consists of one or more reproducible worksheets. Some of the simplest activities designed primarily to develop positive attitudes toward writing may use just one worksheet. Most of the activities will consist of two or three worksheets as required to guide the student through the steps of the writing process.

The directions on each worksheet are clear and easy-to-understand, designed for independent student use as well as teacher-directed class assignments.

Each activity is tied into that month of the year by season, holiday, anniversary, birthday, event, etc., many of which can also be used for interdisciplinary purposes with social studies, science, reading, art, music, physical education, etc. An interdisciplinary listing is included in each month's listing of activities.

Each activity stresses the development of one or more writing skills, i.e., sentence and paragraph construction, essay writing, letter writing, creative writing, poetry or journalism; and/or one or more elements of good writing, i.e., sentence construction, active verbs, vivid description, sensory language, similes and metaphors, plotting and characterization, etc. The skills for each activity are indicated in the activities listing for each month.

Most of these activities are designed to guide the student easily through the steps of the writing process. In their simplest form, these steps are:

1. **PREWRITING**—getting and organizing ideas and information.

2. **WRITING A FIRST DRAFT**—concentrating on getting one's thoughts down quickly without too much concern for spelling, grammar, etc.

3. **REVISING AND WRITING A FINAL COPY**—following specific suggestions designed to produce skills in revising.

These activities are designed for use in grades 4 through 8. Most of them can be adapted to each grade level, and you can easily determine which are best suited to the age, grade, skills level, and interest of any particular group of students.

CONTENTS

ACTIVITIES FOR OCTOBER

ACTIVITIES FOR NOVEMBER

ACTIVITIES FOR DECEMBER

ACTIVITIES FOR JANUARY

ACTIVITIES FOR FEBRUARY

ACTIVITIES FOR MARCH

ACTIVITIES FOR APRIL

ACTIVITIES FOR MAY

ACTIVITIES FOR JUNE

SEPTEMBER

SEPTEMBER

"Up from the meadows rich with corn, clear in the cool September morn."
—John Greenleaf Whittier

LABOR DAY—A METAPHOR FOR THE REALITIES OF JOB AND SCHOOL . . .
NEW BEGINNINGS . . . NEW SCHOOLS . . . NEW JOBS . . . NEW FRIENDS . . .
THE EXCITEMENT AND UNCERTAINTY OF CHANGE AND MOVEMENT . . .
COOLER WEATHER IN MANY AREAS . . . HINTING AT THE WINTER TO
COME

SEPTEMBER EVENTS

September 2, 1945: VJ Day—Allies and Japan signed World War II surrender agreement onboard battleship *Missouri* in Tokyo Bay

September 3, 1894: First Labor Day celebrated as legal holiday

September 4, 1609: Henry Hudson, British sea captain, discovered Manhattan Island

September 4, 1888: George Eastman patented the first hand-held roll-film camera which he called a Kodak

September 11, 1985: Pete Rose broke Ty Cobb's long-standing record as he made career base hit number 4,192

September 16, 1620: Pilgrims set sail from Plymouth, England in the *Mayflower* bound for the New World and religious freedom

September 19, 1928: Walt Disney's Mickey Mouse first appeared in the animated cartoon, *Steamboat Willie*

SEPTEMBER BIRTHDAYS

September 1, 1907: Walter Reuther, American labor leader, President of United Auto Workers

September 7, 1860: Grandma Moses, American primitive painter; Anna Mary Robertson Moses started painting at age 76, painted 25 pictures after her 100th birthday

September 7, 1908: Michael Ellis DeBakey, American heart surgeon noted for pioneering work in treatment of cardiovascular disease

September 12, 1913: Jesse Owens, American athlete, the hero of the 1936 Olympics in Berlin

September 21, 1866: H.G. Wells, English novelist and historian, author of *The Time Machine* and *The War of the Worlds*

September 25, 1931: Barbara Walters, TV personality

September 29, 1948: Bryant Gumbel, American sportscaster and TV host

WRITING ACTIVITIES FOR SEPTEMBER

Name _____ **Date** _____

SAVVY SEPTEMBER SENTENCES

DIRECTIONS: All the sentences below have something to do with the month of September. Complete them with your own words.

1. The Labor Day weekend _____.

2. Last week I shopped for _____.

3. The weather at the beginning of September _____.

4. In September, my family _____.

5. This summer was _____.

6. My school is _____.

7. My new class _____.

8. The kid next to me _____.

9. The weather at the end of September _____.

10. In September I like to _____.

11. In September I don't like to _____.

12. Tonight, I will _____.

13. Next week, I will _____.

14. September mornings are _____.

15. On September afternoons _____.

16. My new teacher _____.

17. This month will be _____.

18. In September, I feel _____.

19. Before September ends, _____.

20. The best thing to do in September is _____.

Name _____ Date_____

NEW BEGINNINGS
PREWRITING

What can make you feel happy and excited and scared and nervous all at the same time? You might answer "a roller coaster" or some other thrilling ride. But isn't the same thing true of many new experiences?

Most of us approach new experiences with mixed emotions. Sometimes, it can be really hard to take a plunge into the unknown. It helps to know more about the new place. It can also help to understand our feelings about it.

One new step you take each year is into a different grade. In this activity, you are going to write about your new class and your feelings about it.

This essay will be a lot easier to write if you first prepare a brainstorming list where you write down and organize your ideas.

Here is a brainstorming list that one new seventh-grader made:

Brainstorming List

GOOD THINGS: My friend, Alex, sits behind me.
It's a nice room with lots of windows.
I know most of the kids.
I really want to learn Spanish.
There are four computers in the room.

BAD THINGS: My best friend, Billy, is in a different homeroom.
There are mostly girls in this class.
I've been assigned a seat right up front.
The teacher is new and looks sort of mean.
I heard that seventh grade math is really hard.

MY FEELINGS: nervous, excited, jumpy, happy to be in seventh grade, afraid of the teacher, annoyed with so many girls, sad about Billy

DIRECTIONS: Prepare your brainstorming list about your new class in the space below. Write down everything you can think of. The more facts on your list, the bigger your choice will be when writing the essay.

Brainstorming List

GOOD THINGS:

BAD THINGS:

MY FEELINGS:

Name _____   **Date** _____

NEW BEGINNINGS
FIRST DRAFT

You are going to write a simple, four-paragraph essay about your new school grade. Here is an example:

I've heard lots of different things about seventh grade. Some are good and some are terrible. That's why I don't know whether to be happy or miserable about the new school year.

The worst thing was when I found out that my best friend, Billy, is in a different homeroom. We've been in the same class since first grade. Then, I couldn't believe it when I saw that there are mostly girls in this class. What a bummer! To make it worse, the teacher put me right in front. I don't like having the teacher's eye on me all the time. It makes me nervous.

At least Alex is sitting right behind me, and I do know most of the kids in the class, even the girls. (Ugh!) It's a nice room, too, with lots of windows and bright walls, and I noticed four computers in the back. I'll be going to Spanish class, too, and that will be fun.

I guess it's natural to have mixed feelings about a new class. Maybe Billy will be in one of my other classes. Maybe the teacher is nicer than he looks. I'll just have to wait and see how things turn out.

DIRECTIONS: On another sheet of paper, write a first draft of your essay. It will be easy if you follow these suggestions:

1. Use the sample essay above as a guide for writing your own essay.

2. Write the title first. You can call it NEW BEGINNINGS or any other appropriate title you like.

3. Introduce the topic in the *first paragraph*. Talk about what the beginning of a new school year is like and how it makes kids feel.

4. In the *second paragraph*, describe the BAD THINGS on your brainstorming list.

5. In the *third paragraph*, tell about the GOOD THINGS you listed.

6. In the *final paragraph*, restate your topic and sum up your essay.

This is just a *first draft*. Don't be concerned about spelling, grammar, etc. Just concentrate on getting your thoughts down on paper.

Use your brainstorming list and the sample above as guides.

Name _____ **Date** _____

NEW BEGINNINGS
REVISING AND WRITING A FINAL COPY

DIRECTIONS: You want the final copy of your essay to be as clear and well-written as possible. Read your first draft carefully. Make all changes right on the first draft. Here are some suggestions that will help you improve it:

1. Are all your sentences complete? Do verbs and nouns agree?

2. Cut out unnecessary words such as *very, so, then, also, therefore.* Sometimes these words are necessary. Usually, an essay is improved when they are cut.

3. Is the topic stated clearly in the first paragraph? Is the beginning of your essay interesting enough to make the reader go on? Try to make the beginning more exciting. Sometimes asking a question or telling a little story helps.

4. Is the middle of the essay clearly organized? Does the second paragraph describe BAD THINGS? Does the third paragraph describe the GOOD THINGS?

5. Does the final paragraph restate the topic and sum up your thoughts. Humor can often be effective here.

Write the final copy of your essay below. Write the title on the first line. Use the back of this worksheet if you need more room.

_____

_____

_____

_____

_____

_____

_____

_____

_____

_____

_____

_____

Name _____ Date _____

GETTING OFF TO A GOOD START
FILL-IN STORY

DIRECTIONS: Complete the story by filling in the blank lines.

It was _____, September _____. My _____ family

had just moved into our _____ new house in the _____ town

of _____ . Now it was time to start school. My brother, _____, and

I put on our _____ new clothes and left the _____ house. My

name is _____. I am _____ years old and going

into _____ grade. My brother is _____ years old. He is

in _____ grade. Our new school was called _____. It

was only blocks away from our _____ house, so we didn't have to take a

bus. It took _____ minutes to get to school. It was a _____

building with _____ steps in front and a _____ door. I thought it

looked like a _____.

My brother said, "_____."

I replied, "_____."

Then we went inside. The hall looked _____ . There

were _____ kids there. They looked at us _____ . One of them

said to my brother, "_____." My brother told him

that _____.

I walked my brother to his _____ room. He went inside with

a _____ look. I continued on down the _____ hall to my

own _____ room, and _____ inside. All the _____ kids

were there. So was the _____ teacher. I felt _____. I wondered if I

should _____. Suddenly, _____

(Continue the story in your own words. Use the back of this paper if you
need more room.)

Name _____ **Date**_____

LOVE THAT JOB!
PREWRITING

On September 3, 1894, LABOR DAY was first celebrated as a legal holiday in the U.S. Which of the following do you think is the reason for having a Labor Day?

> 1. to enjoy one last long weekend at the end of the summer
> 2. to visit the malls and shop for fall and winter clothes
> 3. to honor working men and women of this country and the world

If you chose *3*, you're right! Working people weren't always appreciated. Often, they had to work long hours, 6 or 7 days a week for low pay. Labor Day was created to show the nation's appreciation.

Work is an important part of people's lives. A student's work is going to school and learning. Many boys and girls also work at part-time and summer jobs. Sometimes they find these jobs through "classified ads" in the newspaper. Here are some examples from the Jackson *Tribune*, 20 Main Street, Jackson, NJ 07305:

Baby-sitter for three-year-old twin boys, Saturdays 9–2. Write giving age and experience, Box #54.

Tutor for 8-year-old with learning disabilities. Must be patient and good in math. About 6 hours a week. Box #96.

Summer position assisting elderly lady with indoor and outdoor chores. Mowing, weeding, errands, patio cleanup. Monday–Friday, 4 hours daily. Good pay. Box #67.

Could you write a letter applying for such a job? Angela Grimes wrote this one. Read it, then follow directions in Activity 4B.

```
                                        2 Pine Street
                                        Jackson, NJ 07305
                                        May 20, 19 __

Box #54
Jackson Tribune
20 Main Street
Jackson, NJ 07305
Dear Sir:

I am applying for the job as baby-sitter for your twin boys.

I am twelve years old and an honor student at Jackson Middle School. I am
very responsible and have had lots of experience caring for small children.
Two of the people I baby-sit for regularly are Mrs. Miller, 498-9056, and
Mr. and Mrs. Cates, 498-7785. I know they will give me excellent references.

I think I am the right person to take care of your boys. Three-year-olds
are my favorite age. My telephone number is 498-0101.

                                Yours Truly,

                                Angela Grimes
```

Name _____ **Date** _____

LOVE THAT JOB!
FIRST DRAFT

DIRECTIONS: Choose one of the ads in Activity 4A and write a letter applying for the job. First, read Angela Grimes's letter again. Notice how she:

1. stated what the letter was about in the first paragraph.

2. told about herself in the second paragraph, stressing her qualifications for this job.

3. ended with a positive statement.

Now, write a first draft of your letter. Use the same business letter form as Angela by following the guide below.

This is just a first draft so don't worry about grammar or spelling. Concentrate on organizing and writing down your thoughts.

© 1997 by The Center for Applied Research in Education

_____

(Write your street address here)

_____

(Write your city, state, zip here)

_____

(Write today's date here)

_____

Box # (Copy Box # from the ad)

The Jackson Tribune

20 Main Street

Jackson, NJ 07305

Dear Sir:

_____

_____

_____

_____

_____

_____

Yours truly,

_____

(Write your name here)

Name _____ **Date** _____

LOVE THAT JOB!
REVISING AND WRITING A FINAL COPY

DIRECTIONS: Read your letter of application carefully and try to make it better. Here are some suggestions:

1. Is there a good beginning and ending? Is the information in between clear and well organized?

2. Have you stressed your good qualities and experience that make you right for the job?

3. Does your letter make you seem enthusiastic and willing to work hard?

4. Are all words spelled correctly? If in doubt, check the dictionary.

5. Are your sentences clear. Do nouns and verbs agree?

Write the final copy of your letter below. Be sure to use the correct business letter form shown in Activity 4B.

_____

_____

_____

_____

_____

_____

_____

_____

_____

_____

_____

_____

Name _____ Date _____

NEVER TOO LATE TO DREAM
PREWRITING

Anna Mary Robertson Moses was born on September 7, 1860. Does that name mean anything to you? Probably not. For most of Anna's life, no one had heard of her except her family, friends, and neighbors. She was a hard-working farm wife, busy with household and farm chores and raising her family. Anna had a dream, but no chance to live that dream until she was *76 years old!* That seems old to start a new life, doesn't it? But it was at that advanced age that Anna began to paint pictures of the places and people she knew. Her style of painting was called "primitive." Soon, people realized that she had an immense talent. They began to call her "Grandma Moses." She became famous. Her paintings were shown all over the world. Grandma Moses kept right on painting. She completed 25 pictures after the age of 100!

For 76 long years, it didn't look as though Anna Mary Robertson Moses's dream had any chance of coming true. Many of us have wishes and dreams that seem impossible. Grandma Moses's story tells us that it's never too late to live a dream.

Do you have dreams that seem unrealistic, or too difficult to achieve? Sometimes writing about these wishes can help show a way of making them come true. A brainstorming list like the one set up below can help you collect and organize your thoughts.

DIRECTIONS: In the *first section* of the brainstorming list, write down words and phrases that describe your wishes and dreams.

In the *second section* of the brainstorming list, write down all the reasons why these dreams seem difficult or impossible.

In the *third section* of the brainstorming list, tell what might happen (like a fairy godmother?) or things you could do to make your dream possible. How long might this take? Why?

In the *last section* of the brainstorming list, state your feelings about your dream. Does it seem any more possible than when you first began thinking about it? Why or why not?

(You do not need to use complete sentences on this list—just words or phrases.)

BRAINSTORMING LIST

SECTION 1:

SECTION 2:

SECTION 3:

SECTION 4:

© 1997 by The Center for Applied Research in Education

Name _____ **Date** _____

NEVER TOO LATE TO DREAM
FIRST DRAFT

DIRECTIONS: Your brainstorming list will help you organize and write this essay. In this first draft, don't be concerned with spelling or grammar. Just concentrate on writing down your thoughts. It will be easy if you organize your essay as follows:

1. There will be four paragraphs in your essay. In your *first paragraph*, describe your dream (or dreams) in a vivid, interesting manner.
2. In your *second paragraph*, describe the problems and situations that make your dreams difficult or impossible.
3. In your *third paragraph*, come up with ways that you might overcome these obstacles. These can be realistic or fantastic, or both.
4. In your *last paragraph*, re-state your dream, your feelings about it, and whether or not you think it might ever come true.

Write your first draft on the lines below. (Use the back of this worksheet if you need more room.)

_____

_____

_____

_____

_____

_____

_____

_____

_____

_____

_____

_____

_____

_____

Name _____ **Date** _____

NEVER TOO LATE TO DREAM
REVISING AND WRITING A FINAL COPY

DIRECTIONS: Revise the first draft of your essay. Follow these suggestions for making it more effective.

1. Does your *first paragraph* state the topic clearly and in an interesting manner?
2. Does your *second paragraph* clearly describe the problems?
3. Does the *third paragraph* show positive steps that could be taken?
4. Does the *last paragraph* restate the topic and describe your feelings and conclusions about it?
5. Are your sentences complete? Do subjects and verbs agree?
6. Could the writing be improved with vivid, striking images, such as active verbs, similes, or sensory words?
7. Check spelling with dictionary.

Now, write your final copy below. Indent at the beginning of paragraphs. (Use the back of this worksheet if you need more room.)

NEVER TOO LATE TO DREAM

_____

_____

_____

_____

_____

_____

_____

_____

_____

_____

_____

_____

Name _____   **Date**_____

SCI-FI OR WHAT?
PREWRITING

War of the Worlds, The Time Machine, First Man on the Moon—These sound like titles out of the latest catalog of sci-fi books. Surprisingly, they were written a long time ago by Herbert George Wells. He is better known as H.G. Wells, and was born in England on September 21, 1866. When he started writing exciting stories about the future, no one had ever heard of "science fiction." Yet, these imaginative, thrilling tales are so up-to-date that they are still enjoyed by people of all ages, and are even made into movies. *Some of the things he predicted in these stories have already happened!* Have you read any of these books? If not, you should surely look at them.

Most people enjoy science fiction. For many, it is their favorite kind of book. Others prefer mysteries or sports stories or adventures or fantasies or realistic stories about modern kids.

What kind of books do *you* like best? Why? In this activity, you are going to write about the kind of stories you enjoy most. Before beginning your essay, it helps to organize your thoughts and ideas in a brainstorming list like the one below.

BRAINSTORMING LIST

1. What kind of books do you like best ("Science Fiction," "Mysteries," etc.)? _____ Why do you like them? (You don't need sentences here, just words and phrases.) _____

   _____

2. *Example #1:* Write the title of one of these books that you have read. Then tell what it is about. Keep the story description short—one or two sentences at most.

   Title: _____

   What is it about? _____

   _____

   Now, make a list of words or phrases that tell why you liked this book, such as "exciting," "funny," "weird," "like real life," "wild," "helpful," "inspiring," "sad," "suspenseful," "great characters," etc. List as many words or phrases as you can that might apply to this book.

   _____

3. *Example #2:* Write the title of another book of that kind you enjoyed. Then write a summary of the story in one or two sentences.

   Title: _____

   What is it about? _____

   _____

   Make a list of words or phrases that tell why you liked this book, as in Example #1.

   _____

Name _____ Date _____

Sci-Fi or What?
First Draft

Writing a four-paragraph essay about your favorite kind of books will be a snap! Just use the brainstorming list you prepared in Activity 6A. Keep it in front of you as you follow the directions below. (This is just a first draft, so don't worry about spelling or sentence structure. Concentrate on getting your thoughts down on paper.)

FIRST PARAGRAPH: Introduce your topic here. Try to begin in an interesting way that will make the reader want to continue. Here are some examples: *"Whenever my Mom looks at me in a certain way, I know that she has found my latest sci-fi book under the pillow. She doesn't like me to stay up late reading in bed. But I can't help it. I love science fiction so much! When I open the pages of a good one, I can't seem to stop reading!"* or, *"Guess who is the number-one ghost story fan in the world? I am! I can't help it! I love being scared! A good ghost story will terrify me every time!"*

Now, write your first paragraph here. _____
_____
_____

SECOND PARAGRAPH: Tell about one book of this kind you have enjoyed. Use *Example #1* on your brainstorming list. Tell the title. Copy the description of the story. Use some of the words and phrases on your list to explain why you like this book.

Write your second paragraph here. _____
_____
_____

THIRD PARAGRAPH: Tell about *Example #2* on your brainstorming list. Follow the directions for the second paragraph above.

Write your third paragraph here. _____
_____
_____

FOURTH PARAGRAPH: In the last paragraph, you will state the topic again and sum it up. (Example: *"I know I'll always love to read science fiction. It is exciting and imaginative. It takes me into the world of the future and shows me what it might be like."*)

Write your last paragraph here. _____
_____
_____

Name _____ **Date** _____

SCI-FI OR WHAT?
REVISING AND WRITING A FINAL COPY

It won't be necessary to make a lot of changes on your first draft of this essay if you followed the directions and used your brainstorming list. Here are some things you can do to make your final copy perfect. (Make the revisions right on the draft copy.)

1. Is the topic stated clearly in the first paragraph? Is the beginning interesting enough to make the reader go on? Look at the examples again. Perhaps you can start with a question or use humor for an exciting beginning.
2. Are paragraphs two and three clearly organized? Does each tell about a particular story and why you liked it?
3. Does the final paragraph restate the topic and sum it up? Can you add some strong words such as "exciting," "thrilling," "spine-tingling," "mind-boggling" to make it more forceful?
4. Are all your sentences complete? Do verbs and nouns agree?
5. Check spelling where you are not 100% certain.

Write the final copy of your essay below. Write the title on the first line. Use the back of this worksheet if you need more room. (Indent at the beginning of each paragraph.)

_____

_____

_____

_____

_____

_____

_____

_____

_____

Name _____ Date _____

HOW I GOT MY OWN TV SHOW
PREWRITING

The name Barbara Walters is familiar to everyone. She is one of the best-known interviewers on television. She was born in Boston on September 25, 1931, and was the first woman in broadcasting to receive a salary of a million dollars a year.

Barbara Walters is a co-host on "20/20." How would you like to have *your* own TV show? This is your chance to picture yourself doing just that. You are going to let your imagination *soar*, and write a story about how *you* get your big break and become the star of your own show.

There are lots of ways that could happen (in your imagination, of course!). For example, you might be walking down a street, minding your own business, a talent agent spots you, he thinks you would be perfect for a new sitcom, and the rest is history!

OR . . . You are determined to make it in broadcasting. You haunt TV sets and offices, going back time after time, week after week, year after year; you audition for parts, you make friends with people in the casting offices; you take speech lessons and classes in acting. Finally, just when you are ready to give up, someone finally offers you a part in a sitcom. It is a small role, but you are so good that a month later, you become the star of the show!

OR . . . You are in the audience of a popular talk show; you raise your hand to ask a question; the mike is put in front of you; you begin to talk and . . . well, you fill in the rest!

OR . . . you can come up with your own exciting ideas.

It's easier to write a story like this if you first prepare a summary—a short telling of the plot—something like the brief descriptions above. Your plot summary would have to be a bit longer. It should describe the main character (*you*, but this doesn't have to be the real you; you can become whatever you wish!). It should tell about some of the other characters and how they affect the story. Describe where and how the story begins. Then, tell briefly, step-by-step, what happens, and how the whole thing ends. Your story will be more interesting if the main character has problems finding success or if there are some not-so-nice characters who stand in the way.

Your plot summary should not be longer than *one or two paragraphs*. Save the details for the story itself.

Write your plot summary below. (Use the back of this worksheet if you need more room.)

© 1997 by The Center for Applied Research in Education

Name _____ Date_____

How I Got My Own TV Show
First Draft

DIRECTIONS: Writing a story is easy if you have done a plot summary first. Here are some hints that will help you create a better story.

1. Make your beginning interesting. Start with action (something exciting happening) or dialogue (one or more characters talking).
2. Use strong verbs (action words). Instead of *went*, say *rushed* or *raced* or *sauntered* or *leaped*. Instead of *see*, use *stare* or *glare* or *squint*. Instead of *touch*, say *pat* or *smack* or *grab* or *stroke*.
3. Tell something about the setting. No story takes place in the middle of nowhere. Are you in a small town or a city? Which one? What kind of building? In what kind of room does a scene occur? Always show a little something about the setting.

Now, write your story below. Use your plot summary as a guide. This is just a first draft, so don't be concerned with spelling or sentence structure. Concentrate on getting your story down. (Use the back of this worksheet if you need more room.)

HOW I GOT MY OWN TV SHOW

_____

_____

_____

_____

_____

_____

_____

_____

_____

_____

_____

_____

Name _____ **Date** _____

HOW I GOT MY OWN TV SHOW
REVISING AND WRITING A FINAL COPY

DIRECTIONS: Read and edit the first draft of your story. Ask yourself these questions:

1. Is the beginning interesting enough to grab a reader's interest? How could it be changed to be more exciting?
2. Does the main character's speech and action indicate his or her personality? What can that character do or say to make this clear?
3. Have you used strong active verbs wherever possible? Are there some you can add or change to make the scene more exciting?
4. Are your sentences complete? Do subjects and verbs agree?
5. Are all your words spelled correctly?
6. Are there any other changes that would make your story more exciting or suspenseful?

Write your final copy of this story below. Use the back of this worksheet if you need more room.

Don't forget to indent at the beginning of each paragraph.

HOW I GOT MY OWN TV SHOW

_____

_____

_____

_____

_____

_____

_____

_____

_____

_____

_____

Name _____ **Date**_____

DEAR DOC
PREWRITING

> Michael E. DeBakey was born in Louisiana on September 7, 1908. Dr. DeBakey has been a pioneer in heart surgery. He developed new methods and procedures that give patients many extra years of life. Years ago, there was little that doctors could do for people who had heart and artery disease. The work of Michael DeBakey and other *cardiovascular* surgeons has given new hope to these people.

We don't always appreciate what doctors do for us. After all, how many kids really look forward to a visit to the doctor's office. Be honest now—aren't there a lot of other things you'd rather be doing?

We like being healthy and strong, though. Often, it is the skill and care of our doctors that help keep us that way. Have you ever thanked your doctor for what he or she has done for you?

Just saying, "Hey, thanks a lot, Doc," at your next visit would be great. But there's even a better way.

A *letter* from a grateful patient is something a doctor can keep on his or her desk and look at over and over again. Here is such a letter that was sent to one doctor:

```
                                        25 Elm Street
                                        Pottsville, NY 14601
                                        March 3, 19__

Dr. Kenneth Hiller
24 Mott Road
Pottsville, NY 14601
Dear Dr. Hiller:
   You have been my doctor since I was three. You've always been there when
I needed you. Sometimes I'm grumpy when you give me shots but I know they
help me stay healthy.
   Do you remember two years ago when I fell off my bike and broke my arm?
You met us at the hospital. I was scared, but when I saw you there, I knew
that everything would be okay.
   Thanks for everything. I hope you'll always be my doctor.

                                        Your friend,
                                        Paul Pascal
```

You are going to write a letter to your doctor. Before you begin, it will help to prepare the list below:

1. Write your doctor's name here. Add the address if you know it:

_____

2. What happened the last time you saw the doctor?

_____

3. List illnesses or problems for which you've seen the doctor.

_____

4. List the things about your doctor that you like best.

_____

Name _____ **Date** _____

DEAR DOC
FIRST DRAFT

DIRECTIONS:

1. Read Paul Pascal's letter to his doctor in Activity 8A. It will help you get started with your letter to your own doctor. You'll also be able to use the notes you made on the bottom of that activity sheet.
2. Use correct letter form, just as Paul did. The instructions on this page will show you how.
3. Write a first draft of your letter below. Don't be concerned about spelling and punctuation. Just concentrate on getting down your thoughts. Think how pleased the doctor will be to get your letter.

   Follow the form below. Be sure to indent at the beginning of each paragraph.

_____
(Write your street address here)

_____
(Write City, State, ZIP here)

_____
(Write today's date here)

Dr. _____ (Fill in name of Doctor)

_____ (Doctor's street address)

_____ (City, state, ZIP)

Dear Dr.   :

_____

_____

_____

_____

                                        Your friend,

_____

                                (Write your name here)

Name _____ Date_____

DEAR DOC
REVISING AND WRITING A FINAL COPY

DIRECTIONS: Edit and revise your letter right on your first draft, as follows:

---

1. Have you told the doctor how much you appreciate him or her? Is there any way you could express it better or more clearly?

2. Have you given one or two specific examples of what the doctor has done for you? Can you think of any others that you would like to add?

3. Is your letter form correct?
   RETURN ADDRESS (your address) and DATE on upper right side
   INSIDE ADDRESS (name and address of doctor) at left margin
   GREETING at left margin
   CLOSING at lower right
   YOUR SIGNATURE below CLOSING

4. Is your sentence structure correct? Do subjects and verbs agree? Is there a period at the end of each sentence?

5. Have you always used the best word or phrase? Is there anything you can change to make your writing stronger or clearer?

6. Have you checked all spelling?

7. Did you indent at the beginning of each paragraph?

Is your letter as perfect as you can make it now? If it is, write your final copy on a separate sheet of paper. That way, you can actually mail your letter to the doctor, if you wish.

Be sure to use correct letter form, as indicated on your first draft and also shown in the directions above.

Name _____   Date _____

STAR REPORTER
PREWRITING

September has always been a time for beginnings. An important one occurred in the year 1851 on September 18. That was the day the first issue of *the New York Times* appeared on newsstands! It didn't take long for it to become one of the most important newspapers in the U.S. A reporter who can get a job at the *Times* is at the top of his or her field.

In 1851, newspapers were the only way the public could find out what was going on in the country and the world. Now we have radio and TV, too, but newspapers are still an important source of news.

It is fun to find out what is happening and report on it. Does your school have a newspaper? If not, perhaps you can talk to your teacher or principal about starting one. The things that happen in your school may not be so important as national or world news, but they are important to the teachers and kids who spend their days there.

A reporter needs to be able to tell a story in as few words as possible. That is because it has to fit into limited space in the paper. In fact, the main points of the story must be expressed in a couple of sentences so a reader will know the gist of the story just by reading the first paragraph. Details can come later.

The main points of a news story are:

WHO?   (Who are the people involved?)
WHAT?   (What happened?)
WHERE?   (Where did it happen?)
WHEN?   (Exactly when did it occur?)

The first few sentences of a news story is called the *lead*. The lead must always tell WHO? WHAT? WHERE? and WHEN? The lead should be interesting enough to catch a reader's attention. Many news stories also answer the question WHY?, but this can come later in the story.

There are many things going on in a school that could make interesting stories for a school newspaper, such as class trips, special assemblies, sports information about a school team, special class projects, etc.

Here is an example of a lead for a school newspaper story. Read it, then answer the questions below:

> "Mr. Jackson's seventh-grade science class went to a rain forest on Thursday, March 12. No, they didn't take a trip to South America! They visited the rain forest exhibit at the Botanical Gardens."

Can you name the WHO of this lead? _____

WHAT happened? _____

WHEN did it happen? _____

WHERE did it happen? _____

What phrase makes the lead interesting? _____

Name _____ **Date** _____

STAR REPORTER
FIRST DRAFT

DIRECTIONS: Write a lead for a news story about something that has occurred in your school or class.

You can choose a *real* event in your school and use actual names, dates, etc.
OR, you can make up a story about one of the following:

A special assembly or program
A school or class trip
An interesting class project
A new teacher or program in the school
New foods in the school cafeteria

If you choose a made-up story, you will have to invent names, dates, etc.

Remember, your lead must answer the questions:

WHO?
WHAT?
WHEN?
WHERE?

The example of a lead in Activity 9A includes a humorous comparison with a trip to South America. This makes the lead more interesting. Try to use an exciting or humorous phrase in your lead to make it more interesting.

Write a first draft of your lead on the lines below. It should be no longer than *three* sentences.

Be sure to answer the questions WHO? WHAT? WHEN? and WHERE?

_____

_____

_____

_____

_____

_____

_____

_____

Name _____ **Date** _____

STAR REPORTER
REVISING AND WRITING A FINAL COPY

DIRECTIONS: Edit and revise your news story lead right on the first draft, as follows:

1. Is your lead short and to the point—no more than three sentences?
2. Does your lead answer the questions—WHO? WHAT? WHEN? and WHERE?
3. Have you included something exciting or humorous to catch the reader's attention?
4. Are your sentences complete? Do subjects and verbs agree?
5. Have you checked your spelling?

   Write the final copy of your lead below. Indent at the beginning of the paragraph.

_____

_____

_____

_____

_____

_____

_____

_____

_____

_____

_____

_____

_____

_____

_____

Name _____ **Date**_____

The Sentence Detective
Prewriting

Do you like mysteries? The most important person in a mystery is the detective. Detectives look for clues. Then, if they are good detectives, they will solve the mystery.

In this activity, you will be the detective! The crime you are going to solve is called *The Mystery of the Incomplete Sentences*.

Incomplete sentences are sometimes called *fragments*. The word "fragment" means "piece." That's the opposite of "whole." Fragments make writing choppy and unclear and hard to read.

For example, look at the paragraph below. It tells about an interesting event, but it is spoiled by fragments.

Something amazing happened in the year 1928. On September 18. There was a movie theater in New York City. Called the Colony Theatre. The people who came loved to watch movies. Especially cartoons. That day, they were shown a new cartoon called *Steamboat Willie*. Made by Walt Disney. A new character appeared in that cartoon. Never seen before. A most unusual mouse. This character's name was "Mickey Mouse."

Can you find the fragments (incomplete sentences) in this story? Put on your detective hat! Search for clues! Find all the fragments and *circle them now*. Remember, every sentence must have a subject and a verb. If either of these is missing, it is only a fragment. A sentence must always express a complete thought.

After you have circled the fragments, go to Activity 10B to see if you were a great detective and found all the clues in *The Mystery of the Incomplete Sentences*.

Name _____ **Date** _____

THE SENTENCE DETECTIVE
REVISING AND WRITING A FINAL COPY

Are you a great detective? Was your investigation thorough? Did you circle all the fragments (incomplete sentences) in Activity 10A? Here's what the paragraph should look like:

Something amazing happened in the year 1928. On September 18, There was a movie theater in New York City. Called the Colony Theatre. The people who came loved to watch movies. Especially cartoons. That day, they were shown a new cartoon called *Steamboat Willie.* Made by Walt Disney. A new character appeared in that cartoon. Never seen before. A most unusual mouse. This character's name was "Mickey Mouse."

A detective doesn't only look for clues, but also uses them to solve the mystery. You can "wrap up" your investigations by rewriting this paragraph, making complete sentences out of each fragment. Here are some clues you can use to do this:

1. Add a subject, if it is missing.
2. Add a verb, if that is missing.
3. Combine the fragment with the sentence before.
4. Combine the fragment with the sentence that follows.

DIRECTIONS: Copy the story about Mickey Mouse's first cartoon below. Make it more readable. Fix every fragment and make it whole. The four clues above will help you do this. When every sentence is whole and complete, you will have solved *The Mystery of the Incomplete Sentences.*

_____

_____

_____

_____

_____

_____

_____

_____

_____

_____

© 1997 by The Center for Applied Research in Education

Name _____ **Date** _____

GOING FOR THE GOLD
PREWRITING

September 12 was the birth date of a famous American athlete. His name was Jesse Owens.

In 1936, the Olympic Games were held in Berlin. At that time, Germany was ruled with an iron fist by Adolph Hitler and his National Socialist (Nazi) party. They had declared that Germans were the "Master Race." Other people, such as blacks, Jews, Poles, etc., "were inferior." Americans were called "mongrels." Then along came Jesse Owens. He was an African-American and a member of the U.S.A. track team.

Jesse ran as no athlete had run before him. In one day, he set three world track records, and became the hero of the Olympics. His skill and courage showed up the falseness of Hitler's racial ideas.

How did Jesse Owens become one of the greatest athletes of all time? Some people say that a great athlete is born that way. Others believe it is determination and hard work that make the difference.

What do you think? Are some people born to be athletes while others are destined to be clumsy at sports? Can *anyone* who works hard and long enough become a skilled athlete?

You are going to write an opinion essay telling what you think about this question. Before you begin, it is wise to first prepare a brainstorming list, where you can write down and organize your ideas.

BRAINSTORMING LIST

1. What *physical skills* does a person need to be successful at sports? *Coordination* is one. *Strength* is another. Can you think of any others? List them on the lines below:

   _____   _____   _____

2. What *mental skills* are needed to be successful at sports? *Willpower* is one. *Not giving up* is another. Can you add more? List them below:

   _____   _____   _____

3. Can you think of any athletic skills that a person is born with? List them below:

   _____   _____   _____

4. What athletic skills can a person acquire? List them below:

   _____   _____   _____

5. Check the statement below that most closely matches your opinion:

   Good athletes are born that way.
   Hard work and willpower will bring about success in sports.
   Both natural ability and hard work are important to an athlete.

Name _____ **Date** _____

GOING FOR THE GOLD
FIRST DRAFT

DIRECTIONS: You are going to write a three-paragraph essay telling your opinion about how good athletes are made. It will be easy if you follow the directions below. Since this is a first draft, don't worry about spelling or grammar—just concentrate on getting down your thoughts.

The first paragraph states the topic in two or three sentences. You could begin with one of the sentences at the bottom of your brainstorming list, or you can make your essay more interesting by starting with a question or something personal, as in these examples:

> "What makes a great athlete? No one knows for sure. I think most really good athletes are born that way."
>
> "I was never good at sports. Everyone thought I was a nerd. Last year, my gym teacher helped me train. It took a lot of time and effort, but now I do okay at sports. I believe anyone who works hard enough can become a good athlete."

Write the first paragraph of your essay below:

_____

_____

_____

In the second paragraph, you will give reasons to support your opinion. Use the words and phrases on your brainstorming list as a guide. Here is one example of a second paragraph:

> "An athlete needs strength. Anyone can become stronger by exercising and working out. Coordination is also important in sports. It takes lots of work, but if you practice pitching or batting a ball long enough, you can improve your skills a lot. Mental attitude makes a difference, too. A person who is determined to learn athletic skills will usually succeed."

Write the second paragraph of your essay below:

_____

_____

_____

The third paragraph restates and sums up your opinion. Example:

> "My experience is proof that an athlete is made, not born. The important ingredients are hard work and determination. With these, anyone can become successful at sports."

Write the third paragraph of your essay below:

_____

_____

_____

Name _____ **Date** _____

GOING FOR THE GOLD
REVISING AND WRITING A FINAL COPY

DIRECTIONS: First, revise your first draft right on the paper, as follows:

1. In the first paragraph, did you introduce the topic in an interesting way? Can you make it more exciting with a question or interesting story?
2. Does your second paragraph give at least three convincing reasons for your opinion?
3. Does the third paragraph restate and sum up the topic clearly?
4. Are your sentences complete? Do all subjects and verbs agree?
5. Can you make your essay more exciting by using some strong, active verbs, such as *run, leap, jump, strain, sweat*?
6. Check your spelling whenever in doubt.

Write the final copy of your essay below. Indent at the beginning of each paragraph. (Use the back of this worksheet if you need more room.)

_____

_____

_____

_____

_____

_____

_____

_____

_____

_____

_____

_____

_____

_____

Name _____ **Date** _____

FALL INTO RHYME
PREWRITING

The season of autumn (also called Fall) usually begins on September 22. It is a colorful time of year. Here is how an English poet named Shelley described autumn:

I love all that you love,
  Spirit of Delight;
The fresh Earth in new leaves dressed,
  And the starry night;
Autumn evening and the morn
When the golden mists are born.

Not all poetry has to rhyme, but rhyming can add to the enjoyment of writing and reading poetry. There are many rhyming patterns that work well. Not all lines have to rhyme. In the poem above, can you find the lines that rhyme?

If you said lines 2 and 4, then lines 5 and 6, you are right!

It can be fun to play with words and create rhymes. Autumn is a good subject because there are so many colorful words that can be used to describe it. Fill the box below with as many words you can think of that have something to do with the season of Autumn. A few words have already been put in the box for you. Add as many as you can.

gold   brown   chilly

How many words were you able to put into the box? If you wish, you can share with your classmates. You can add some of their words to your box, and they can use yours.

Let's take some of your Autumn words and find rhymes for them. Choose at least ten words. Write them on the lines below. Then, next to each, write down as many rhymes as you can think of. The first two are done for you.

	Autumn Word	Rhyming Words
1.	gold	bold, hold, fold, cold, scold, tolled
2.	fall	ball, mall, call, hall, wall, tall
3.		
4.		
5.		
6.		
7.		
8.		
9.		
10.		

Name _____ Date_____

FALL INTO RHYME
FIRST DRAFT

There are many rhyme schemes you could use in a poem about Autumn. One is to have the *first two* lines rhyme with each other, and then to rhyme lines *three* and *four*. This is called AABB, as in this verse:

Autumn is a lovely season,	**A**
And that is the only reason	**A**
Why I write this silly verse—	**B**
Winter, summer, spring are worse!	**B**

Or, line *one* could rhyme with line *three*, and line *two* rhyme with line *four*. This is called ABAB, as in this poem:

Rainbow-colored leaves are falling from the trees,	**A**
They do a little dance upon the air,	**B**
Shimmering and whirling, twisting in the breeze,	**A**
Breaking off until the limbs are bare.	**B**

These are the simplest rhymes. Choose one of these (or any other kind of rhyme you like) to write a poem about Autumn, as follows:

1. Your poem should have at least four lines. You can make it much longer, if you wish.
2. Look at your list of rhyming words in Activity 12A. These will give you lots of ideas for your poem.
3. Your poem can be serious or it can be silly as in the first example above.
4. Write a first draft of your poem below. Concentrate on getting down your ideas and rhymes. You can edit and fix it up later. (You can put a title on the first line.)

Name _____ **Date** _____

FALL INTO RHYME
REVISING AND WRITING A FINAL COPY

Here are some suggestions for making changes in your poem about Autumn:

1. Use sensory language. Words that appeal to the five senses (sight, sound, touch, taste, smell) can make a poem more vivid. Colors are good—they involve sight. Examples of other sensory words are *ring, chime, soft, velvety, sweet, smoky,* etc. Can you add any sensory words to your poem?
2. Strong, active verbs such as *whirl, twirl, dance, shimmer, leap,* etc., can make your poem exciting. Can you add any active verbs?
3. Do at least some of the lines in your poem rhyme? Try reading it aloud to get a better sense of how well the rhyme works.

Write the final copy of your poem below. (If you like, you can illustrate it in the space below.)

_____

_____

_____

_____

_____

_____

_____

_____

Name _____ **Date** _____

BUILDING BLOCKS
SENTENCES

Babies play with building blocks. Construction workers use another sort of block to construct tall buildings.

Sentences are constructed, too. They are built up from building blocks such as *subjects and predicates, nouns and verbs, adjectives and adverbs*, etc.

Here is a fun way to build a sentence beginning with a single block:

First block:	The clock
Add adjectives:	The big, round clock
Add a verb:	The big, round clock ticks
Add an adverb:	The big round clock ticks loudly.

Building sentences can be exciting and creative!

The following words represent objects found in most classrooms. Can you add building blocks, as directed, to create a complete sentence? (If you are not sure what to do, look at the example above again.)

1. First block: A pencil

   Add adjectives:_____

   Add a verb: _____

   Add an adverb: _____

2. First block: The desk

   Add adjectives:_____

   Add a verb: _____

   Add an adverb: _____

3. First block: The book

   Add adjectives:_____

   Add a verb: _____

   Add an adverb: _____

Name _____ **Date** _____

BUILDING BLOCKS
PARAGRAPHS

In Activity 13A, you used words as building blocks to create sentences.

What kind of building blocks would you need to construct a paragraph?

If you answered "sentences," you are correct. Sentences are the building blocks for paragraphs.

The first building block is the *beginning* or *topic sentence*:

I saw a strange sight this morning.

The next three or four building blocks give more details about the topic:

I was on my way to school when I heard a baby's loud cries.
I rushed ahead to see what was happening.
There were two cats on a fence yowling.

The last building block sentence completes and sums up the thoughts in the paragraph:

It is weird that cats can sound so much like human babies.

DIRECTIONS: Choose *one* topic sentence block and build it into a paragraph by adding three or four detail sentences and one concluding sentence.

Begin your paragraph by *copying one* of the following sentences on the lines below. Then, create your own building blocks to write a complete paragraph as in the example above. (Use the back of this worksheet if you need more room.)

TOPIC SENTENCES (choose *one*)
My favorite video game is lots of fun.
Sometimes, everything seems to go wrong at the same time.
Some school subjects are more interesting than others.
I have a really great friend.

_____

_____

_____

_____

_____

_____

OCTOBER

OCTOBER

"It was night in the lonesome October
  Of my most immemorial year."
  —Edgar Allan Poe

CRISP DAYS . . . A RIOT OF AUTUMN COLORS . . . CHILDREN JUMPING IN PILES OF CRACKLING LEAVES . . . COLUMBUS DAY . . . AND WHAT MANY CHILDREN SEE AS THE MOST IMPORTANT HOLIDAY OF THE YEAR: HALLOWEEN (OCTOBER 31st)!

OCTOBER EVENTS

October 1, 1903: Baseball's first World Series in Boston between Boston and Pittsburgh; won by Boston, 5 games to 3

October 1, 1908: The famous Model-T Ford, known as the "Tin Lizzie," was first put on sale by Henry Ford at a price of $850.00

October 12, 1492: Christopher Columbus landed in the New World (celebrated on the second Monday of the month)

October 16, 1845: Edgar Allen Poe read his new poem, "The Raven," to a Boston audience who walked out on him

October 19, 1781: British general Cornwallis surrendered to General Washington at Yorktown, Virginia, ending the Revolutionary War

October 19, 1879: Thomas A. Edison invented the electric light bulb

October 23, 1915: 25,000 women marched in New York City demanding the right to vote

October 24, 1945: The United Nations was formally established

October 28, 1886: The Statue of Liberty was dedicated in New York harbor

OCTOBER BIRTHDAYS

October 6, 1914: Thor Heyerdahl, Norwegian adventurer and writer who sailed across the ocean on a raft, author of *Kon-Tiki* (1950)

October 8, 1941: Jesse Jackson, American civil rights leader

October 9, 1940: John Lennon, British pop singer, musician and songwriter who rose to fame with The Beatles

October 13, 1969: Nancy Kerrigan, American Olympic iceskating champion

October 16, 1758: Noah Webster, American educator who compiled *Webster's Dictionary*

October 18, 1956: Martina Navratilova, Czech-born American tennis champion who won nine Wimbledon women's single titles

October 27, 1858: Theodore Roosevelt, 26th U.S. President

October 28, 1914: Jonas Salk, American physician who developed the first polio vaccine

WRITING ACTIVITIES FOR OCTOBER

Name _____ Date _____

A RAFTING ADVENTURE
PREWRITING

> Thor Heyerdahl was born on October 6, 1914. He was a Norwegian explorer who had a daring adventure. He believed that the people of Tahiti had arrived there thousands of years ago by sailing on a primitive raft across the Pacific Ocean. The experts said this was impossible. So, Thor Heyerdahl himself set sail on a raft from South America 5,000 miles across the dangerous Pacific to an island near Tahiti. He proved it could be done and wrote a book about his trip called *Kon-Tiki* (after the name of his raft).

Mark Twain also wrote about a journey on a raft in his book *Huckleberry Finn*. *Kon-Tiki* told about something that had really happened. *Huckleberry Finn* is fiction. Mark Twain made it up. Now, you are going to be an author and make up your own story about a trip on a raft. You can let your imagination run wild and have all sorts of incredible things happen. Before you begin, it will be helpful to prepare a brainstorming list organizing information about the people in your story and what happens to them.

DIRECTIONS: Complete the brainstorming list as follows:

1. In the first section, write down the names of your characters. Next to each name, list some important facts about that person's age, appearance, personality, and character.

2. In Section 2, describe the place or places where your story happens.

3. In Section 3, describe the raft and why the characters go off on it. Then write a beginning sentence for your story.

4. In Section 4, list some of the adventures the characters will have on the raft.

5. In Section 5, tell how the story will end.

Except for the beginning sentence, you can use just words and phrases in your brainstorming list.

BRAINSTORMING LIST

SECTION 1 (CHARACTERS):

SECTION 2 (SETTING):

SECTION 3 (BEGINNING):

SECTION 4 (ADVENTURES):

SECTION 5 (ENDING):

Name _____ **Date**_____

A RAFTING ADVENTURE
FIRST DRAFT

DIRECTIONS: Write the first draft of your story below. First, copy the beginning sentence. Then, it should be easy to write your story using your brainstorming list. This is just a first draft, so don't worry about grammar or spelling. Just concentrate on getting down your thoughts. (Use the back of this paper if you need more room.)

Here is one outline you can follow, if you wish:

1. In the first paragraph, write your beginning and introduce your characters.
2. In the second paragraph, tell how they get the raft. Where do they decide to go on it? Why?
3. The third and fourth paragraphs can describe their adventures along the way.
4. In the last paragraph, tell where they end up and what happens to them there.
5. Try to include some dialogue (conversations) in your story.

A RAFTING ADVENTURE

_____

_____

_____

_____

_____

_____

_____

_____

_____

_____

_____

_____

_____

_____

Name _____ Date _____

A RAFTING ADVENTURE
REVISING AND WRITING A FINAL COPY

DIRECTIONS: Revise your first draft. Make any changes needed to improve your story. Here are some suggestions:

1. Is your beginning interesting enough to make the reader want to continue? Can you make it more exciting?
2. Do you tell enough about the characters so the reader can see them in his or her mind? Can you add more details, using vivid words?
3. Change boring verbs such as *go, say,* or *see* to more active verbs like *leap, shout,* or *stare.*
4. Do you use dialogue (conversation)? It's fun for the writer and the reader. Is the dialogue the way people really talk?
5. Are your sentences complete? Do subjects and verbs agree?
6. Check spelling with a dictionary.

When your story is as good as you can make it, write your final copy below. Indent at beginning of paragraphs. Use the back of this worksheet if you need more room.

A RAFTING ADVENTURE

_____

_____

_____

_____

_____

_____

_____

_____

_____

_____

_____

Name _____ **Date**_____

TOWN WITHOUT LIGHTS
PREWRITING

> Something very important happened on October 19, 1879. Thomas A. Edison invented the electric lightbulb!
>
> Before that date, there were no electric lights! Can you imagine what it was like to live in a world without electric lights? That's what you are going to do now. You are going to imagine you live in such a world, and describe how your life would be different.
>
> It will be easier to write your essay if you first organize your ideas with a brainstorming list.

DIRECTIONS: Prepare a brainstorming list for an essay called "Town Without Lights."

1. In the first space below, make a list of words and phrases describing how your HOME would be different without electric lights.

2. In the second space, make a list of words and phrases describing how your SCHOOL would be different without electric lights.

3. In the third space, make a list of words and phrases describing how SHOPPING in stores and malls would be different.

4. In the fourth space, list words and phrases that describe how STREETS and HIGHWAYS and TRAVEL might be different.

5. In the fifth space, list words and phrases that describe how SPORTS and HOBBIES and RECREATION might be different.

6. In the sixth space, write a beginning for your essay. Use one or two sentences to introduce the topic in an interesting way.

BRAINSTORMING LIST

1. HOME:

2. SCHOOL:

3. SHOPPING:

4. TRAVEL:

5. SPORTS AND RECREATION:

6. BEGINNING SENTENCES:

Name _____ **Date** _____

TOWN WITHOUT LIGHTS
FIRST DRAFT

DIRECTIONS: Write a draft for a five-paragraph essay about a "Town Without Lights." It will be easy if you use the information in your brainstorming list.

1. Introduce the topic in your first paragraph. Use the beginning sentences on your brainstorming list. Then add one or two sentences with additional details.
2. Choose three of the headings on your brainstorming list where you have the most details. Then add three paragraphs to your essay. Discuss one subject (HOME, SCHOOL, SHOPPING, TRAVEL, or SPORTS AND RECREATION) in each paragraph. Introduce the topic at the beginning of each paragraph.
3. In your last (fifth) paragraph, state the main topic again and tell how you feel about living in a "Town Without Lights."

(It would be nice if you mention Thomas A. Edison and how his wonderful discovery of October 19, 1879 changed our lives. You can do this in either the first or the last paragraph.)

Write your essay on the lines below. This is just a first draft, so don't be concerned with spelling or grammar. Just concentrate on writing down your thoughts. (Use the back of this worksheet if you need more room.) Indent at the beginning of each paragraph.

TOWN WITHOUT LIGHTS

_____

_____

_____

_____

_____

_____

_____

_____

_____

Name _____ **Date** _____

TOWN WITHOUT LIGHTS
REVISING AND WRITING A FINAL COPY

DIRECTIONS: Revise your first draft. Here are some suggestions for making it better:

1. Does your first paragraph introduce the topic? Sometimes an outrageous question or statement at the beginning can make it more exciting.
2. Do the next three paragraphs *each* discuss one subject? Is it clearly described at the beginning of each paragraph? Can you add details to make these paragraphs more interesting?
3. Does the last paragraph sum up the topic and your feelings about it? Can you add anything that would be fun for the reader to think about?
4. Are your sentences complete? Do subjects and verbs agree?

Write the final copy below. Indent at the beginning of each paragraph. (Use the back of this worksheet if you need more room.)

TOWN WITHOUT LIGHTS

_____

_____

_____

_____

_____

_____

_____

_____

_____

_____

_____

_____

_____

_____

Name _____ Date _____

DICTIONARY WRITER

What do you do when you don't know the meaning of a word or how to spell it? You go to the dictionary, of course!

Dictionaries haven't always been around for us to use. An American educator named Noah Webster was born on October 16, 1758. He compiled *Webster's Dictionary,* one of the best-known dictionaries of the English language.

Can you be a "Noah Webster" and put together your own dictionary?

DIRECTIONS: Write your own definition for each of the words below. (All the words have something to do with the month of October!) When you finish, compare your "dictionary" with those of your classmates. It will be fun to see how your definitions are the same or different.

1. discover _____

2. sail _____

3. Columbus _____

4. baseball _____

5. diamond_____

6. autumn _____

7. tree _____

8. leaves _____

9. sweater _____

10. ghost_____

11. skeleton _____

12. witch_____

13. candy _____

14. party_____

15. trick-or-treat _____

16. Halloween _____

17. mask_____

Name _____ **Date** _____

SPECTATOR SPORTS
PREWRITING

Are you a baseball fan? Do you know when and where the very first World Series took place?

Baseball's first World Series began on October 1, 1903. It was played in Boston between Boston and Pittsburgh. Boston won that Series, 5 games to 3.

Do you know what a spectator sport is? The word *spectator* means someone who watches. A spectator sport is one that people watch. You may play baseball or soccer or basketball yourself, but when you attend a professional game, you become a *spectator*.

Would you rather watch a pro game, or play the sport yourself? Why? Are there things you like about both activities? What are the main differences?

You are going to write a paragraph comparing spectator sports with those that you play yourself. First, you can organize your ideas by preparing a brainstorming list.

DIRECTIONS: Complete the brainstorming list below.

1. In the first column, list your two or three favorite sports to *do*. In the space beneath each sport, write down as many words and phrases you can think of that describe that sport and what it feels like to PLAY.

2. In the second column, list two or three of your favorite sports to *watch*. In the space beneath each, write words and phrases to describe that sport and what it feels like to *watch*.

3. In the third column, write down words and phrases that might be used to describe the *differences* between playing and watching.

BRAINSTORMING LIST		
SPORTS I LIKE TO PLAY	*SPORTS I LIKE TO WATCH*	*DIFFERENCES*
1.	1.	
2.	2.	
3.	3.	

Name _____ **Date** _____

SPECTATOR SPORTS
FIRST DRAFT

Here is a paragraph that one student wrote comparing spectator sports with games he played himself:

> I like to watch professional sports sometimes, but I would much rather be playing. My favorite sports to watch and play are baseball and hockey. I'm a *Devils* fan in hockey and root for the *Yankees* in baseball. It's fun to watch the pros on TV or in the ballpark and see how great athletes perform. It is even more exciting, however, when I feel myself streaking across the ice or facing the pitcher on my own local teams. There is nothing like the thrill of making a goal or smashing a home-run yourself. Spectator sports are okay, but I'm happiest on the field.

DIRECTIONS:

1. Read this paragraph again. Note how the writer:
   - → Introduced the topic in the first sentence. ←
   - → Described his own favorite sports. ←
   - → Compared watching a game with playing it oneself. ←
   - → Summed up the topic in the last sentence. ←

2. On the lines below, write two *possible* beginning sentences for your paragraph:
   _____
   _____

Which sentence introduces the topic in the more interesting way? That's how you will begin the first draft of your paragraph below. Use your brainstorming list to write the rest of your paragraph. Be sure to restate the topic in the last sentence.

> This is just a first draft, so don't be concerned with spelling or grammar. Concentrate on getting your thoughts down on paper.

_____

_____

_____

_____

_____

_____

_____

Name _____ **Date** _____

SPECTATOR SPORTS
REVISING AND WRITING A FINAL COPY

DIRECTIONS: Revise the first draft of your paragraph. Here are some suggestions:

1. Does your first sentence state the topic? Can you think of any words or phrases to make it more interesting?
2. Are your sentences complete? Do subjects and verbs agree?
3. Are there any vivid words or phrases on your brainstorming list that you didn't use? Can you find a place for them in your paragraph?
4. Can you make your writing strong by cutting unnecessary words such as *so*, *very*, *maybe*, *then*?
5. The sample paragraph in Activity 4B used strong, active verbs such as *play*, *root*, *streaking*, *smashing*. Can you replace any of the verbs in your paragraph with strong, more active ones?
6. Check your spelling with a dictionary.

Write the final copy of your paragraph below. Indent at the beginning.

SPECTATOR SPORTS

_____

_____

_____

_____

_____

_____

_____

_____

_____

_____

_____

_____

Name _____ Date _____

SCARY VERSES
PREWRITING

Everyone loves to be scared on Halloween! It is a great time to read spooky stories and poems.

There is a well-known, scary poem called "The Raven." It was written by Edgar Allan Poe. On October 16, 1845, he read this poem for the first time to an audience in Boston. The people hated it so much that they walked out in the middle. Now, "The Raven" is one of the most famous poems ever written. Here are some lines from this poem:

"Once upon a midnight dreary, while I pondered, weak and weary,
Over many a quaint and curious volume of forgotten lore—
While I nodded, nearly napping, suddenly there came a tapping,
As of some one gently rapping, rapping at my chamber door.
'Tis some visitor,' I muttered, 'tapping at my chamber door—
Only this and nothing more.' "
"And the silken, sad, uncertain rustling of each purple curtain
Thrilled me—filled me with fantastic terrors never felt before;"

The visitor turns out to be a huge, black bird. The Raven speaks only one word—"NEVERMORE!" The poet wonders

"What this grim, ungainly, ghastly, gaunt and ominous bird of yore
Meant in croaking 'Nevermore.' "

The bird never explains, just keeps croaking, "NEVERMORE." At the end,

"And the Raven, never flitting, still is sitting, still is sitting
On the pallid bust of Pallas just above my chamber door;
And his eyes have all the seeming of a demon's that is dreaming,
And the lamplight o'er him streaming throws his shadow on the floor;
And my soul from out that shadow that lies floating on the floor
Shall be lifted—nevermore!"

There are a lot of fun words and phrases in this poem that make it scary, such as *midnight dreary*, *rapping*, *tapping*. Can you find at least five more vivid or scary words? Copy them here: _____

_____

You are going to write a poem for Halloween called "The Scary Visitor." The "visitor" in your poem might be a weird bird or animal, a ghost, a skeleton, a witch, or any other scary thing. On the brainstorming list below, write down as many words and phrases you can think of that might help make your poem scary. (You can use some of the same ones as Edgar Allen Poe did.)

BRAINSTORMING LIST OF SCARY WORDS

_____

_____

© 1997 by The Center for Applied Research in Education

Name _____ **Date**_____

Scary Verses
First Draft

Before you begin to write your poem about "A Scary Visitor," it will help if you know in advance what is going to happen. In "The Raven," Edgar Allan Poe tells about someone who hears a strange, tapping on his door that doesn't stop. A huge, black raven flies in, perches on a statue in the room and says, "Nevermore." The person keeps begging the bird to explain what that means, but the bird only keeps repeating, "Nevermore." The man is too terrified to leave and stays there forever with that horrible bird croaking, "Nevermore."

On the lines below, write a short summary of what is going to happen in your poem, like the one above about "The Raven."

_____

_____

_____

Now you are ready to write a first draft of your poem. Follow the summary you just wrote and use the scary words or phrases from your brainstorming list. Your poem can rhyme, like "The Raven," or it doesn't have to rhyme.

This is a first draft, so just concentrate on putting your thoughts and ideas into a poem. (Use the back of this worksheet if you need more room.)

A SCARY VISITOR

_____

_____

_____

_____

_____

_____

_____

_____

_____

Name _____ **Date** _____

Scary Verses
Revising and Writing a Final Copy

DIRECTIONS: Revise the first draft of your poem. Here are some suggestions:

1. Have you made clear to the reader just what is happening? If something is not clear, it might help to add extra lines.
2. Could you add any more suspense at the beginning?
3. Each word counts in a poem! Have you always used the best word or phrase, or can you think of others that might be better?
4. Unnecessary words can cause clutter and confusion. Can you cut any words that do this?
5. Would your poem be more effective with more active verbs, such as *stare, tremble, freeze, shiver, scream, screech, groan,* etc.?
6. Is your poem as *scary* as you can make it?

Write your final copy on the lines below. (If you wish, you can draw illustrations in the margins or at the bottom.)

A SCARY VISITOR

_____

_____

_____

_____

_____

_____

_____

Name _____ **Date** _____

IF I WERE PRESIDENT
PREWRITING

Theodore Roosevelt, the 26th president of the United States, was born on October 27, 1858. He was a forceful and active person with many strong opinions. He worked to pass laws to limit the power of large corporations and provide better conditions for workers. He had a deep interest in ecology and conservation. Under his guidance, millions of acres of forest land were made national forest land, to be preserved and used for the benefit and enjoyment of the public. He wanted the U.S. to be fair but strong in its relations with other nations. His policy was to "speak softly and carry a big stick."

A hundred years later, the U.S. is still faced with some of the same problems as well as new ones. Suppose you were president: What changes would you like to see? How would you do this? Before you write an essay setting out your ideas, you are going to first prepare a brainstorming list. Follow the directions below.

DIRECTIONS: There are two columns in this brainstorming list. In the first column, *list at least three things* you think are wrong in this country and should be changed. In the second column, *list the steps* you would take, as president, to improve these conditions. For example, in the first column you might mention "too much crime." In the second column, you could list possible remedies such as, "build more prisons," "better education," "create more jobs," etc.

Write your brainstorming list below. You don't need sentences—words or phrases are fine. The more ideas you can get down, the easier it will be to write your essay.

BRAINSTORMING LIST

PROBLEMS	STEPS FOR IMPROVEMENT
1. _____	_____
	_____
	_____
2. _____	_____
	_____
	_____
3. _____	_____
	_____
	_____

Name _____ **Date** _____

IF I WERE PRESIDENT
FIRST DRAFT

DIRECTIONS: Write a three-paragraph essay titled "If I Were President." It will be a snap if you use your brainstorming list and follow these directions. (This is just a first draft, so don't worry about spelling or grammar. Concentrate on getting down your ideas.)

FIRST PARAGRAPH—This is the topic paragraph. It introduces the subject. This can be simple and to the point, as *"If I were president, I would try to make this a better country. Some of the problems I would work on are crime, unemployment, and education. Here are some changes I would make."* Or, you can try to make your introduction more interesting with a question or unusual statement in the first sentence like, *"Are you satisfied with conditions in our country? Not me! If I were president, there are lots of things that would be different."* Write your first paragraph below:

_____

_____

SECOND PARAGRAPH—Your second paragraph will describe the changes you plan to make as president. Example: *"The first thing I would do is build more prisons so we can get the criminals off the streets. People have a right to feel safe in their neighborhoods. Then I would make sure that all children have good schools. They need small classes, good teachers, enough books and computers. I would also lower taxes because parents need more money to support their families."* Write your second paragraph below:

_____

_____

_____

_____

LAST PARAGRAPH—The last paragraph restates and sums up the topic. Example: *"This is a great country, but there are still many problems. If I were president, I would see to it that there were less crime, better schools, and lower taxes."* Write your last paragraph below:

_____

_____

Name _____ **Date** _____

If I Were President
Revising and Writing a Final Copy

DIRECTIONS: First, edit and revise your first draft right on the paper. Here are some suggestions for improving your essay.

1. Does your first paragraph clearly state the topic. Could you begin in a more interesting way that will catch the reader's attention?
2. Does your second paragraph give enough details? Can you add anything to make it more persuasive?
3. Does your last paragraph restate and sum up the topic clearly?
4. Are sentences complete? Do subjects and verbs agree?
5. Are your sentences smooth and clearly written? Are there choppy sentences that would be better combined or lengthened? Are any sentences too long?
6. Are there any unnecessary words? Would your writing be clearer if they were removed?
7. Check spelling where necessary.

When your first draft is as good as you can make it, write your final copy below. Indent at the beginning of each paragraph. (Use the back of this worksheet if you need more room.)

IF I WERE PRESIDENT

Name _____ **Date** _____

Breathing Free
Prewriting

> "Give me your tired, your poor,
> Your huddled masses yearning to breathe free."

These lines, written by poet Emma Lazarus, appear on the Statue of Liberty. This remarkable sculpture was a gift to the people of America from the people of France. On October 28, 1886, the Statue of Liberty was dedicated in New York Harbor.

Through the years, "Lady Liberty" with her raised torch has welcomed visitors and immigrants from across the sea. It is an awesome symbol of the country many thought of as a "golden land."

Most of our ancestors came to this continent from somewhere else, seeking a better life. Where did your ancestors come from? Here is what one twelve-year-old wrote:

> My great-grandparents came from Ireland, where they were starving. There was a terrible famine and not enough food. They hoped their lives would be better in America.
>
> At first, they were very poor. They lived in a tiny apartment with their four children. But there was food to eat. They found jobs and worked hard. So did their children.
>
> My family lives in a comfortable house. We cannot imagine what it is like to be starving. I am lucky that my great-grandparents decided to emigrate to this country.

Can you write a short essay about how *your* family came here? It will be easy if you first complete the brainstorming list.

BRAINSTORMING LIST

1. On the line below, list the country or countries where your ancestors lived before coming here.

   _____

2. On the lines below, write two or three sentences to describe what you know about that country and their lives there. (If you listed more than one country for number 1, you can write about all of them or choose just one.)
   (1)_____
   (2)_____
   (3)_____

3. On the lines below, write two or three sentences to describe their lives in this country.
   (1)_____
   (2)_____
   (3)_____

4. Write two or three sentences about your family's life now, and how you feel about this country.
   (1)_____
   (2)_____
   (3)_____

Name _____ **Date** _____

BREATHING FREE
FIRST DRAFT

DIRECTIONS: Write a simple, three-paragraph essay about where your ancestors came from and why they left that country. It will be easy if you follow these directions:

1. This is a first draft, so don't worry about spelling or grammar. Just concentrate on getting down your thoughts.

2. FIRST PARAGRAPH—The first paragraph introduces the topic in an interesting way. Read the first paragraph of the sample letter in Activity 7A. Read your answers to the first two questions on the brainstorming list. Then, write your first paragraph here. (It should contain two to four sentences.)

3. SECOND PARAGRAPH—The first paragraph introduced your ancestors and their homeland. The second paragraph can tell about their lives in this country. Read the second paragraph of the sample letter in Activity 7A. Read your answer to the third question on the brainstorming list. Then write your second paragraph here. (It should contain three to five sentences.)

4. FINAL PARAGRAPH—The final paragraph restates the topic and sums it up. This is a good place for you to describe your own feelings about living in this country. Read the last paragraph of the sample letter. Then, read your answer to the fourth question on the brainstorming list. Write your final paragraph here. (It should contain two to four sentences.)

Name _____ **Date** _____

BREATHING FREE
REVISING AND WRITING A FINAL COPY

DIRECTIONS: Edit and revise your first draft right on the worksheet. Here are some suggestions.

1. Does your first paragraph introduce the topic in an interesting way? Can you think of a beginning sentence that would excite the reader?
2. Does the second paragraph continue and expand the topic? Are there any more interesting details you could add?
3. Does the third paragraph restate and sum up your topic?
4. Can you tighten your writing by cutting unnecessary words?
5. Can you add some colorful adjectives or sensory words to make your writing more vibrant?
6. Can you make your writing more interesting by substituting active verbs for passive ones? (Examples: *leap, fly, creep, dash* instead of *go*; *pat, stroke, punch, rub* instead of *touch*.)
7. Are your sentences complete? Do subjects and verbs agree?
8. Check your spelling!

When your essay is as well-written and interesting as you can make it, write your final copy below. Indent at the beginning of each paragraph. (Use the back of this worksheet if you need more room.)

_____

_____

_____

_____

_____

_____

_____

_____

_____

_____

_____

Name _____ Date_____

OCTOBER BIRTHDAY BASH

Birthday parties are fun! The famous people below were all born in October. Let's celebrate their birthdays with a word game!

How many words can you make using the letters in the names of these well-known people? Write the words on the lines below each name. You can use letters from both the first and last name. Each list of words is your birthday gift to a famous person. The more words you can come up with, the greater the value of your gift.

In case you don't recognize these names, a description of each is included, along with their birthdate. (Do not use the letters in the description. Use only the letters in each name!)

The first is done for you. Can you add any additional words?

1. **Thor Heyerdahl** (Norwegian adventurer and writer who sailed across the ocean on a raft; October 6, 1914)

the, there, they, ore, tore, lore, yore, are, dare, rare, hare, eye, ray, day, hay, lay

ray, tray, had, lad, tad, ear, year, dear, hear, tear, rear, head, lead, tread, eel, heel,

ere, here, hat, that, rat, thread, reed, heed, tree, hard, lard

2. **Jesse Jackson** (American civil rights leader; October 8, 1941)

_____

_____

_____

3. **John Lennon** (British singer and songwriter with The Beatles; October 9, 1940)

_____

_____

_____

4. **Nancy Kerrigan** (American skater and Olympic medal winner; October 13, 1969)

_____

_____

_____

5. **Noah Webster** (compiled *Webster's Dictionary*; October 16, 1758)

_____

_____

_____

6. **Theodore Roosevelt** (26th U.S. President, October 27, 1858)

_____

_____

_____

7. **Jonas Silk** (developed first polio vaccine; October 28, 1914)

_____

_____

_____

Name _____ **Date** _____

DEAR CHRISTOPHER COLUMBUS
PREWRITING

Everybody knows that Christopher Columbus landed in the New World on October 12, 1492. He set out from Spain and sailed across the ocean through dangerous seas when no one thought it could be done. But Columbus didn't know where he was! He thought he had arrived in India. That's why he called the native population "Indians."

That was more than 500 years ago. A lot has changed on the continent he discovered. Wouldn't he be astonished to see the America of today? Well, you are going to tell him about it in a letter. Before you write your letter to Christopher Columbus, you will use this worksheet to organize your ideas into a brainstorming list.

DIRECTIONS:

In the first column below, write all the words and phrases you can think of to describe the world of Columbus's time.

In the second column, write all the words and phrases you can think of to describe the America of today.

BRAINSTORMING LIST	
The World of Columbus	The America of Today

Name _____ Date_____

DEAR CHRISTOPHER COLUMBUS
FIRST DRAFT

DIRECTIONS: Write a letter to Christopher Columbus, describing the differences between his world of 1492 and America today.

Use the brainstorming list you prepared in Activity 9A as a guide. Your letter should have at least three paragraphs.

> In the first paragraph, tell who you are and where you live.
>
> In the second paragraph, describe how America today is very different from the way it was in 1492.
>
> In the third paragraph, tell whether or not you think all these changes are good and why you are happy (or not so happy) to be living in today's world.

Follow the directions below for correct letter form. Be sure to indent at the beginning of each paragraph. (This is just a first draft, so don't worry about spelling or grammar. Just concentrate on getting down your ideas.)

(Write your street address here)

(Write City, State, ZIP here)

(Write today's date here)

Christopher Columbus
The World of 1492

Dear Christopher Columbus,

Your friend,

(Write your name here)

Name _____ **Date** _____

DEAR CHRISTOPHER COLUMBUS
REVISING AND WRITING A FINAL COPY

DIRECTIONS: Edit and revise the first draft of your letter to Christopher Columbus. Here are some suggestions:

1. Did you introduce yourself in the first paragraph? Is there any way you can make the beginning more interesting?
2. Did you describe the differences between the world of 1492 and today in your second paragraph? Can you change any words or phrases to make it more exciting?
3. Did you sum up your own feelings in the third paragraph?
4. Is your writing clear? Can you cut unnecessary words?
5. Are your sentences complete? Do subjects and verbs agree?
6. Check your spelling.

Write the final copy of your letter below. Use correct letter form as shown in Activity 9B. Indent at the beginning of each paragraph.

Name _____ **Date** _____

ACE REPORTER
PREWRITING

On October 23, 1915, 25,000 women marched in New York City demanding the right to vote. Does it seem possible that half the U.S. population could not vote as late as the twentieth century?

The fact is that it was not until 1920 that Congress passed the 19th Amendment to the Constitution that gave women the vote.

Before this victory was achieved, there were many marches like that October one in New York City. The women who took part in them were called *suffragettes*. ("Suffrage" means the right to vote.)

The suffragettes were front-page news. Journalists today report on current topics of interest. In this activity, you are going to write a news article about a recent event. It should be something that happened recently in your town or neighborhood or school.

A good reporter makes notes before writing an article. This is what you are going to do. Follow the instructions below.

NEWS NOTES

1. Write a one-sentence description of a recent event in your school or neighborhood or town. Don't include any details—just one sentence covering the main point. (Examples: "There was a bomb scare at our school last Thursday." **or** "A teenager on my street won an award from the Governor on Friday for saving two children from drowning." **or** "A new town law goes into effect next week saying that people can no longer burn leaves on their property." Write your sentence here: _____

_____

2. The beginning of a news article is called the *lead*. It answers the questions WHO?, WHAT?, WHEN?, WHERE? by stating briefly WHO did WHAT, WHEN it happened, and WHERE. A good reporter tries to grab the reader's interest by making the beginning interesting or exciting. The sentences above could be changed into more interesting leads, as follows: "We're still in shock!' said Robert Sills, a student at the Park Street School, referring to the bomb scare there last Thursday." **or** "Who says that young people are irresponsible? Not the Governor, who presented an award at Town Hall on Friday to a Stanley Street teenager." **or** "Homeowners who burn leaves on their property will have to find a new way to dispose of them or face prosecution, according to a town law that goes into effect next week." Write a new lead for your article in one or two sentences. Use the information in the sentence above but try to introduce it in a more exciting way._____

_____

_____

3. List more details about the news event—exactly what happened, describe the people involved and what they said. You don't need sentences—words and phrases are good enough _____

_____

Name _____ **Date** _____

ACE REPORTER
FIRST DRAFT

The news notes you made in Activity 10A will make it easy to write your news article. First, check the lead you wrote for question #2 in your news notes. Does it tell WHO? WHAT? WHEN? WHERE? in an interesting way? If so, copy it here as your first paragraph.

_____

_____

The second paragraph of your news article will add additional important details. Here is an example.

"At a luncheon ceremony attended by officials and a cheering crowd of neighbors, Governor Watt presented sixteen-year-old Jim Wood with a Good Citizenship Award for his courage and quick thinking last August when he saved two toddlers from drowning. Jim noticed four-year-old Troy Potts and his two-year-old brother, Sean, playing near a stream that runs behind their townhouse development. When he realized the boys were no longer in sight, Jim rushed over, saw them struggling in the water, and jumped in to pull them to safety."

Select the most important details from number 3 in your news notes and write the second paragraph of your article in three or four sentences. (This is a first draft so don't be concerned with spelling or grammar. Just concentrate on getting down your thoughts.)

_____

_____

_____

_____

The last paragraph of a news article does not sum up a topic as in an essay. It just continues telling more about the story. In a news story, the least important details come at the end. That way, if there is not enough room for the whole article, the editor can cut out the end without omitting important facts. Your final paragraph might include some quotations from people involved, descriptions of them, or more details about the event itself. Write your final paragraph here. It should contain two to five sentences.

_____

_____

Name _____ **Date**_____

ACE REPORTER
REVISING AND WRITING A FINAL COPY

DIRECTIONS: Edit and revise the first draft of your news article. Here are some suggestions:

1. Readers like articles that are clear and to the point. Are there any unnecessary words you can cut from your story?
2. Can you make your article more exciting by using strong, active verbs, such as *leap, plunge, shout, jump, rush,* etc.?
3. Is your lead interesting and exciting enough to "hook" the reader? Does it answer the questions WHO?, WHAT?, WHEN?, WHERE?
4. Are the details of your story in order of importance—most important, first; least important, last?
5. Are your sentences complete? Have you checked all spelling?

Write the final copy of your news article below. First, write a short, exciting headline, using at least one active verb. (Example: Governor presents award to teenage hero.)

Indent at the beginning of each paragraph. Use the back of this worksheet if you need more room.

_____

_____

_____

_____

_____

_____

_____

_____

_____

_____

_____

Name _____ Date _____

SPOOKY SKELETONS

What would the English language be like without *adjectives?* It would be a lot less fun! There would be no way to describe things as they really are. "Busy, noisy, city street" tells a lot more than "street." The reader can picture a "cluttered, dusty, wooden desk" a lot better than "desk."

Halloween is a time for lots of exciting adjectives. *Spooky, scary, terrifying*—these are just a few adjectives that fit this trick-or-treat holiday.

How many Halloween adjectives can you think of? List them in the box below. Try to come up with at least ten.

Adjectives are usually attached to *nouns.* Here are a list of Halloween nouns. Attach one adjective in front of each noun. You can use adjectives from the box above, or choose new ones.

1. _____ Halloween

2. _____ skeleton

3. _____ jack-o'-lantern

4. _____ ghost

5. _____ candy

6. _____ pumpkin

7. _____ devil

8. _____ witch

9. _____ ghoul

10. _____ broomstick

11. _____ bonfire

12. _____ costume

Name _____ **Date**_____

MORE SPOOKY SKELETONS

Most stories would be boring without adjectives. In Activity 11A, you came up with lots of adjectives for Halloween. Can you use these adjectives (and others) to make this story more interesting?

DIRECTIONS: Circle every noun in the story below. Then, copy the complete story, putting at least one adjective in front of each noun that you circled.

Ken and his friend, Luke, were out on Halloween. Their bags were almost full. Suddenly, Luke stopped.

"I'm not going into that house!" he said.

"Why not?"

"My sister told me it's haunted." Luke shook his head. "I don't want to see ghosts."

"Get real!" said Ken. "There are no such things as ghosts."

"Oh, no? What's that?" Luke pointed to a shadow on the porch of the house."

Ken's eyes widened. "It looks like a ghost!"

The shadow moved. It came down the steps. A moan seemed to come from its head.

The boys were too scared to move. The shape came closer. It shouted, "Boo!" and ripped off its sheet. It laughed and laughed because it wasn't a ghost at all. It was Luke's sister, Laurie.

Copy this story, putting at least one adjective before each noun.

_____

_____

_____

_____

_____

_____

_____

_____

_____

Name _____ **Date** _____

Good as Gold
Sentences

A *simile* is a comparison, using the words *as* or *like*. Here are some common similes:

cold as ice; green as grass; sweet as sugar

Similes that are not so common are even more interesting:

cold as the peak of Mt. McKinley; green as my brother's face after he ate a worm; sweet as chocolate ice cream on a hot summer day

The following sentences all have something to do with the month of October. Can you complete each, using a simile?

1. In the fall, I am as busy as _____.

2. My Halloween candy was as delicious as _____.

3. I got as excited as _____ when I watched the World Series.

4. Some autumn leaves are as yellow as _____.

5. Thomas A. Edison must have been as smart as _____ to have invented the electric light on October 19, 1879.

6. Columbus was as brave as _____ to have sailed across the ocean in a sailing ship.

7. During a storm, the *Santa Maria* must have tossed upon the ocean like _____.

8. If I had been on that rolling ship, I would have been as frightened as _____.

9. Halloween parties are as much fun as _____.

10. On a crisp October day, I wear a sweater that is as warm as _____.

11. Autumn leaves are as colorful as _____.

12. Sometimes, October evenings are as cold as _____.

13. Apple cider tastes as cool and sweet as _____.

© 1997 by The Center for Applied Research in Education

Name _____ Date_____

GOOD AS GOLD
PARAGRAPHS

DIRECTIONS: The following paragraphs could be improved by adding similes. Copy each paragraph below, adding at least three similes to each. (You can use similes you wrote for Activity 12A or make up new ones.)

In 1492, it was commonly believed that the Earth was flat. Christopher Columbus said it was round. Lots of people thought he was crazy. Columbus set out to prove he was right by sailing westward across the Atlantic ocean. They warned him that he would topple off the edge of the Earth. But Columbus was brave and confident. The journey was dangerous, but he kept going. On October 12, land was sighted. Columbus and his crew safely landed in the New World.

_____

_____

_____

_____

_____

_____

October is a great month. Everyone seems to be busy. The weather gets cool. The trees are colorful. Some leaves turn brown. Others are gold or red. Sometimes there are bonfires. You can't go too close because the flames are hot. Halloween comes at the end of October. I get excited waiting for it. Our pumpkin is always big. Trick-or-treating is exciting. It is scary, but fun.

Name _____ Date _____

ROCKETING TO NEW WORLDS
PREWRITING

On October 12, 1492, Christopher Columbus landed in the New World. Nowadays we travel across the ocean easily on planes or huge ships. In 1492, it was a dangerous trip. The ships were tiny, easily overturned by the great waves of the Atlantic. Columbus and his crews braved the fury of the ocean and discovered a New World.

New worlds of the twentieth and twenty-first centuries are out in space. Would you like to be a modern Columbus and discover one? Perhaps you will someday, but for now, your imagination is enough. In this activity, you are going to write a story about an expedition into space to discover new worlds. It will be easy to do if you first prepare a brainstorming list by following the directions below.

BRAINSTORMING LIST

1. Write a title for your story here. You can make one up or use one of these: *Rocketing to New Worlds*; *Journey Into the Unknown*; *Raider of Lost Planets*; *Out of the Galaxy*.

    Your Title: _____

2. Choose one main character. Tell that character's name and what he or she does. (Examples: Angus McGuff, pilot; Laurel White, scientist; etc.)

    Name: _____ Job: _____

3. Describe your main character. (You don't need complete sentences here, just words and phrases. _____

    _____

4. Decide on two more characters. One should be *good*. The other should be *bad*. Write in a name for each character. Next to that, list words and phrases to describe him or her.

    GOOD CHARACTER—Name: _____
    Description: _____

    BAD CHARACTER—Name: _____
    Description: _____

5. THE JOURNEY: Write a list of words and phrases describing possible events on the trip. (Examples: getting lost, something breaking on spaceship, fights onboard; illness; etc.) _____

    _____

6. NEW WORLD: Give a name to the new world discovered. Write as many words and phrases as you can think of to describe it.

    NAME OF NEW WORLD: _____

    DESCRIPTION: _____

    _____

Name _____ **Date** _____

ROCKETING TO NEW WORLDS
FIRST DRAFT

GETTING STARTED: Often, the most difficult part of writing a story is getting started. Here are some sample beginnings for a story about discovering new worlds in space. You can use one of these beginnings, or create one of your own.

Without any warning, the ship suddenly began to shake and bobble. Kate was flung into a corner.

"What's happening?" Kate rubbed her head where it had banged against a wall.

Mike, the lead pilot, shook his head. "I don't know." He struggled with the controls. "We're too close now for anything to go wrong."

The takeoff was perfect. Angus unbuckled his seat belt and set the controls on automatic pilot.

"We're on our way," he said.

Jason Friend, the navigator, gave a thumbs-up sign. Dr. Laurel White, the anthropologist, grinned. These three were the complete crew.

DIRECTIONS: Write a first draft of your story. Begin with one of the examples above or make up your own. Then, use the information on the brainstorming list you prepared in Activity 13A to go on with your story. This is just a first draft, so don't be concerned about spelling or grammar—just concentrate on getting your thoughts down on paper. Use the back of this worksheet if you need more room. (Write your title on the first line.)

_____

_____

_____

_____

_____

_____

_____

_____

_____

Name _____   **Date** _____

ROCKETING TO NEW WORLDS
REVISING AND WRITING A FINAL COPY

DIRECTIONS: Edit and revise your first draft right on the paper. Here are some suggestions:

1. Does the beginning grab the reader's attention? Can you make it more exciting?
2. Are each of the characters clearly described? Are their personalities and characters shown by what they say and do? Can you add anything that will make this clear to the reader?
3. Are the thoughts and feelings of the main characters shown?
4. Can you add striking adjectives to make a scene more vivid?
5. Would the action be more exciting with strong, active verbs?
6. Are all sentences complete? Do subjects and verbs agree?
7. Check spelling.

Write the final copy below. Indent at the beginning of each paragraph. Write the title on the first line. (Use the back of the worksheet if you need more room.)

_____

_____

_____

_____

_____

_____

_____

_____

_____

_____

_____

_____

Name _____ Date_____

Hero Worship
Prewriting

October 18 is the birthday of Martina Navratilova, one of the greatest tennis players of all time. She was born in Czechoslovakia in 1956 and was ranked the number-one tennis player there by 1972. She moved to the U.S., became a citizen in 1981, and continued to set records, winning all major tennis competitions. Her courage and skill are an inspiration. For many young athletes, she is a heroine.

Is there anyone you want to be like, who inspires you to become the best you can be? It might be somebody famous, but it could also be a friend, teacher, or someone in your family. This person would like to know how you feel. In this activity, you are going to write a letter to one of your heroes. Here is one written by a seventh grader:

```
                                                        25 Elm Street
                                                        Benton, NJ 05893
                                                        October 20, _____

Matthew Gallo
25 Elm Street
Benton, NJ 05893

Dear Matt,

    Hi! I'll bet you're wondering why you are getting a letter from "the
pest." I know that's what you call me. I guess I am a pest. You can be a
big pain, too, sometimes, but most of the time, you are okay.
    That's why I'm writing this letter. It's to let you know that even
though we fight a lot, I really think you're the best. It's not just that
you are popular and great at sports, which you are. It's mostly the way you
always have time to show me how to do things and how to solve my problems.
I know we fight a lot, but the next time I'm being a pest, remember that
you are my hero.
                                                        Your brother,

                                                        Luke
```

Before writing your letter, it will help to organize your thoughts by answering these questions.

1. Write your hero's name and address here:_____

_____

2. List the things he or she does that are important to you:_____

_____

_____

3. Write a beginning sentence for your letter: _____

_____

_____

Name _____   **Date** _____

HERO WORSHIP
FIRST DRAFT

DIRECTIONS: Your answers to the questions in Activity 14A will help you organize and write a letter to your hero. Use correct letter form, as shown in the example in Activity 14A. The directions below will also help you get the letter form correct. Begin the message with the sentence you wrote for question #3. This is a first draft, so just concentrate on getting your thoughts down.

_____ (Write your street address here)

_____ (Write City, State, ZIP here)

_____ (Write today's date here)

_____ (Write your hero's name here)

_____ (Street address here)

_____ (City, state, ZIP here)

Dear _____ :

_____

_____

_____

_____

_____

_____

_____

_____

_____

_____ (Write closing here)

Name _____ **Date**_____

Hero Worship
Revising and Writing a Final Copy

DIRECTIONS: You want your letter to your hero to be just right! Revise your first draft carefully! Here are suggestions for improvement.

---

1. Do you begin by telling who you are and why you are writing this letter? This would make a good first paragraph.
2. Do you clearly state why you admire this person? Are there any reasons you left out? If so, insert them now. This would make a good second paragraph.
3. In your last paragraph, do you sum up who you are and what you admire about this person?
4. Did you follow correct letter form as shown in the example in Activity 14A and the directions in 14B?
5. Did you indent at the beginning of each paragraph?
6. Sometimes too many words are confusing. Can you make your meaning clearer by cutting unnecessary words?
7. Are your sentences complete? Do subjects and verbs agree?
8. If you are not completely sure about spelling, check with a dictionary.

When your letter is as clear and well-written as possible, write a final copy. Use a separate sheet of paper, so that you can mail this letter if you wish to do so.

Be sure to use correct letter form.

NOVEMBER

NOVEMBER

"November's sky is chill and drear,
November's leaf is dead and sear."
—Sir Walter Scott

> POLITICAL CAMPAIGNS CULMINATE WITH ELECTION DAY (FIRST TUES-
> DAY AFTER FIRST MONDAY) ... THE CHILL OF LATE AUTUMN ... BOUN-
> TIFUL HARVESTS ... BONFIRES AND FOOTBALL GAMES ... VETERANS
> DAY (NOVEMBER 11) ... PILGRIMS AND INDIANS ... THANKSGIVING
> (FOURTH THURSDAY) ... JOYS AND FAMILY TOGETHERNESS

NOVEMBER EVENTS

November 2, 1936: The world's first regular high-definition TV service was started by
the British Broadcasting Corporation, beginning the modern TV age

November 7, 1916: Jeanette Rankin of Montana became the first female member of
Congress

November 8, 1966: Edward Brooke of Massachusetts became the first African-
American senator in U.S. history

November 19, 1863: Abraham Lincoln delivered the Gettysburg Address

November 21, 1877: Thomas A. Edison announced his invention of a "talking machine"
(the phonograph)

November 22, 1963: President John F. Kennedy was shot at 12:30 P.M. in Dallas, Texas
while riding in a motorcade; he died at 1 P.M.

November 29, 1641: The first English newspaper was published.

NOVEMBER BIRTHDAYS

November 2, 1734: Daniel Boone, American frontiersman and hunter

November 10, 1483: Martin Luther, German religious reformer who began the
Reformation

November 12, 1961: Nadia Comaneci, Romanian gymnast who won three Olympic
gold medals at age 14

November 14, 1948: Prince Charles of England

November 25, 1914: Joe DiMaggio, American baseball star

November 29, 1832: Louisa May Alcott, author of *Little Women*

November 30, 1835: Mark Twain (born Samuel Langhorne Clemens), author of *Tom
Sawyer* and *Huckleberry Finn*

WRITING ACTIVITIES FOR NOVEMBER

Name _____ **Date** _____

LAST LEAF ON THE TREE
PREWRITING

Do plants have feelings? Some experiments indicate that this might be true. Flowers seem to grow better when they are cared for lovingly and spoken to with affection. Plants, flowers, and trees aren't able to tell us how they feel, but maybe we can guess.

> How do you think you would feel if you were a leaf in November when most trees are becoming bare?
> How would the cold autumn breezes feel on your "leafskin"?
> What would you think about while all the other leaves were falling?
> How might it feel to be the last leaf left on the tree?
> And what about when your stem snaps loose and you begin to drop down, down to the ground?

You're going to write a paragraph as though you were this last leaf. It will be easier to write if you first prepare a brainstorming list.

DIRECTIONS: The Brainstorming list below is divided into four sections.

In the *first section*, write all the words and phrases you can think of that could describe how cold autumn winds might feel to a leaf.

In the *second section*, write words and phrases to describe a leaf's thoughts while all the other leaves are falling.

In the *third section*, write words and phrases to describe the feelings and thoughts of the last leaf on the tree.

In the *fourth section*, write words and phrases to describe how it feels to snap off the tree and drop down to the ground.

BRAINSTORMING LIST

1. (COLD, AUTUMN WINDS):

_____

2. (OTHER LEAVES FALLING):

_____

3. (LAST LEAF ON THE TREE):

_____

4. (FALLING DOWN TO THE GROUND):

_____

Name _____ **Date** _____

Last Leaf on the Tree
First Draft

DIRECTIONS: Write a paragraph telling how it feels to be the last leaf on the tree. Use the words and phrases from your brainstorming list. Here are suggestions that will make this paragraph easy to write:

1. Introduce the topic in your first sentence (or sentences). Here are some possible ways to begin: "It's tough to be the last leaf on the tree." "I spent a happy spring and summer with my brother and sister leaves. How could I have known that I would lose them in the fall?"

   You can use one of these beginnings. It would be even better if you made up one of your own.
2. The next sentence might tell about the cold winds of autumn. Then, describe your feelings as the other leaves begin to fall. What are your thoughts when you are the last leaf left on the tree? Then, tell how it feels to break loose and drop down to the ground.
3. Your last sentence should sum up the topic. Here are some examples: "I sank into the soft ground knowing that the last leaf had finally fallen." "The last leaf on the tree had finally joined its brothers and sisters." You can use one of these endings or make up one of your own.

Write your paragraph below. This is only a first draft, so don't be concerned with spelling or grammar. Concentrate on organizing and writing your ideas.

LAST LEAF ON THE TREE

_____

_____

_____

_____

_____

_____

_____

_____

Name _____ **Date** _____

LAST LEAF ON THE TREE
REVISING AND WRITING A FINAL COPY

DIRECTIONS: Here are some things to look for when revising your first draft.

1. Does the beginning state the topic in an interesting way?
2. Is the rest of the paragraph arranged in a logical order?
3. Are some sentences too long and rambling? Would they be sharper if you shortened them?
4. Can you add any vivid adjectives to describe the appearance of the leaves and trees?
5. Do you clearly show the thoughts and feelings of this leaf? Could anything be added to make it more real?
6. Are your sentences complete? Do subjects and verbs agree?
7. Does your last sentence restate and sum up the topic?

Write the final copy of your paragraph below.

LAST LEAF ON THE TREE

_____

_____

_____

_____

_____

_____

_____

_____

_____

_____

_____

Name _____ **Date** _____

VOTE FOR JOE!
PREWRITING

ELECTION DAY in the United States always falls on the first Tuesday after the first Monday in November. In this country, the government is elected by the people. That's not true everywhere. In many parts of the world, the people have no power. They must obey a government and laws they did not choose.

Good citizens vote for their representatives, but first they find out as much as they can about the candidates.

You can begin practicing good citizenship by taking an interest in your school elections. Sometimes a school newspaper can be a good way to find out about those who are running for office.

The Lawrence Middle School is holding an election. Two candidates are running for president of the School Council. Their names are Joey Lassiter and Joanne Merino. You are going to write an *editorial* about them for the school newspaper.

An editorial is an *opinion article*. In this editorial, you are going to:

1. Describe the candidates and their qualifications.
2. Announce which candidate you recommend.
3. Explain why you have made this choice.

Before you can write this editorial, you will first have to decide who these people are, what they are like, and why you think one is better suited for the job. You can organize your information by answering the questions below. Include as many details as you can. (This information is just to help you write the article. You don't have to use complete sentences—words and phrases are fine.)

---

1. Who is Joey Lassiter? (age, grade, class, personality, character, interests, hobbies, accomplishments in and out of school, etc.)

2. Who is Joanne Merino? (age, grade, class, personality, character, interests, hobbies, accomplishments in and out of school, etc.)

3. Which one would be a better Student Council president? Why? (Give at least two reasons—three or four would be even better.)

Name _____ **Date** _____

VOTE FOR JOE!
FIRST DRAFT

DIRECTIONS: You are going to write an editorial (opinion article) about the upcoming election for president of the Student Council of the Lawrence Middle School. Your editorial should have two goals:

1. to give students all the information they need about *both* candidates, and
2. to recommend your choice for Student Council president and give your reasons for that decision.

Your editorial will be easy to write if you organize it as follows:

1. In the *first paragraph*, introduce the topic, your reason for writing abut it, and your choice. Here is one possible beginning: "We have an important election coming up at our school next week. Two excellent candidates are running for president of the Student Council. We believe that Joanne Merino would be the better choice."
2. In the *second paragraph*, describe one of the candidates, using the information you compiled in Activity 2A.
3. In the *third paragraph*, describe the other candidate.
4. In the *last paragraph*, list the reasons for your choice and sum up your article.

Write your editorial below. This is only a first draft, so just concentrate on getting down your ideas. Indent at the beginning of each paragraph. (Use the back of this worksheet if you need more room.)

_____

_____

_____

_____

_____

_____

_____

_____

_____

Name_____ **Date**_____

Vote for Joe!
Revising and Writing a Final Copy

DIRECTIONS: Here are some ideas for revising your first draft.

---

1. Does the first paragraph introduce the topic in an interesting way? Sometimes a question or humor can make the beginning better. Does your first paragraph state your choice for election?
2. Do you describe both candidates fully in the following paragraphs? Can you think of any additional personal details?
3. Do you give several *good reasons* for your choice in the final paragraph? Can you add anything that would make it stronger?
4. Are your sentences complete? Do subjects and verbs agree?
5. Are any sentences too long and rambling? If so, cut them.
6. Check spelling with a dictionary.

Write the final copy of your editorial below. Indent at the beginning of each paragraph. (Use the back of this worksheet if you need more room.)

_____

_____

_____

_____

_____

_____

_____

_____

_____

_____

_____

_____

_____

Name _____ **Date** _____

TAKE A POLL!
PREWRITING

What does the public think about issues and people in the news? Polls are one way to find out. It's fun to watch the polls before Election Day. Almost every day, a new poll appears, telling which candidate is ahead and by how many points.

Polls are used for many purposes in addition to elections. People are asked what TV programs they watch and what brand of clothes they prefer. In this activity, *you* are going to be a polltaker and discover trends among people you know.

Everyone is interested in FOOD! That is what your poll will be about. You can do this poll with your friends and classmates, with family and neighbors, or any combination. You must include at least ten people in your poll; twenty would be even better. The greater the number, the more accurate your poll will be.

Ask each person the following questions. Put a check (✓) next to an item each time it is chosen.

FOOD POLL

1. WHAT IS YOUR FAVORITE ICE CREAM FLAVOR?

vanilla _____	rocky road _____
chocolate _____	chocolate chip _____
strawberry _____	other _____

2. WHAT IS YOUR FAVORITE MEAL?

pizza _____	hamburgers _____
tacos _____	pasta _____
hot dogs _____	chicken _____
sandwich _____	other _____

3. WHAT IS YOUR FAVORITE DRINK?

soda _____	cola _____
milk _____	chocolate milk _____
juice _____	other _____

4. WHAT IS YOUR FAVORITE FRUIT?

grapes _____	bananas _____
apples _____	pears _____
oranges _____	grapefruit _____
cherries _____	other _____

Now, count up the number of checks and write the total next to each item. Then, move ahead to Activity 3B.

Name _____ **Date** _____

TAKE A POLL!
FIRST DRAFT

Congratulations! You have completed your assignment as a polltaker! Now you are going to write an article about it. This is a first draft, so just concentrate on getting your ideas down.

The first paragraph states the topic (food preference poll) in an exciting way that will make the reader want to continue, as in this example:

> Would it amaze you to know that seventh graders like grapes better than bananas or apples? That was the result of a recent poll of fifteen students in Mr. Murdoch's 7C homeroom. Some of their other food choices were just as surprising.

Write your first paragraph here:

_____

_____

_____

The second paragraph gives details, as in this example:

> Grapes were the favorite fruit of eight people. Bananas and apples each received three votes, and only one person chose oranges. Pizza came in as the overwhelming food favorite, getting twelve out of fifteen votes. Soda and colas tied for favorite drink, far ahead of all others. As for ice cream, something we all love, chocolate narrowly edged out rocky road seven to six. Vanilla and strawberry were far behind with only one vote each.

Write your second paragraph here:

_____

_____

_____

The last paragraph restates and sums up the topic, as in this example:

> It wasn't hard to get seventh graders to take part in this poll. They liked talking about food. They all had strong opinions about their favorites. Some of the results, like favorite fruit, were surprising, but most were what we expected.

Write your last paragraph here:

_____

_____

_____

Name _____ **Date** _____

TAKE A POLL!
ADVISING AND WRITING A FINAL COPY

DIRECTIONS:

1. Revise and edit your first draft right on the worksheet:

> a. Does the *first paragraph* introduce the topic (taking a poll on food preferences)? Can you make the beginning more interesting with a question or startling statement?
>
> b. Does the *second paragraph* supply details? Are there any unnecessary or boring details that could be deleted? Did you omit any important or exciting details?
>
> c. Does the *last paragraph* restate and sum up the poll and its results?
>
> d. Do you have a variety of long and short sentences? If ALL the sentences are too long, shorten a few. If ALL the sentences are too short, combine some of them.
>
> e. Are all sentences complete? Do subjects and verbs agree?
>
> f. Check spelling with a dictionary where you are unsure.

2. Write the final copy of your article below. Indent at the beginning of each paragraph. (Use the back of this worksheet if you need more room.)

_____

_____

_____

_____

_____

_____

_____

_____

_____

_____

_____

Name _____ Date_____

A Sense-Ative Place
Prewriting

Everybody has places that are special where they like to visit, to see things, or just to get away by themselves. Some of these spots are great only at certain seasons of the year, like a beach in summer or ski slope in winter.

Do you have a place that's especially nice in November? It's great to play in the cool, crisp outdoors, but maybe you like the warmth of a fire on cold evenings.

Ask yourself, "Where would I like to be on a bright November day?" "Why do I like to go there?" Try to picture this place in your mind. Then, think about how this place affects each of your five senses.

SIGHT, SOUND, SMELL, TOUCH, TASTE

Think about things that you **see** in this place, and list some of them below:

Now, think about sounds you can **hear** in this special place. List them below:

Are there any special odors or **smells** in your special place? It might be something you never even think about, like the smell of dusty boxes. List these smells below:

What can you **feel** or **touch** in this place? Is there a special breeze on your skin or face? What can your hands touch? List these below:

Are there any special **tastes** connected with this place? It might be ice cream at a carnival or toasted marshmallows at a bonfire. List these tastes below:

Name _____ Date _____

A SENSE-ATIVE PLACE
FIRST DRAFT

DIRECTIONS: Write a paragraph about a special place where you like to be in November. Describe how this place affects each of your five senses. Use the lists you wrote in Activity 4A.

Organize your paragraph as follows:

1. Begin by naming your special place and telling where it is.
2. Use one or two sentences for *each* of your senses. First, tell what you see, then what you hear, then smell, then touch, then taste. There will be at least five sentences describing these sensory experiences.
3. The last sentence should again state what this special place is and, perhaps, why you like it so much.

Write your paragraph below. This is only a first draft, so don't worry about mistakes in spelling or grammar. Just write down your ideas as quickly as you can. (Use the back of this worksheet if you need more space.)

_____

_____

_____

_____

_____

_____

_____

_____

_____

_____

_____

_____

_____

Name _____ Date _____

A Sense-Ative Place
Revising and Writing a Final Copy

DIRECTIONS: Here are some ideas for revising the first draft of your paragraph about your special place.

1. Does your first sentence introduce the topic? Can you think of any way to make it more interesting?
2. Are there any words or phrases you can add to show how this place affects your five senses?
3. Are all your sentences complete? Do subjects and verbs agree?
4. Check spelling with a dictionary.

Write the final copy of your paragraph here. (Use the back of this worksheet if you need more space.) If you wish, you can use the box at the bottom of this worksheet to draw a picture of your special place.

_____

_____

_____

_____

_____

_____

_____

_____

_____

Name _____ **Date** _____

A World Without TV
Prewriting

Can you imagine a world without TV? Sounds impossible, doesn't it? Yet, the fact is that before 1936, most people on Earth had never heard the word "television."

Everything changed on November 2 of that year, when the world's first high-definition TV service was started by the British Broadcasting Corporation. This was the beginning of the modern TV age.

What if that had never happened? *What if* no inventor had ever come up with the idea of TV? *What if* no one had ever been successful in making it work? How would life be different today? Would the world be worse? Are there ways in which life would actually be better?

In this activity, you are going to write an essay about this "world without TV." First, organize your thoughts and ideas by preparing a brainstorming list, as follows:

1. In the first space, list as many things you can think of that would be different without TV.
2. In the second space, list ways in which life might be worse.
3. In the third space, list ways in which life might be better.

BRAINSTORMING LIST

1. THINGS THAT WOULD BE DIFFERENT WITHOUT TV:

2. WAYS IN WHICH LIFE MIGHT BE WORSE:

3. WAYS IN WHICH LIFE MIGHT BE BETTER:

Name _____ **Date** _____

A World Without TV
First Draft

DIRECTIONS: Use the brainstorming list you prepared for Activity 5A to write a 4-paragraph essay about a world without TV. On this page, you will write a first draft. Concentrate on getting down your thoughts.

In the first paragraph, introduce the topic in an interesting way, as in this example:

> Is it possible that a time existed when people lived without TV? It doesn't seen believable, but before 1936, there was no such thing as television broadcasting. What would our lives be like if TV had never been invented?

Write your first paragraph here:

_____

_____

_____

In the second paragraph, describe how your life might be worse, using the ideas from your brainstorming list. Write your second paragraph here:

_____

_____

_____

In the third paragraph, describe how your life might be better. Use the ideas from your brainstorming list. Write your third paragraph now:

_____

_____

_____

In the fourth paragraph, restate and sum up the topic, as in this example:

> The invention of television changed the world. It made life better in lots of ways. It also created new problems. For good or bad, however, we now live in the television age.

Write your fourth (last) paragraph here:

_____

_____

_____

Name _____ **Date** _____

A World Without TV
Revising and Writing a Final Copy

DIRECTIONS: Revise and edit your first draft. Here are some suggestions:

---

1. Does your first paragraph introduce the topic? Can you make it more interesting so the reader will want to continue?
2. Does your second paragraph show how the world would be worse without TV? Can you think of anything to add?
3. Does your third paragraph tell about problems that have been created by TV?
4. Does your last paragraph restate the topic and sum it up?
5. Are your sentences complete? Do subjects and verbs agree?
6. Are you positive all words are spelled correctly?

Write the final copy of your essay below. Indent at the beginning of each paragraph. Use the back of this worksheet if you need more room.

A WORLD WITHOUT TV

_____

_____

_____

_____

_____

_____

_____

_____

_____

_____

_____

Name _____ **Date** _____

A 21st-Century Invention
Prewriting

Do you enjoy listening to your stereo, your tapes, or your CD? These things did not exist for most of the time that mankind has been on the Earth. We can thank Thomas A. Edison for starting the whole world listening to recorded music. It happened on November 19, 1863. That was when he announced his invention of a "talking machine." Later, it was called a phonograph, then a record player, then a hi-fi, then a stereo.

Edison invented many things that changed the way people lived. He was always coming up with new ideas. What do you think Edison might invent if he lived today? What new creations could he think up for the people of the upcoming 21st century?

What do *you* think people need today that they don't have? How about a robot teacher programmed with every bit of information known on a particular subject? Would you like to own a vision enhancer that enables you to see through solid objects like walls? What if someone invented a time machine and people could travel back and ahead through time?

You are going to write an essay about an invention for the 21st century. This will be easier if you prepare a brainstorming list first.

BRAINSTORMING LIST

DIRECTIONS:

1. Think of an idea for an invention for the 21st century. You can choose one of the examples above, or, even better, come up with one of your own.

   → WRITE THE NAME OF YOUR INVENTION HERE: _____ ←

2. There are two columns in the chart below.

   In the *first column*, write all the words and phrases you can think of that describe your invention. Give as many details as possible. You don't need sentences here—just words and phrases.

   In the *second column*, write down what sort of people would use your invention and list as many reasons you can think of why your invention would be useful.

DESCRIPTION	USEFULNESS

Name _____ Date _____

A 21ST-CENTURY INVENTION
FIRST DRAFT

DIRECTIONS: Write a 4-paragraph essay about your 21st-century invention. Keep your brainstorming list in front of you and follow these directions. (This is just a first draft, so don't be concerned with spelling or grammar; just concentrate on getting down your thoughts.)

The *first paragraph* introduces the topic in an interesting way, as in this example: "Wouldn't it be thrilling to take a trip into the past and walk the streets that your ancestors traveled centuries ago? Even better, how would you like to be able to see the world of the future? You can experience both of these exciting adventures in a time machine."
Write your first paragraph here (2 to 4 sentences):

_____

_____

The *second paragraph* describes the invention in detail, as in this example: "The time machine looks like a combination automobile and electric chair. The outside is made of indestructible metal, shaped like an oval sportscar. Inside are two high-backed wooden seats, with heavy leather straps extending from both sides. A large dashboard is crowded with levers, buttons, and small computer screens . . ."
Write your second paragraph here (3 to 5 sentences):

_____

_____

The *third paragraph* tells who might operate these machines and how they would be used, as in this example: "A time machine would help writers of history see what really happened a long time ago. Children could travel back in time to see what their parents were like when they were young. The President and congresspeople could see into the future, and then take steps to prevent bad things from happening."
Write your third paragraph here (3 to 5 sentences):

_____

_____

The *last paragraph* restates and sums up the topic, as in this example: "Many writers and inventors have dreamed of creating time machines. Someday, one of them will finally succeed. Then, can you imagine what amazing journeys we will be able to take?"
Write your last paragraph here (2 to 4 sentences):

_____

_____

_____

Name _____ **Date** _____

A 21ST-CENTURY INVENTION
REVISING AND WRITING A FINAL COPY

Did you write about amazing things in your essay about a 21st-century invention? Before writing the final copy, try to make it even better by following these suggestions. (Revise right on the first draft.)

1. Does your first paragraph clearly introduce the topic in a way that will make the reader want to continue? Can you make it more interesting by beginning with a question or a startling statement?
2. Does your second paragraph describe the invention in detail? Can your reader really *see* what it looks like? Can you make the word picture more vivid by using more adjectives, sensory language, and active verbs?
3. Does the third paragraph tell how the invention will be used? Are the people and uses described in clear details?
4. Does the last paragraph sum up the topic? Can you insert a humorous statement that would make it more interesting to the reader?
5. Are your sentences complete? Do subjects and verbs agree?
6. Do you vary your sentences, making some short and others long?
7. Check spelling wherever you are not 100% sure.

Write the final copy of your essay below. Write a title on the first line. Indent at the beginning of each paragraph. (Use the back of this worksheet if you need more room.)

_____

_____

_____

_____

_____

_____

_____

_____

_____

Name _____ Date _____

WAR AND PEACE
PREWRITING

November 11 is Veterans Day. That is when we say "thank you" to the men and women who have fought for our country. Beginning with the War of Independence in 1776, brave people have risked their lives so that we can live in freedom and peace.

This activity is about a different kind of battle—a battle of words! We are going to pretend that nouns and adjectives have declared war. They have separated into two armies—NOUNS on one side; ADJECTIVES on the other.

Here are their armies. The nouns are lined up on the left side of the page. They are shaped like rectangles. The adjectives are lined up on the right side. They are circle-shaped.

	Nouns	Adjectives
1.	shoes	sturdy
2.	building	enormous
3.	computer	useful
4.	flower	fragrant
5.	bedroom	messy
6.	socks	smelly
7.	moonlight	bright
8.	candy	chocolate

The troops are facing each other. They are ready to fight, but you are going to stop them. You are the peacemaker. You must show both armies that they should be together. Nouns and adjectives need each other. You can prove this by combining each set of opposing soldiers into a sentence. Then they will know that they should live together in peace. Write a sentence for each set of soldiers. The first one is done for you.

1. <u>Sturdy shoes are good for hiking.</u>

2. _____

3. _____

4. _____

5. _____

6. _____

7. _____

8. _____

Name _____ **Date** _____

WAR AND PEACE
FIRST DRAFT

In Activity 7A, you were able to end a war between nouns and adjectives by combining them into sentences.

Now the nouns are at it again! This time, they have declared war on verbs. Their troops are lined up on opposite sides of the page. The NOUN soldiers are on the left. They are still shaped like rectangles. The VERB soldiers are on the right. They are circles. Here are their armies.

	Nouns	Verbs
1.	ballplayer	raced
2.	parents	love
3.	sun	rises
4.	doorbell	rang
5.	train	chugged
6.	lion	roars
7.	artist	painted
8.	ghost	frightened
9.	ship	sailed

Now, it's your job to be a peacemaker again. Show the NOUNS and VERBS how peacefully they can live together. Combine each set of nouns and verbs into a sentence. The first one is done for you.

1. The ballplayer raced to the outfield to catch the fly ball.

2. _____

3. _____

4. _____

5. _____

6. _____

7. _____

8. _____

9. _____

Name _____   Date _____

CHOPPING WOOD

This sentence is short.

There's nothing wrong with a short sentence except when there are too many of them. A paragraph of all short sentences reads in a choppy, jerky fashion, like this one:

> Thanksgiving is coming. It is one week away. I love this holiday. My whole family is together. Uncle Jack lives in Texas. Aunt Sophie lives in Michigan. Grandma is in Florida. They all come to our house on Thanksgiving.

Doesn't it sound smoother and better like this:

> Thanksgiving is just one week away. I love this holiday because my whole family is together. Uncle Jack lives in Texas, Aunt Sophie lives in Michigan, and Grandma is in Florida. They all come to our house on Thanksgiving.

It gets cold in many places at the end of November. Thanksgiving is a busy time for woodchoppers, but a paragraph is not a log of wood.

The following paragraph reads as though a woodchopper got to it. Can you rewrite the paragraph on the lines below, combining some of the sentences to make it sound smoother?

> Thanksgiving dinner is great. It is the best part of Thanksgiving. My mom cooks. She roasts a turkey. She bakes sweet potatoes. She makes several desserts. Her apple pie is delicious. So are the cupcakes. We all eat a lot. Then we feel full and happy.

Rewrite this paragraph below. Take out the choppiness by combining sentences. (HINT: Sometimes, it is necessary to remove words or add them when you combine sentences, as in the example.)

_____

_____

_____

_____

_____

_____

_____

© 1997 by The Center for Applied Research in Education

Name _____ **Date** _____

CHOPPING MORE WOOD

Do you sometimes sit by a glowing fireplace after Thanksgiving dinner? A fire is cozy, but first it is necessary to chop up the logs.

In Activity 8A, you edited paragraphs that were *too* choppy because of many short sentences. Paragraphs can be just as unpleasant to read when all the sentences are *too long*, as in this example:

> After Thanksgiving dinner, we all help clear the table, put away the leftovers, scrape the dishes and stack them in the dishwasher, and afterwards go into the family room to relax and play games. My brothers and I have a hockey pinball game that is lots of fun to play, especially for me since I'm the one who usually wins. Mom is tired after all her work, so she puts up her feet and relaxes in front of the TV, with Aunt Sophie sitting next to her and watching, too, while Uncle Jack almost always takes a nap on the couch.

Doesn't it sound better when some of these overly long sentences are broken up, like this:

> After Thanksgiving dinner, we all help clear the table. We put away the leftovers, scrape the dishes, and stack them in the dishwasher. Afterwards, we go into the family room to relax and play games. My brothers and I have a hockey pinball game. It's lots of fun to play, especially for me since I'm the one who usually wins. Mom is tired after all her work. She puts up her feet and relaxes in front of the TV. Aunt Sophie sits next to her and watches, too. Uncle Jack almost always takes a nap on the couch.

The following paragraph is difficult to read because ALL the sentences are too long. Can you chop some of them up into shorter sentences, and rewrite the paragraph on the lines below? (HINT: It may be necessary to remove or change some words as in the example.)

> Another great thing about Thanksgiving is that we get to stay up late because Uncle Jack and Aunt Sophie are there and we don't see them too often because they live so far away. They like to hear about all the things that are going on in our lives, how we're doing at school, what our friends are like, and what books we are reading. We let them listen to music we are into and talk about our favorite singers and rock groups, and we also discuss movies we've seen that we like best, and we don't go to sleep until the fire dies down.

_____

_____

_____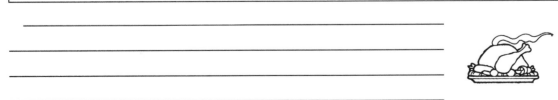

_____

Name _____ Date _____

Happy Haiku
Prewriting

It's interesting to watch the changes in the seasons of the year—the first flowers of spring, the iciness of winter, the heat and outdoor fun of summer. November brings late autumn when there is a chill in the air and piles of fallen leaves upon the ground.

For hundreds of years, the Japanese people have been writing little poems about nature in all its seasons. These poems are called *haiku*. They are popular in this country too, because they are fun and easy to write.

Each haiku has only 3 lines, with 17 syllables, divided as follows:

The first line has FIVE syllables.
The second line has SEVEN syllables.
The third line has FIVE syllables.

Here are examples of haiku about different seasons:

Cruel winter wind Blowing snow upon the fields Chasing us indoors

Sudden spring shower Nourishes expectant buds Red tulip pop up!

Say each of these haiku aloud. Count the syllables as you say them. Can you hear the pattern for each line: 5, 7, 5?

Haiku are usually about nature, but they don't have to be. You could even write a haiku about a sports event:

Thrilling football game The quarterback grabs the ball And streaks down the field

Here are some possible subjects for November haiku. Next to each one, write as many words and phrases you can think of that could describe that subject. The first two are begun for you.

1. THANKSGIVING: turkey, family, Pilgrims, _____

_____

2. PILES OF LEAVES: brown and gold, children jumping, _____

_____

3. FOOTBALL GAME: _____

_____

4, CHILLY WIND: _____

_____

5. BIRDS FLYING SOUTH: _____

_____

Name _____ **Date** _____

HAPPY HAIKU
FIRST DRAFT

Haiku can be happy like this:

> Here comes Thanksgiving
> Jolly, laughing family
> Mom's tasty stuffing

Or sad, like this:

> All the leaves are gone
> The trees are bare and lonely
> Weeping in the wind

Say these haiku aloud. Count the syllables in each line—5, 7, 5.

On the lines below, write three haiku about this time of year. Select three of the subjects in the list in Activity 9A, or choose any others that seem appropriate. Examine your lists of words and phrases and use those that best fit the mood of your poems. (This is just a first draft, so don't worry if the words are not perfect—you can change them later.) To make it easier, the first one is begun for you.

REMEMBER: Line One—   5 Syllables
                       Line Two—   7 Syllables
                       Line Three— 5 Syllables

HAIKU #1.   <u>Birds are flying south</u>

_____

_____

_____

HAIKU #2. _____

_____

_____

_____

HAIKU #3. _____

_____

_____

_____

Name _____ **Date** _____

HAPPY HAIKU
REVISING AND WRITING A FINAL COPY

DIRECTIONS: Edit and revise your three haiku poems right on the first draft. There are not many words in a haiku, so it is really important that each word and phrase be the best. Here are some suggestions:

1. Read each haiku aloud to be sure you have the correct number of syllables in each line. Remember, the first line has *5* syllables, the second line has *7* syllables, and the last line has *5* syllables.

2. Sensory language works well in haiku. Have you used words that appeal to the senses of *sight, sound, smell, touch,* and *taste*? Can you think of any that would sound better than the words you have used?

3. Active verbs can help bring your poems to life. Use *dash* or *leap* instead of *go*. *Gobble* or *stuff* are more interesting than *eat*. Can you change your passive verbs to active ones?

4. Unusual phrases such as *waterfall music* or *dimpled raindrops* can make your haiku more colorful. Can you think of any unusual phrases to improve your poems?

When your haiku are as perfect as you can make them, write your final copy on the lines below. If you wish, you can draw illustrations in the spaces around each poem.

HAIKU #1: _____

_____

_____

HAIKU #2: _____

_____

_____

HAIKU #3: _____

_____

_____

Name _____ **Date**_____

FUNNYBONE TICKLING
PREWRITING

A great American writer was born on November 30, 1835. His name was Samuel Langhorne Clemens. Never heard of him? That's because he is better known by his pen name—Mark Twain.

Mark Twain wrote many stories and books. Some of his best-known works are *Tom Sawyer*, *The Prince and the Pauper*, *A Connecticut Yankee in King Arthur's Court*, and *The Adventures of Huckleberry Finn*.

Mark Twain loved humor. Here are some of his amusing sayings:

> "The only way to keep your health is to eat what you don't want, drink what you don't like, and do what you'd rather not."
>
> "Never run after your own hat—others will be delighted to do it; why spoil their fun?"
>
> "Nothing helps scenery like ham and eggs."
>
> "Put all thine eggs in one basket and—watch that basket!"
>
> "As to the Adjective; when in doubt, strike it out."

Humor is not easy to write. In fact, it can be a lot harder to write a funny paragraph than a serious one. However, that is what you are about to do! First, read Mark Twain's humor again as inspiration, and then complete the brainstorming list below.

BRAINSTORMING LIST

DIRECTIONS: Choose one of the following topics for your humorous paragraph. (Check the one you have selected.)

❑ 1. A Lesson With a Substitute Teacher
❑ 2. The Day I Tried to Bake a Cake
❑ 3. The Cat That Came to Dinner
❑ 4. The Turtle That Got Away During the Pet Show
❑ 5. The Overloaded Shopping Bag
❑ 6. _____ (Write a subject of your own choice here.)

Write a beginning sentence on the line below. (Try to make it funny, or startling or even silly.)

_____

On the lines below, list some of the amusing things that might happen. You don't need sentences—words and phrases are enough.

_____

_____

_____

Name _____ Date _____

FUNNYBONE TICKLING
FIRST DRAFT

> "Part of the secret of success in life is to eat what you like and let the food fight it out inside."

That is another of Mark Twain's amusing sayings. Now, let's see how funny *you* can be!

Here is one example of a humorous paragraph:

> "I think I'll become a substitute teacher when I am grown. It seems like so much fun! At what other job can you begin your day by entering a classroom where the noise is as loud as a den full of roaring lions? When you take attendance, students answer to the wrong name and you never find out who they really are. The best part is when you turn your back to write on the chalkboard. That's the moment for paper airplanes and gumballs to go flying across the room. What a wonderful experience! That's the job for me!

The writer of this paragraph has found humor by stating the opposite of what he really means. This is called *irony*. You can use this technique in your own paragraph, or you can search for your own style of humor. It shouldn't be hard because you've already done most of the work in your brainstorming list.

DIRECTIONS: Write your humorous paragraph below. This is a first draft, so just concentrate on getting your ideas on paper, as follows:

1. Write the title on the first line.
2. Indent at the beginning of the paragraph. Write your introductory sentence first.
3. The next three or four sentences should develop the topic and add details.
4. Sum up the topic, in a humorous way, in the last sentence.

_____

_____

_____

_____

_____

_____

_____

Name _____ **Date** _____

FUNNYBONE TICKLING
REVISING AND WRITING A FINAL COPY

DIRECTIONS:

1. Revise and edit the first draft of your humorous paragraph. Here are some suggestions for improving it:

---

a. Does your introductory sentence state the topic? Is it interesting and exciting? Does it make the reader want to continue? Does it set the mood for humor? Can you think of a funnier or more startling way to begin?

b. Do the next three or four sentences develop the theme with humor? Are the details interesting and fun to read? Can you think of sillier or more surprising details?

c. Does your concluding sentence sum up the topic? Is it funny? Will it make the reader smile?

d. Are there unnecessary words or phrases you can take out to make the paragraph sharper and stronger?

e. Can you think of any funny word images to add?

f. Are your sentences complete? Do subjects and verbs agree?

g. Check your spelling.

---

2. When you are satisfied that your paragraph is as humorous and readable as you can make it, write the final copy below. Write the title on the first line. Indent at the beginning of the paragraph.

_____

_____

_____

_____

_____

_____

_____

_____

Name _____   **Date** _____

ATHLETIC WORDS

The birthdays of several great athletes occur in November. Nadia Comaneci, Romanian gymnast, was born on November 12, 1961. When she was only 14 years old, she electrified the Olympic Games with her amazing performance and won three gold medals.

One of America's best-loved baseball stars, Joe DiMaggio, was born on November 25, 1914. He played outfield for the New York Yankees from 1936 to 1942 and from 1946 to 1951. In both 1939 and 1940, he led the American League in batting and held a lifetime batting average of .325. In 1941, he set a major league record by hitting safely in 56 consecutive games. He played in 10 World Series and was three times chosen the American League's most valuable player. Fans, impressed by his modesty and good nature as well as his athletic prowess, affectionately called him the "Yankee Clipper."

Have you ever heard broadcasts of sports events on radio or TV, or read newspaper articles about them? If you have, you've probably noticed a variety of active verbs and other striking language.

In the first column below, you will see a list of vivid words or phrases that have been used to describe sports events. Can you put each one into a sentence in the second column?

WORDS / PHRASES	SENTENCES
1. flied out	_____
2. drove in	_____
3. hurled	_____
4. slid	_____
5. sped	_____
6. tackled	_____
7. grabbed	_____
8. scored	_____
9. raced	_____
10. swung	_____
11. fumbled	_____
12. smashed	_____

Name _____ Date _____

A TERRIBLE DAY
PREWRITING

November 22, 1963 was one of the most tragic dates in American history. It was on that day that President John F. Kennedy was shot and killed while riding in a motorcade in Dallas, Texas.

Most people who were alive then can remember exactly where they were and how they felt when they first heard the news. A few days later, people of all political beliefs grieved as they watched the funeral on TV. Assassinations do not happen often in the United States. In a democracy, if you don't approve of a president, you can always vote him out in the next election. During those dark November days in 1963, the entire country mourned for its lost young president. Many people have written about their deep feelings of sorrow.

The death of a president is a dreadful occasion for a country, but everyone also has times of personal unhappiness. In this activity, you are going to write about a time when you felt sad. It might have been the death of a pet, when your friend moved away, an illness that lasted a long time, a bad report card, not getting what you wanted most for your birthday, or any other event that made you feel sad.

First, complete this brainstorming list.

BRAINSTORMING LIST

1. In the box below, write one or two phrases *naming* the event (such as "dog got run over by car" or "in bed for a week with the flu" or "broke my arm" or "grandma died," etc.).

   ```
   [                                                                    ]
   ```

2. In the box below, tell *where* and *when* this occurred. (You don't need complete sentences here—words and phrases will do.)

   ```
   [                                                                    ]
   ```

3. In the box below, list words or phrases that you will be able to use to *describe* what happened.

   ```
   [                                                                    ]
   ```

4. In the box below, list words or phrases that show your feelings at that time.

   ```
   [                                                                    ]
   ```

Name _____ **Date** _____

A Terrible Day
First Draft

Use your brainstorming list and follow these directions to write about a sad day in your life.

1. The first paragraph should introduce the topic and set the mood, as in this example:

> March 10, 1995 was the saddest day of my life. That was when I lost my best friend. His name was Monster and he was my dog.

Write your first paragraph here. It should have 2 to 4 sentences.

_____

_____

2. The second paragraph should describe the event, as in this example:

> Monster was only one year old. He was playful and frisky and didn't always come when called. We were careful to keep him on a leash outside. One day, a plumber came to the house to fix a leaky pipe. He left the door open, and Monster raced out into the street, right in front of a car. He was killed instantly.

Write your second paragraph here (4–7 sentences).

_____

_____

3. The third paragraph describes your feelings, as in this example:

> I got Monster for a birthday present when he was only six weeks old. He always met me at the door with a waggy tail when I got home from school. He loved me and I loved him. I cried when he died. I felt as though I had lost my best friend.

Write your third paragraph here (2–6 sentences).

_____

_____

4. The last paragraph should restate and sum up the topic, like this:

> I hope I never have another day as terrible as that one in March of 1995. I still get a lump in my throat when I think about Monster. I'll never forget him or the way I lost him.

Write your last paragraph here (2–4 sentences).

_____

_____

_____

Name _____ **Date** _____

A TERRIBLE DAY
REVISING AND WRITING A FINAL COPY

DIRECTIONS

1. Revise and edit your first draft, as follows:

a. Does your first paragraph introduce the topic in an interesting way? Can you change anything to make it more exciting for the reader?

b. Does your second paragraph state clearly the details about what happened? Can you add any active verbs or sensory words to paint a vivid word picture?

c. Does the third paragraph describe your feelings?

d. Does the last paragraph restate and sum up the topic in an interesting way?

e. Are your sentences complete? Do subjects and verbs agree?

f. Is all spelling correct?

2. Write your final copy below. Indent at the beginning of each paragraph. (Use the back of this worksheet if you need more room.)

A TERRIBLE DAY

_____

_____

_____

_____

_____

_____

_____

_____

_____

_____

_____

_____

Name _____ **Date** _____

DANGEROUS JOURNEYS
PREWRITING

Would you be brave enough to go on a dangerous journey? What if you knew ahead of time that you might never get to your destination, and that even if you got there, you might not survive? Would you go?

Most people would not take such a chance. In 1620, however, there were 102 courageous men, women, and children. They set sail from Plymouth, England in a small ship called the "Mayflower," across the treacherous waters of the Atlantic Ocean toward an unknown continent. These Pilgrims were seeking a new home where they could follow their religion in peace. The terrible trip lasted almost four months. Even after they arrived in the New World, their troubles were not over. The first year in the new settlement of Plymouth was harsh. Many of the settlers died. With the help of friendly native Americans, however, and their own hard work, they made it to a good harvest in the autumn of 1621. They celebrated the occasion with a feast of thanksgiving.

Like the Pilgrims, we, too, celebrate Thanksgiving every November. Life today is much easier than it was for the Pilgrims, but we like to believe that we, too, could be strong and brave if it were necessary.

You don't have to prove your courage now. In this activity, you are only going to *pretend* that you are going on a dangerous journey. Here are some suggestions. Check (✓) the one you would like to write about or write in your own choice on the last line.

❏ A Journey on the "Mayflower"

❏ Rocket to the Moon

❏ Spaceship to Mars

❏ To the Bottom of the Sea in a Submarine

❏ Journey Through Time in a Time Machine

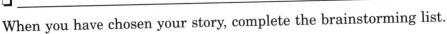

❏ Around the World in a Balloon

❏ Climbing the Highest Mountain

❏ _____ (own choice)

When you have chosen your story, complete the brainstorming list.

BRAINSTORMING LIST

1. Write names for your main characters below. Next to each, write some words and phrases that describe who they are and what they do.

2. List words and phrases describing where/when the story takes place.

3. Write words and phrases describing the dangers encountered.

4. Tell briefly how the journey ends.

5. Write a first sentence for your story.

Name _____ **Date** _____

DANGEROUS JOURNEYS
FIRST DRAFT

The Pilgrims had to be brave and clever to survive in the New World. Their "Dangerous Journey" was real. Your "Dangerous Journey" has to exist only in your imagination. It should be easy to write with the help of your brainstorming list. Here are some suggestions:

1. Use the first sentence from your brainstorming list to begin your story.
2. Tell the story through the eyes of the main character. Use the words and phrases in your brainstorming list to describe that person as well as the others in your story.
3. Make it clear where and when your story takes place.
4. Make the dangerous parts as exciting as you can.
5. Use some dialogue (conversations between the characters).
6. It should be clear how the story ends.

Write your story below. Put the title on the top line. Indent at the beginning of paragraphs. (This is just a first draft, so don't be concerned with spelling and grammar—just concentrate on getting it down.) Use the back of this worksheet if you need more room.

_____

Name _____ **Date** _____

DANGEROUS JOURNEYS
REVISING AND WRITING A FINAL COPY

DIRECTIONS

1. Edit and revise your first draft right on the paper.

---

a. Can you make the beginning more exciting so the reader will want to continue?

b. Are all the characters described clearly? Will the reader know who they are and what they are like?

c. Is the story seen through the eyes of the main character?

d. Are the events shown clearly? Will the reader be able to follow?

e. Can the dangers be even more frightening?

f. Can you add some dialogue?

g. Is your story cluttered with too many words? Take out any that won't be missed.

h. Can you make a scene more striking by using active verbs?

i. Are sentences complete? Do subjects and verbs agree?

j. Is all the spelling correct?

---

2. Write your final copy below. Put the title on the top line. Indent at the beginning of paragraphs. (Use the back of this worksheet if you need more room.)

_____

_____

_____

_____

_____

_____

_____

_____

_____

_____

DECEMBER

December

"What freezings have I felt, what dark days seen!
What old December's bareness everywhere!
—William Shakespeare

WINTER BEGINS . . . CHILLS AND ICE . . . HEAVY COATS AND BOOTS . . . WARM CAPS AND GLOVES . . . FIRST SNOW SPARKLING ON BARE TREES . . . SLEDDING AND ICESKATING . . . SCHOOL VACATIONS . . . HOLIDAY CELEBRATIONS, SONGS, AND GAMES . . . SANTA AND REINDEER . . . CHRISTMAS, CHANUKAH, AND KWANZAA . . . NEW YEAR'S EVE!

December Events

December 1, 1955: Rosa Parks, an African-American woman, sat on a front bus seat usually reserved for whites, in Montgomery, Alabama, which started the civil rights movement led by Dr. Martin Luther King, Jr.

December 3, 1967: South American surgeon, Dr. Christiaan Barnard, performed the first human heart transplant in Capetown, South Africa on 55-year-old Louis Washkansky

December 7, 1941: Japanese naval and air forces suddenly attacked Pearl Harbor, plunging the U.S. into World War II

December 15, 1791: The U.S. Bill of Rights became law, having been ratified by the states

December 16, 1773: The "Boston Tea Party" protest against British tax on tea took place in Boston Harbor

December 17, 1843: Charles Dickens published *A Christmas Carol*, one of the most famous stories ever written

December 18, 1969: Great Britain abolished capital punishment

December 28, 1869: Chewing gum was patented by William F. Semple, a dentist from Ohio

December 29, 1890: The Wounded Knee massacre took place in South Dakota; over 200 Sioux men, women, and children were killed by U.S. troops

December Birthdays

December 5, 1901: Walt Disney, American cartoonist; creator and producer of animated cartoons

December 14, 1503: Nostradamus, French astrologer and physician; famous for his prophecies

December 18, 1947: Steven Spielberg, American motion picture director (*Jaws, ET, Raiders of the Lost Ark, Schindler's List*)

December 27, 1822: Louis Pasteur, great scientist and originator of the process of pasteurization

WRITING ACTIVITIES FOR DECEMBER

Name _____ **Date** _____

CHILLS AND THRILLS
PREWRITING

December is a cold month in many areas. Temperatures fall to freezing or below, icy winds blow, and many places see the first snow. Winter begins on December 21. Brrrr!

Does this mean that outdoor fun time has ended? *No way!* Winter can be just as much fun as summer. Just bundle up in warm clothes and try some of these activities:

> TAKE A WALK IN THE SNOW
> BUILD A SNOWMAN
> HAVE A SNOWBALL FIGHT WITH YOUR FRIENDS
> GO ICE SKATING ON THE POND (Be sure it's safe)
> GO SKIING

What are your favorite winter activities? What do your classmates like to do on cold winter days? (If you live in a warm climate, pretend it gets cold.) It will be fun to write about your winter "chills and thrills" and then compare your essays.

First, complete the brainstorming list below:

BRAINSTORMING LIST

1. Choose two of your favorite winter activities and write them here:

   _____

   _____

2. In the space below, write as many words and phrases you can think of that describe your *first* favorite winter activity:

3. In the space below, write as many words and phrases you can think of that describe your *second* favorite winter activity:

4. In the space below, write as many words and phrases you can think of that describe the winter season:

5. The first sentence in an essay must do two things. It should tell what the essay is about and it should spark interest so the reader will want to continue reading. One way to do this is to start with a question, such as "Is it possible to have fun in the winter?" Another way is to make a startling statement, such as "Frosty chills can lead to thrills." Write a first sentence (or sentences) for your essay below:

   _____

   _____

   _____

Name _____ Date _____

CHILLS AND THRILLS
FIRST DRAFT

Write a 4-paragraph essay about your favorite kinds of winter fun. This is a first draft, so don't worry about spelling or grammar. Keep your brainstorming list handy, and follow these directions.

1. FIRST PARAGRAPH: The first paragraph introduces the topic in an interesting way, as in this example:

   "Is it possible to have fun in the winter? I think so. In fact, some of my favorite outdoor activities take place in cold weather."

Write your first paragraph here (2–4 sentences).

_____

_____

2. SECOND PARAGRAPH: Choose one winter activity you like and describe it in the second paragraph, as in this example:

   "We have a pond near our house. When it freezes over, all the neighborhood kids go ice skating. It feels great to glide across the ice with the wind blowing on your face. Sometimes we choose teams and play hockey there."

Write your second paragraph here (3–6 sentences).

_____

_____

_____

3. THIRD PARAGRAPH: Describe your second winter activity. Example:

   "Everything looks different after the first good snowfall. My brother and I rush right out and build a snowman. Sometimes we wrap a scarf around its neck and put a hat on its head. Every year, our snowman gets bigger and better."

Write your third paragraph here (3–6 sentences).

_____

_____

_____

4. LAST PARAGRAPH: The last paragraph restates and sums up the topic. Example:

   "Some kids moan and groan when the weather gets frigid, but I love it. Winter fun is the best kind of fun there is!

Write your last paragraph here (2–4 sentences).

_____

_____

Name _____ **Date** _____

CHILLS AND THRILLS
REVISING AND WRITING A FINAL COPY

DIRECTIONS:

1. Revise and edit your first draft. Here are some suggestions:

---

a. Does your first paragraph introduce the topic? Can you make it more interesting so the reader will want to continue?

b. Does your second paragraph describe the first example? Did you use vivid words and phrases from your brainstorming list?

c. Does your third paragraph tell about the second example? Do you include your feelings about it? Would active verbs make it more exciting?

d. Does the last paragraph restate and sum up the topic? Can you think of an ending that would be more interesting?

e. Are your sentences complete? Do subjects and verbs agree?

f. Check all spelling.

---

2. Write the final copy here. Indent at the beginning of each paragraph. If you wish, you can draw winter illustrations in the margins or below the essay. (Use the back of this worksheet if you need more room.)

_____

_____

_____

_____

_____

_____

_____

_____

_____

_____

_____

Name _____ Date_____

REMEMBER PEARL HARBOR
PREWRITING

> "December 7, 1941, a date which will live in infamy."

These words were spoken by President Franklin D. Roosevelt after the sneak attack on Pearl Harbor by the Japanese. Pearl Harbor is a large U.S. Naval base in Hawaii. Thousands of people were killed on that terrible day and a large part of the American Navy was destroyed. This event brought the U.S. into World War II to fight the Axis powers.

These were uncertain and scary times for the people of the U.S. and the rest of the free world. Germany, Italy, and Japan seemed unbeatable in their quest to dominate the world. But America and its allies pulled together. Our young men and women fought in the armed forces. Those left at home worked day and night in factories to produce the weapons and tools that were needed. It took years. Many soldiers and civilians were killed in addition to the millions who perished in the Holocaust. Finally, the Axis was defeated and the world set free.

> In this activity, you are going to pretend you are living during the difficult days of World War II. Many countries have been conquered by cruel dictators. Perhaps your neighbor, parent, another family member, or older brother or sister are fighting or serving in far-off lands. They are tired and sad.
>
> Letters from home helped a lot to make the servicepeople a little less lonely. You want to help, too. Your job for the war effort is to write a letter to someone in the armed forces.
>
> Close your eyes for a moment and try to imagine yourself living in the 1940s during World War II. Are you there? Now, think about what you might write.

Your letter will be easier to compose if you first complete a brainstorming list.

BRAINSTORMING LIST

1. You can write a letter to any one of the following: a relative, neighbor, friend, or friend's relative away at war. You can make up a name or use a real one. Write the name of the person to whom you are writing on the line below and tell who he or she is.

   _____

2. In the space below, list words and phrases you could use to describe what the people at home, including yourself, are doing.

3. In the space below, list words and phrases to describe your feelings about the person to whom you are writing and what he or she is doing.

Name _____ **Date** _____

REMEMBER PEARL HARBOR
FIRST DRAFT

Can you pretend you are living during the difficult days of World War II? A soldier who is fighting or serving far from home will love getting your letter. He or she will feel less lonely. So, make your message cheerful and positive. Use the information you prepared on your brainstorming list to write a first draft of your letter. Here are some other suggestions:

1. Begin with a joke or an amusing incident. This should cheer the person.

2. In the second paragraph, describe things going on at home. You can talk about yourself, your friends, or family. *REMEMBER*—This is the 1940s. There is no television, no VCR's, no computers, no digital clocks, no microwaves. (Yes, there are radios and movie theaters and ballparks.)

3. In the third paragraph, talk about feelings (like missing that person).

4. Follow correct form for a personal letter as shown below.

_____

(Write your street address above)

_____

(Your city, state, ZIP above)

_____

(Write today's date above)

Dear _____, (This is the Greeting)

(Write the person's name above)

_____

(Begin your message above)

_____

_____

_____

_____

_____

_____ ,

(Write the closing above)

_____

(Sign your name above)

Name _____ **Date** _____

REMEMBER PEARL HARBOR
REVISING AND WRITING A FINAL COPY

Did you feel as though you were living during World War II when you wrote the first draft of your letter? Here are some suggestions for editing and revising before you write the final copy:

1. Did you write your address and date in the upper right?

2. Did you write the greeting at the left margin, followed by a comma?

3. Did you indent at the beginning of each paragraph?

4. Did you write the closing (*Love, Your friend, Your brother*, etc.) at the lower right, followed by a comma?

5. Did you sign your name below the closing?

6. Is your letter cheerful and newsy? Were you able to pretend that it was the 1940s?

7. Are your sentences complete? Do subjects and verbs agree?

8. Is all spelling correct?

Now, write the final copy of your letter below. Use the correct form for a personal letter as shown on the first draft.

Name _____ **Date** _____

JINGLE BELLS
PREWRITING

> "Jingle bells, jingle bells, jingle all the way,
> Oh what fun it is to ride in a one-horse open sleigh."

When people think about December and holiday time, a word that sometimes comes to mind is "bells."

Bells are often associated with winter activities, as in these lines by Alfred, Lord Tennyson:

> "Ring, happy bells, across the snow;
> The year is going, let him go;"

Bells are not just for winter. Here is a poem by James Robinson Planche about some different kinds of bells:

> "Ching-a-ring-a-ring-ching! Feast of lanterns!
> What a crop of chop-sticks, hongs and gongs!
> Hundred thousand crinkum-crankums
> Hung among the bells and ding-dongs!"

How many kinds of bells are there? List below as many kinds of bells as you can think of. Can you write at least five? One is given for you.

1. sleigh bells _____   5. _____
2. _____   6. _____
3. _____   7. _____
4. _____   8. _____

Bells are fun to write about because they make so many sounds. Look at the 4-line poem by James Robinson Planche above. Underline the words that *sound* like bells.

Did you underline *ching-a-ring, hongs, gongs, crinkum-crankums*, and *ding-dongs*?

> On the lines below, write all the words and phrases you can think of that make you think of bells. These can be kinds of bells, the sounds that are made by bells, or any other words that remind you of bells.
>
> _____
>
> _____
>
> _____
>
> _____

© 1997 by The Center for Applied Research in Education

Name _____ Date_____

JINGLE BELLS
FIRST DRAFT

> "Hear the sledges with the bells—Silver bells!
> What a world of merriment their melody foretells!
>   How they tinkle, tinkle, tinkle,
>   In the icy air of night!
>   While the stars, that oversprinkle
>   All the heavens seem to twinkle
>   With a crystalline delight;
>   Keeping time, time, time
>   In a sort of Runic rhyme,
> To the tintinnabulation that so musically wells
>   From the bells, bells, bells, bells,
>   Bells, bells, bells—
>   From the jingling and the tinkling of the bells."

This is from the most famous poem ever written about bells. It's title is "The Bells," by Edgar Allan Poe. You don't have to know the meaning of every word to feel how all the lines sound like bells.

"The Bells" is a long poem. It describes many kinds of bells, like wedding bells, alarm bells, and church bells. Here are a few more lines:

> ". . . the swinging and the ringing
>   Of the bells, bells, bells,
> To the rhyming and the chiming of the bells."
>
> "By the twanging and the clanging,
>   In the jangling and the wrangling . . .
> In the clamour and the clangour of the bells!"

There is a special word for the use of words or phrases that imitate or suggest the sound being described. It is called *onomatopoeia*. You don't have to remember that word (unless you want to amaze your friends!). You can understand what it means just by reading "The Bells."

> On the lines below, you are going to write a poem about bells. Try to make it sound like the bells themselves. You can use some of Poe's words and the ones you listed in Activity 3A. Your poem can be about one kind of bell, such as sleigh bells, or many kinds. It does not have to rhyme. You can use rhyme if you wish, but it is not necessary.
>
> Read Poe's lines a few times to get in the mood. Then write a first draft of your poem. (Use the back of this worksheet if you need more room.)

_____

_____

_____

Name _____ **Date** _____

JINGLE BELLS
REVISING AND WRITING A FINAL COPY

> "Hear the loud alarum bells—Brazen bells!
> What a tale of terror now their turbulency tells!
> In the startled ear of night
> How they scream out their affright!
> Too much horrified to speak,
> They can only shriek, shriek . . ."
> (from "The Bells" by Edgar Allan Poe)

Did you have fun writing the first draft of a poem about bells? Now it's time to revise and edit it. Here are some suggestions:

1. Do the lines in your poem sound like bells? Read some of Poe's lines again. Does he use any words that you can use in your poem?
2. Can you add any exciting active verbs such as *startle*, *scream*, or *shriek*?
3. Would the poem be better if you put in additional striking lines?
4. Would the poem be better if you cut out boring words or lines?
5. Check your spelling.

Write the final copy of your poem below. Put a title on the first line. If you wish, you can illustrate your poem in the side and bottom margins.

_____

_____

_____

_____

_____

_____

_____

_____

_____

_____

Name _____ **Date** _____

PRO OR ANTI?
PREWRITING

> On December 18, 1969, Great Britain abolished capital punishment (the death penalty). That meant that no one could ever be executed, no matter how terrible their crime.
>
> In the U.S., some states also do not permit capital punishment. Other states allow it for certain crimes.

For many years, there has been much debate on this subject. Those who are *pro capital punishment* (for it), say:

—Murderers can get out of jail by escaping or by completing their sentences. Then they commit more crimes.

—Criminals would hesitate to commit capital crimes if they knew they could get the death penalty. Therefore there would be fewer murders.

—People who commit premeditated (planned) murders deserve to die.

—The victims of murderers want justice.

Those who are *anti capital punishment* (against it), say:

—Killing is immoral even if it is done by the State.

—Sometimes innocent people are convicted and executed.

—It has not been proven that the crime rate goes down in places that have capital punishment.

—A life sentence without parole would keep murderers off the streets.

> What do you think? Are you for or against the death penalty? You can share your thoughts in an opinion essay. Perhaps you can even convince others of the rightness of your views.

An opinion essay will be easier to write if you first complete a brainstorming list.

> ### *BRAINSTORMING LIST*
>
> 1. On the line below, write whether you are PRO (for) or ANTI (against) capital punishment.
>
> _____
>
> 2. List at least three reasons to support your opinion. (You don't need sentences here—words or phrases are enough.)
>
> _____
> _____
> _____
> _____

Name _____ **Date** _____

PRO OR ANTI?
FIRST DRAFT

DIRECTIONS: Using your brainstorming list as a guide, write a 3-paragraph opinion essay *for* or *against* capital punishment.

1. In the first paragraph, introduce the topic, as in this example:

> Would you like to die for a crime you did not commit? This has happened! People have been executed who were later discovered to be innocent. This is only one of several reasons why I am against capital punishment.

Write your first paragraph here (2–4 sentences). Make the beginning as interesting as you can.

_____

_____

_____

_____

2. In the second paragraph, tell *at least three reasons* why you are *for* or *against* the death penalty. (Copy from your brainstorming list, using sentences.) Write the second paragraph here (3–7 sentences).

_____

_____

_____

_____

_____

3. In the third paragraph, sum up the topic, as in this example:

> For these reasons, I believe there should be no capital punishment. The death penalty does not belong in a civilized country.

Write your third (last) paragraph here (2–4 sentences).

_____

_____

_____

Name _____ Date _____

PRO OR ANTI?
REVISING AND WRITING A FINAL COPY

DIRECTIONS:

1. Revise and edit the first draft of your opinion essay. Here are some suggestions for improvement:

---

a. Does the first paragraph introduce the topic? Can you make it more interesting by beginning with a question or a startling statement?

b. Does the second paragraph develop the topic? Do you list at least three reasons to support your opinion? Can you add additional facts? Is there anything that could be said in a more convincing way?

c. Does the third paragraph restate and sum up your opinion? Do you finish the essay in an assured and convincing manner?

d. Read the whole essay again. Is there anything you could add to make your point stronger in a way that might change a reader's mind?

e. Could you add *vivid language* such as active verbs and *sensory words* to make your argument more powerful?

f. Are your sentences complete? Do subjects and verbs agree?

g. Are all words spelled correctly?

---

2. When your essay is as strong and well-written as you can make it, write your final copy here. Indent at the beginning of each paragraph. Use the back of this worksheet if you need more room.

_____

_____

_____

_____

_____

_____

_____

_____

_____

Name _____ Date _____

TENTH MONTH

Did you know that "December" means "tenth month"? The calendar we use is based on one developed by the ancient Romans. The word "decem" meant ten in Rome. For a long time, there were only ten months in the Roman calendar. When they saw it wasn't working too well, they added two additional months, "Januarius" and "Februarius," but these new months came at the end. The year began in March ("Martius" to the Romans), so December was still the tenth month to them. And that is how a word that means "tenth month" came to signify "twelfth month" to us.

Here are some word games you can play with the word December.

WORD SEARCH

How many words can you make from the *letters* in DECEMBER. Write them in the box below. (You should be able to find at least five!)

DECEMBER SENTENCE GAME

Write a sentence beginning with each of the letters in DECEMBER. The first one is done for you.

D— Don't we have fun in December? _____

E— _____

C— _____

E— _____

M— _____

B— _____

E— _____

R— _____

Name _____ **Date**_____

YOU ARE A FILM CRITIC
PREWRITING

Two famous movie-makers were born in December. Walt Disney was born on December 5, 1901; Steven Spielberg's birth date is December 18, 1947.

These two have brought much pleasure to millions of people. Disney's films are animated. Everybody knows Mickey and Minnie Mouse and their friends, and have enjoyed other Disney movies such as *Pinocchio, Snow White*, and *Fantasia*. Steven Spielberg's adventure films, such as *Raiders of the Lost Ark, Jaws*, and *Star Wars*, have thrilled movie-goers.

Movies become successful only if they get good reviews in newspapers, radio, and TV. The people who do the reviewing are called "film critics." In their reviews, they usually do three things:

1. They describe the film (title, director, actors, plot, characters, and setting).
2. They list good points and bad points of the film.
3. They recommend, or don't recommend, the movie, and sometimes give it a rating, such as one to four stars.

DIRECTIONS: In this activity you are going to become a film critic, and review a movie you have seen. (If you prefer, you can review a TV show.) Before you begin your review, complete this *BRAINSTORMING LIST*.

1. Write the title of the movie or show you are reviewing.

_____

2. Who are the actors and the director (if you know their names)?

_____

3. Describe two or three of the main characters.

_____

_____

4. Tell the plot in a few sentences.

_____

_____

5. What are the good things about this movie or show?

_____

6. What are the bad things about this movie or show?

_____

7. How would you rate this movie or show?

_____

Name _____ Date _____

YOU ARE A FILM CRITIC
FIRST DRAFT

Do you ever read movie or TV show reviews in newspapers or magazines? Before you become a film critic, it would be a good idea to read several reviews. If you do that and then use your brainstorming list, it will be easy to become a film critic yourself. Just follow these directions.

1. In the first paragraph, tell the name of the film or show, the actors, and the director (if you know). A startling or surprising beginning will make the reader want to go on. Write your first paragraph here.

_____

_____

_____

2. In the second paragraph, describe the characters in the story, where it takes place, and what happens (the plot).

_____

_____

_____

3. In the third paragraph, describe the *good* and *bad* points of the film or show.

_____

_____

_____

4. In the last paragraph, tell whether or not you recommend this movie or show, and the reasons for this decision.

_____

_____

_____

_____

© 1997 by The Center for Applied Research in Education

Name _____ **Date** _____

YOU ARE A FILM CRITIC
REVISING AND WRITING A FINAL COPY

DIRECTIONS

1. Revise and edit the first draft of your movie or TV show review, as follows:

---

a. Does your first paragraph introduce the topic and give necessary information (title, actors, etc.)? Can you make the beginning more interesting so that the reader will want to go on, by using humor, an unusual question, or a startling statement?

b. Does the second paragraph tell all about the characters, plot, and setting? Can you make it more exciting by using vivid language such as active verbs and sensory words?

c. Does the third paragraph analyze the good and bad features of the film or show in a clear and logical way?

d. Does the last paragraph clearly state your recommendation and the reasons for it?

---

2. When your review is as good as you can make it, write the final copy below. Indent at the beginning of each paragraph. Use the back of this worksheet if you need more room.

_____

_____

_____

_____

_____

_____

_____

_____

_____

_____

_____

Name _____ Date _____

HOLIDAY FAMILY FUN
PREWRITING

December is holiday time—Christmas, Chanukah, Kwanzaa, New Year's Eve. Lights twinkling on evergreens in the snow. Shoppers laden with packages. Colorfully-wrapped gifts with streaming ribbons. Decorations and candles and greeting cards. Special music and celebrations.

Each family has its own way of enjoying this exciting time of year. Some attend religious services. Some have lots of parties with music and dancing. Some share huge, delicious dinners with relatives and friends. Some prefer quiet times exchanging gifts by the fire. Some go on trips to warm beaches. Some have special traditions that are all their own.

What does your family do during this holiday season? In this activity, you are going to write a description of what the month of December is like in your family. When you have finished, all who wish can share their essays with each other.

First, complete this brainstorming list.

BRAINSTORMING LIST

1. List the names of all who live in your house. Next to each name, write a description of that person (or pet). You don't need sentences here—just words and phrases.

_____
_____
_____
_____
_____
_____

2. List *at least three* things your family likes to do during the holiday season, such as shopping, exchanging gifts, going to see "The Nutcracker," visiting relatives and friends, decorating the house, etc.

_____
_____
_____
_____

3. In the space below, write as many words and phrases as you can think of that can be used to describe December and its holidays:

_____
_____
_____

© 1997 by The Center for Applied Research in Education

Name _____ **Date**_____

Holiday Family Fun
First Draft

DIRECTIONS: Write a first draft for a 4-paragraph essay telling what your family does during the holidays. Use your brainstorming list as a guide.

1. In the first paragraph, introduce the topic in an interesting way, as in this example:

> "The people in my family are usually serious and calm. In December they change, as though touched by a magic wand. They become eager and excited and laugh a lot."

   Write your first paragraph here (2–4 sentences).

_____

_____

_____

_____

2. In the second paragraph, describe the members of your family (3–7 sentences).

_____

_____

_____

_____

3. In the third paragraph, describe three of your favorite things to do at this time of year (3–7 sentences).

_____

_____

_____

_____

4. Your last paragraph should restate the topic and sum it up, as in this example:

> "December is a happy month for my family. We all share in the excitement and joy. Sometimes I wish it would never end."

   Write your last paragraph here (2–4 sentences).

_____

_____

_____

Name _____ **Date** _____

HOLIDAY FAMILY FUN
REVISING AND WRITING A FINAL COPY

1. Revise and edit your first draft. Here are some suggestions:

> a. Does your first paragraph introduce the topic? Can you find a way to make it more interesting and exciting for the reader?
>
> b. Does the second paragraph describe your family? Can you make the descriptions more vivid with sensory words and active verbs?
>
> c. Does the third paragraph describe the three December activities you like best? Are your descriptions clear and vivid?
>
> d. Does the last paragraph clearly restate and sum up the topic?
>
> e. Can you add any words or phrases that give the reader the feeling of the season?
>
> f. Are your sentences complete? Do subjects and verbs agree?
>
> g. Are you sure that all spelling is correct?

2. When your essay is as perfect as you can make it, write your final copy below. Indent at the beginning of each paragraph. Use the back of this worksheet if you need more room.

_____

_____

_____

_____

_____

_____

_____

_____

_____

_____

_____

_____

Name _____ Date_____

Bah! Humbug!
Prewriting

A Christmas Carol by Charles Dickens is one of the most famous stories ever written. It was published on December 17, 1843. It is about Ebenezer Scrooge. He is miserly, greedy, and mean. When anyone wishes him a happy holiday, he replies, "Bah! Humbug!" He learns to be a better person after dreaming about a terrifying adventure with three ghosts. One of the lovable characters in *A Christmas Carol* is Tiny Tim Cratchit, a poor, lame boy who is always cheerful and sees the good in everyone.

Charles Dickens had a gift for creating characters that people remember. We can't all write like Charles Dickens, but we can learn how to make the characters in our own stories more interesting.

In this activity, you are going to make up your own story about a scary dream. The brainstorming list below will help you think up and organize your story.

BRAINSTORMING LIST

1. First, decide upon a character who will have the dream. Is it a boy, a girl, an adult? How old? Write his or her name below. Next to this main character's name, write words and phrases to describe him or her.

   _____

   _____

2. There should be one or two other characters (friends, enemies, relatives, etc.). Write each one's name and a description below.

   _____

   _____

3. Describe a scary dream for your main character. Tell at least three frightening things that happen in the dream.

   _____

   _____

4. Describe how the dream changes the main character.

   _____

   _____

5. How does he or she show these changes to the other characters?

   _____

   _____

Name _____ **Date** _____

Bah! Humbug!
First Draft

DIRECTIONS: Write a first draft of your story below. Use your brainstorming list as a guide. Here are some suggestions:

1. Decide upon a title for your story, such as *A Dreadful Dream*, *The Dream Ghosts*, *Ghosts in December*, *Holiday Horror*, or any other. Write it on the first line below.

2. Begin the story in an interesting way that will make the reader want to go on. You might start with a conversation between two of the characters, or an unusual question, or a startling event.

3. Describe the characters fully, and show what kind of people they are by their actions.

4. The story will be easy to write if you follow the order suggested on your brainstorming list, but you don't have to do this if you would rather tell it in a different way. Just be sure the plot is logical and clear so the reader will know what is going on.

5. The ending of the story can be surprising or sad or joyful. That is up to you—the author. Just be sure that everything happening in the story leads naturally to this ending.

Write the first draft below. Indent at the beginning of each paragraph. Use the back of this worksheet if you need more room.

_____

_____

_____

_____

_____

_____

_____

_____

_____

© 1997 by The Center for Applied Research in Education

Name _____ Date_____

Bah! Humbug!
Revising and Writing a Final Copy

DIRECTIONS:

1. Revise and edit the first draft of your story, as follows:

a. Can you make the beginning more interesting and exciting?

b. Can you describe the characters more vividly with similes such as "He was as strong as a bull" or "Her eyes glowed like burning coals"?

c. Can you make the dreams more striking by using active verbs and sensory language?

d. If you use dialogue, do you begin a new line (and indent) each time a character speaks?

e. Is the ending satisfying? Should anything be added to complete the story?

f. Have you corrected any errors in sentence structure and spelling?

2. Write the final copy of your story below. Put the title on the first line. Indent at the beginning of each paragraph. Use the back of this worksheet if you need more room.

_____

_____

_____

_____

_____

_____

_____

_____

_____

_____

_____

Name _____ Date _____

BOSTON TEA PARTY
SENTENCES

On December 16, 1773, an amazing event took place in Boston Harbor. At that time, Boston was not a city in the state of Massachusetts in the United States of America. There *was* no United States of America. There were only thirteen colonies, belonging to England. Massachusetts was one of those colonies.

The American colonists were different from their English cousins. There was lots of room on this continent. There were many opportunities for hard-working people. England was far away, and the colonists got used to doing things on their own. They became free-thinking and independent. When the King of England began to burden them with heavy taxes, they protested. Instead of listening to their complaints, the King imposed even more taxes, one of the worst being on tea.

On December 16, 1773, workmen and merchants, dressed in native American clothing, boarded a ship bringing tea into Boston Harbor and dumped the tea overboard. This came to be known as the "Boston Tea Party." The American colonists liked tea, but they valued their freedom more.

The English rulers thought that Americans were rowdy, disobedient, and contrary, *just like the sentences below!* Each sentence is contrary or opposite to the truth and contains at least one wrong fact. *Rewrite each sentence on the line below*, using the correct facts. (You can find the real facts by reading this section again.)

1. Nothing important happened in Boston Harbor on December 16, 1773.

_____

2. The American colonies belonged to France then.

_____

3. The colonists liked to obey orders.

_____

4. The King of England did not tax the colonies.

_____

5. The colonists did not protest against the taxes.

_____

6. The King reduced the tax on tea.

_____

7. The colonists bought the tea and paid the tax.

_____

Name _____ **Date** _____

BOSTON TEA PARTY
PARAGRAPH WRITING

DIRECTIONS: Write a paragraph about the Boston Tea Party. You can do it one of two ways:

1. Just copy the sentences you corrected in Activity 9A. They can be combined into a paragraph.
2. OR, write your own paragraph about the Boston Tea Party. Use the information in Activity 9A. If you wish, you can do research about the Boston Tea Party and add more facts.

Write your paragraph below. Indent at the beginning of the paragraph. If you wish, you can illustrate the paragraph in the space beneath.

THE BOSTON TEA PARTY

_____

_____

_____

_____

_____

_____

_____

Name _____ **Date** _____

THE GIANT SNOWMAN
FILL-IN-STORY

DIRECTIONS: Complete this story by filling in the blanks.

Jeremy opened his eyes. He sat up in his _____ bed. Something felt

_____ different. He _____ out of bed and _____ out the window. It had

snowed during the _____! Snow was everywhere. It covered the _____.

Jeremy felt very _____. He _____ his teeth and got dressed. He wore his

_____ and his _____, and put on a warm _____. Then he woke up his

sister, _____.

"It's _____ outside!" he told her.

Jeremy's sister got dressed as _____ as she could. They rushed downstairs.

They put on their _____ jackets and their _____ boots and went outside.

The snow felt _____ on their _____ faces.

"Let's build a _____ snowman!" said _____.

Jeremy and _____ set to work. They worked for _____ hours. At last, it

began to look like a _____ snowman. It had a _____ body and a _____

head. They decorated it with buttons and _____, and put a _____ on top.

"It's the _____ snowman ever!" exclaimed _____.

Suddenly, the _____ snowman began to grow. It kept getting bigger and

_____.

"Hey!" exclaimed _____. "This is really _____."

They stared at the _____ snowman. It was now as tall as _____, and

still growing _____. **(Finish the story in your own words. Use the back of**

this worksheet.)

Name _____ **Date**_____

SCRAMBLED HISTORY

On December 1, 1955, Rosa Parks, an African-American woman, sat on a front bus seat in Montgomery, Alabama. These seats were usually reserved for white people only. Mrs. Parks's brave action was the spark that started the civil rights movement led by Dr. Martin Luther King, Jr.

Paragraphs have a beginning, a middle, and an end. The *beginning* introduces the topic. The *middle* develops the topic and the *end* concludes it.

In the paragraph above, the beginning introduces the subject—Mrs. Rosa Parks's brave act on December 1, 1955. The middle adds more information about the meaning of this event. The end shows how this act resulted in the civil rights movement.

The sentences below are from another paragraph about this event, but they are not in the correct order—they are scrambled! Can you decide which sentence belongs at the beginning, which should be at the end, and how those in the middle should be arranged?

Put these sentences in the correct order into a paragraph. Write the paragraph on the lines below.

1. Rosa Parks was tired, and there were no empty seats in the back of the bus.

2. This anniversary is often called the beginning of the civil rights movement.

3. This event became front-page news all over the country.

4. December 1, 1955 is an important date in the history of civil rights.

5. Rosa Parks sat down on it.

6. There was an empty seat in the front of the bus.

7. It was the day that Rosa Parks, an African-American woman, demanded equal rights.

8. In Montgomery, Alabama, in 1955, the front seats of buses were reserved for white people.

Write the paragraph here:

_____

_____

_____

_____

_____

(See Activity 11B for the correct solution.)

Name _____ **Date** _____

SCRAMBLED HISTORY

Here is the correct solution to the scrambled sentences in Activity 11A:

"December 1, 1955 is an important date in the history of civil rights. It was the day that Rosa Parks, an African-American woman, demanded equal rights. In Montgomery, Alabama, in 1955, the front seats of buses were reserved for white people. Rosa Parks was tired, and there were no empty seats in the back of the bus. There was an empty seat in the front of the bus. Rosa Parks sat down on it. This event became front-page news all over the country. This anniversary is often called the beginning of the civil rights movement."

Is your paragraph correct? If not, rewrite it on the back of the worksheet for Activity 11A.

Here is another scrambled paragraph. These sentences can be combined into a paragraph about a different historical event in December. Can you unscramble them and put them into a paragraph?

1. It was a terrible massacre.
2. The complete story of this bloody day is told in a book called *Bury My Heart at Wounded Knee.*
3. December 29 is the anniversary of a terrible event in U.S. history.
4. It took place in the year 1890 in South Dakota.
5. On that day, U.S. troops killed more than 200 Sioux men, women, and children at Wounded Knee.

Write the paragraph below:

_____

_____

_____

_____

_____

_____

_____

_____

Name _____ Date_____

BILLION-DOLLAR GIFT LIST
PREWRITING

> December is a time for gift-giving. It's great to get presents. Giving them can also be a lot of fun.

What presents would you give to the people you know if you had billions of dollars to spend? That's what you are going to write about in this activity. You can really let your imagination go wild! But, first, organize your ideas in this brainstorming list.

BRAINSTORMING LIST

1. Write a beginning sentence (or sentences) for your essay. Try to make it interesting with a question or a startling statement, such as, "Wouldn't it be great to be a billionaire?" or "I'm looking forward to the day when I am the richest person in the world." Write your sentence (or sentences) here.

2. The chart below is divided into three columns. In the first column, list the names of *at least* three people for whom you would like to buy gifts. In the second column, tell who they are (brother, aunt, friend, parent, neighbor, teacher, etc.). In the third column, write the gift you want to get for each one:

	NAME	*RELATIONSHIP*	*GIFT*
1.			
2.			
3.			
4.			
5.			

Name _____ **Date** _____

Billion-Dollar Gift List
First Draft

> *DIRECTIONS:* Write a first draft of your essay about being a gift-giving billionaire. Use your brainstorming list as a guide.

1. Use the first sentence from your brainstorming list to begin the first paragraph. Then tell what you are going to do, as in this example: "Wouldn't it be great to be a billionaire? If I had lots of money, I could buy wonderful presents for the people I care about." Write your first paragraph here (2–4 sentences).

    _____

    _____

    _____

2. The second paragraph can describe one of the people on your list, what you would like to give him or her, and why, as in this example: "The first person on my billionaire's gift list would be my mom. She always buys us whatever we need, even if she has to do without new clothes. If I had a billion dollars, I would take her to the most expensive shop in town and buy her a complete set of clothes for all seasons of the year." Write your second paragraph here (3–4 sentences).

    _____

    _____

    _____

3. Paragraphs three and four: Choose *two* other people from your list. Write a separate paragraph (3–4 sentences) for each of them.

    _____

    _____

    _____

    _____

4. The last paragraph should restate and sum up the topic, as in this example. "I'll probably never become a billionaire. It's just a dream. But it's fun to plan how I could use that money to make other people happy." Write your last paragraph (2–3 sentences) here.

    _____

    _____

    _____

Name _____ **Date** _____

Billion-Dollar Gift List
Revising and Writing a Final Copy

DIRECTIONS:

1. Revise and edit your first draft. Here are some suggestions:

---

a. Is the beginning as interesting as you can make it? Will the reader want to go on?

b. In the second, third, and fourth paragraphs, do you tell about the people on your list? Do you describe their gifts vividly? Do you explain why you want to give these gifts?

c. Does the last paragraph restate and sum up the topic?

d. Are your sentences complete? Do subjects and verbs agree?

e. Can you cut unnecessary words to make your writing sharper?

f. Check spelling where necessary.

---

2. When your first draft is as good as you can make it, write your final copy below. Indent at the beginning of each paragraph. (Use the back of this worksheet if you need more room.)

_____

_____

_____

_____

_____

_____

_____

_____

_____

_____

_____

Name _____ **Date** _____

DECEMBER DECORATIONS

In December, we see colorful decorations in stores, homes, schools, and offices. *Adjectives* are words that can be used to decorate a sentence and make it shine more brightly. Look at these two sentences:

The snow glittered beneath the sun.
The silvery snow glittered beneath the December sun.

Can you underline the adjectives in the second sentence that make it more colorful? If you underlined *silvery* and *December*, you are correct!

DIRECTIONS: The following sentences are dull. Can you "decorate" them by adding adjectives (at least one adjective for each sentence)? Write the new, colorful sentences on the lines below.

1. The school bus sometimes has trouble on the roads in December.

_____

_____

2. My dog hates to go out on winter evenings.

_____

_____

3. I pulled the sweater over my head.

_____

_____

4. I glide over the pond with my ice skates.

_____

_____

5. I like to look at decorations in the shops.

_____

_____

6. The hat hung down over her eyes.

_____

_____

7. Snow is on the ground.

_____

_____

8. I like to walk in the park on a winter day.

_____

_____

Name _____ **Date** _____

REVEALING THE FUTURE
PREWRITING

One who can see into the future is called a fortuneteller or *seer*. December 14 marks the birth of the most famous seer of all time. His name was Nostradamus and he was born in France in the year 1503. His prophetic books are still being read today. His followers claim that his predictions have come true in the past and will continue to do so.

Most people do not believe it is possible to see into the future. Even so, it can be fun to try. After all, you have a chance of being right at least part of the time!

In this activity, you will write an article (essay) making predictions for the next two months. First, complete this brainstorming list.

BRAINSTORMING LIST

1. Write a sentence introducing yourself as a great fortuneteller. You can use your real name or make up an unusual one.

   _____

2. List some of the things you think might happen to your *family* (including you) during the next two months. These predictions can be silly or serious, possible or ridiculous, good or bad, sad or happy. You don't need sentences here; words or phrases will do.

   _____
   _____
   _____
   _____

3. List things that could happen in your *school* in the next two months.

   _____
   _____
   _____
   _____

4. List things that could happen in *your country* and *the world* in the next two months.

   _____
   _____
   _____
   _____

Name _____ Date _____

REVEALING THE FUTURE
WRITING A FIRST DRAFT

DIRECTIONS: Using your brainstorming list, write the first draft of an article revealing your predictions for the next two months, as follows:

1. In the first paragraph introduce yourself as an expert fortuneteller, as in this example:

> I am Marvelo the Great. In my crystal ball, I can see the past, the present, and the future. Like Nostradamus of old, I know everything that has happened and all that will happen.

Write your first paragraph below. (This is just a first draft).

_____

_____

2. In the second paragraph, make predictions for yourself and your family, as in this example:

> On the first day of the new year, my parents will win the lottery and we'll become instant millionaires. Later that month, a talent scout will see me walking down the street and offer me the lead in a new TV sitcom. Best of all, my brother will disappear into his room and never come out.

Write your second paragraph below.

_____

_____

3. In the third paragraph make predictions for your school or the world or both, as in this example:

> On January 15, a strange spaceship will land on the White House lawn in Washington, D.C. Aliens from a far-off galaxy will take over the country and the world. They will teach humans how to live in peace. There will be no more wars.

Write your third paragraph below.

_____

_____

_____

4. In the last paragraph, sum up the topic, as in this example:

> Marvelo is the greatest fortuneteller ever. That is why everything I predict will come true. Just wait and see!

Write your last paragraph below.

_____

_____

_____

Name _____ **Date** _____

REVEALING THE FUTURE
REVISING AND WRITING A FINAL COPY

DIRECTIONS:

1. Revise and edit the first draft of your article, as follows:

> a. Does your first paragraph introduce the topic in an interesting way? Can you change or add anything to make it more strange or unusual?
>
> b. Does your second paragraph make predictions for you and your family? Can you change any words to make it more exciting to the reader?
>
> c. Does the third paragraph make predictions for your school or the world or both? Will the reader understand them clearly? Can you find ways to make them funnier or more exciting?
>
> d. Does the last paragraph restate the topic and sum it up?
>
> e. Can you add any active verbs to make your writing vivid?
>
> f. Is sentence structure correct? Do subjects and verbs agree?
>
> g. Check spelling.

2. When your article is as perfect as you can make it, write your final copy below. First, make up a title and put it on the first line. Indent at the beginning of paragraphs. Use the back of this worksheet if you need more room.

_____

_____

_____

_____

_____

_____

_____

_____

_____

_____

JANUARY

JANUARY

"Ring out the old, ring in the new,
Ring, happy bells, across the snow:
The year is going, let him go;
Ring out the false, ring in the true."
—*Alfred, Lord Tennyson*

JANUS, THE TWO-FACED GOD, LOOKS TOWARD PAST AND FUTURE . . .
FATHER TIME . . . NEW YEAR'S DAY . . . PARTIES AND RESOLUTIONS . . .
JANUARY SALES . . . LONG WINTER NIGHTS . . . SHORT GREY DAYS . . .
SNOW, ICE, BLIZZARDY AND BLUSTERY . . . SUPERBOWL . . . PRESIDENTIAL
INAUGURATIONS . . . MARTIN LUTHER KING, JR. DAY (3RD MONDAY)

JANUARY EVENTS

January 1, 1863: The Emancipation Proclamation freeing the slaves was issued by President Lincoln in accordance with his preliminary proclamation of September 22, 1862

January 7, 1789: The first national election was held in the U.S.

January 11, 1935: Amelia Earhart became the first woman to make a solo flight across the Pacific Ocean

January 20, 1933: U.S. Congress passed a resolution setting January 20 as the date for the inauguration of a president every four years

January 20, 1892: First official basketball game, invented by Dr. James Naismith, is played by students at the International YMCA Training School in Springfield, Massachusetts

January 24, 1848: Gold was discovered in California, setting in motion the great gold rush of 1849

JANUARY BIRTHDAYS

January 4, 1642: Sir Isaac Newton, one of the world's great scientists, discoverer of the law of gravity

January 8, 1935: Elvis Presley, innovative king of rock-and-roll

January 11, 1757: Alexander Hamilton, American statesman and first Secretary of the Treasury; was born in the West Indies

January 17, 1706: Benjamin Franklin, American printer, journalist, scientist, inventor, philosopher, statesman, diplomat, and author

January 19, 1809: Edgar Allan Poe, American poet, critic and short story writer; wrote the first modern detective stories

January 19, 1807: Robert E. Lee, commander-in-chief of Confederate armies during the Civil War; was born in Stratford, Virginia

January 27, 1756: Wolfgang Amadeus Mozart, great musician and composer

January 30, 1882: Franklin Delano Roosevelt, 32nd president of the U.S.

WRITING ACTIVITIES FOR JANUARY

Name _____ **Date** _____

HAPPY NEW YEAR
PREWRITING

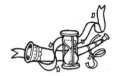

> "Ring out the old, ring in the new,
> Ring, happy bells, across the snow;
> The year is going, let him go;
> Ring out the false, ring in the true."

These lines were written by Alfred, Lord Tennyson, a famous English poet. The beginning of a new year is greeted with celebrations and merrymaking all over the world. Many writers and poets have been inspired by it. Some of them wrote jolly verses like the one above. Others are more serious, such as the Persian poet, Omar Khayyam, who wrote:

> "Now the New Year reviving old Desires,
> The thoughtful Soul to Solitude retires."

Both of these poems use rhyme, but the rhymes are different. In the first poem, the *first and last* lines rhyme, and the *second and third* lines rhyme. This can be shown as ABBA, which means that *Line 1 (A) rhymes with Line 4 (A); Line 2 (B) rhymes with Line 3 (B).*

The two lines in Omar Khayyam's verse rhyme with each other (AA). If you added a third and fourth line that rhymed, this would be shown as BB, as in this example:

"New Year's Day will always fall	**A**
On January first, and all	**A**
Around the world, the bells will ring,	**B**
While folks make merry, feast and sing."	**B**

The rhyme scheme for this poem is AABB. *Lines 1 and 2 rhyme (AA),* as do *lines 3 and 4 (BB).* This is the easiest kind of rhyme. Can you write a 4-line verse about the New Year, using the rhyme scheme AABB?

Before writing your verse, it will help to prepare a list of rhyming words that could be used in a poem about the New Year. Then you can choose the ones that will best fit into your poem.

DIRECTIONS: Next to each word below, write as many rhyming words as you can. The first few are started for you.

1. year: <u>clear, ear, hear,</u> _____
2. new: <u>few, true,</u> _____
3. ring: <u>ding,</u> _____
4. chill: _____
5. snow: _____
6. day: _____

Name _____ **Date** _____

HAPPY NEW YEAR
FIRST DRAFT

Here is another example of a 4-line poem using the rhyme scheme AABB (lines 1 and 2 rhyme; lines 3 and 4 rhyme).

> "Wake up! Wake up! Rise up and hear
> The happy bells ring in the year,
> All is fresh and new and bright,
> And winter birds have taken flight."

DIRECTIONS: Now it's your turn to be a rhyming poet. Use the rhyming words you prepared in Activity 1A. Use the AABB rhyme scheme, where the first two lines rhyme with each other, and the last two lines rhyme.

Write the first draft of a 4-line verse about the New Year on the lines below.

_____

_____

_____

_____

See how easy it is to write a poem? Now that you've done it once, why not try it again! This time, write a 4-line poem about the winter season. The AABB rhyme scheme is easy to use, but if you want to use a different rhyme scheme, you may do so. Here are some winter rhymes that may be of help:

> snow, glow; chill, still; ice, twice; ski, free; sleet, street; freeze, sneeze; cold, hold; frost, glossed; mitten, bitten

Write the first draft of your 4-line poem about winter on the lines below:

_____

_____

_____

_____

Name _____ **Date** _____

HAPPY NEW YEAR
REVISING AND WRITING A FINAL COPY

DIRECTIONS:

1. Most poets rewrite their poems over and over again before they get it exactly right. Revise and edit the two poems you wrote for Activity 1B. Here are some suggestions for improvement:

   a. Is the rhyme scheme in the first poem correct? It should be AABB. Do the first two lines rhyme with each other? Do the last two lines rhyme?

   b. Are the rhymes you used in both poems the best you can do? Can you think of any that would work better?

   c. When we try to use rhyme, sometimes the language becomes awkward. Is this true of any of your lines? Can you reword them to flow more smoothly?

   d. Have you used the best words to fit the mood and theme of your poems? Can you find other words or phrases that might be better?

2. When your poems are as good as you can make them, write your final copies in the boxes below. If you wish, you can use the extra space around each poem for illustrations.

Name _____ **Date** _____

LOOKING BOTH WAYS
PREWRITING

The month of January gets its name from the ancient Roman god, Janus, a two-faced god. With his two faces, Janus could look back into the old year and forward into the new one at the same time.

What did Janus see when he looked back? What did he see when he looked ahead?

What do you remember best about the old year just passed? What do you think will happen in the year to come? In this activity, you will be able to pretend you are the god, Janus, looking both ways!

Before beginning your essay, first write down and organize your ideas in a brainstorming list.

DIRECTIONS:

In the *first column* of **Box A** below, list three events of the past year that were important, interesting, or exciting for you.

In the *second column* next to each item, write some details about that event. (You don't need sentences here—words and phrases are enough.)

In the *third column* next to each item, write words and phrases that explain why this event is important.

BOX A		
EVENT #1:		
EVENT #2:		
EVENT #3:		

In the *first column* of **Box B** below, list three interesting, important, or exciting things you think will happen in the coming year.

In the *second column* next to each item, write details about that event (words and phrases are enough).

In the *third column* next to each item, write words and phrases that explain why this event is important, interesting, or exciting.

BOX B		
EVENT #1:		
EVENT #2:		
EVENT #3:		

Name _____ **Date** _____

LOOKING BOTH WAYS
FIRST DRAFT

Your brainstorming list will help you write an essay about looking both ways. Just keep it in front of you and follow these directions.

1. The first paragraph introduces the topic in an interesting way, as in this example:

> The Roman god, Janus, had two faces. He could look at the year past and the year to come. If Janus were around today, this is what he might see.

Write a first draft of your first paragraph below (2–4 sentences).

_____

_____

_____

2. The second paragraph will tell about three events you remember from the year past. Describe each event briefly and tell why it is important. Write a first draft of your second paragraph below (4–7 sentences).

_____

_____

_____

3. In the third paragraph, mention three events you think will happen in the year ahead. Describe each event briefly and tell why it is important. Write a first draft of your third paragraph below (4–7 sentences).

_____

_____

_____

4. The last paragraph restates and sums up the topic, as in this example:

> Last year's events have already happened. Since I am not Janus, I don't know if my predictions for the year ahead will come true. The months to come will prove me right or wrong.

Write a first draft of your last paragraph below (2–4 sentences).

_____

_____

_____

© 1997 by The Center for Applied Research in Education

Name _____ **Date** _____

LOOKING BOTH WAYS
REVISING AND WRITING A FINAL COPY

DIRECTIONS:

1. Revise and edit the first draft of your essay about looking both ways.

> a. Does your first paragraph introduce the topic? Can you find a way to make it more interesting to the reader?
>
> b. Does the second paragraph describe three things that happened last year? Does it explain why they are important or interesting to you?
>
> c. Does the third paragraph describe three things that will occur in the year ahead and explain why they are important or interesting?
>
> d. Does the last paragraph restate and sum up the topic?
>
> e. Are your sentences complete? Do subjects and verbs agree?
>
> f. Are your sentences cluttered with too many words? Cut out any unnecessary ones.
>
> g. Can you add any vivid language, such as active verbs or sensory words to make your writing more interesting?

2. When you are satisfied with your revisions, write your final copy below. Put a title on the first line—you can use *looking both ways*, or another title of your own choosing. Indent at the beginning of paragraphs. (Use the back of this worksheet if you need more room.)

_____

_____

_____

_____

_____

_____

_____

_____

Name _____ **Date** _____

Promises! Promises!
Prewriting

Do you make New Year's resolutions?

What is a resolution? A *resolution* is a promise. It is a promise that you make to yourself!

It is a tradition for people to make resolutions at the beginning of a new year. There are different kinds of resolutions.

One sort of resolution has to do only with oneself. You might decide to lose weight, to stop eating candy, to exercise more, or to watch less TV. Other resolutions might involve family or friends. You could resolve to be more patient with your little brother, to be more helpful to your mom, or not to get into fights with your friends.

Some resolutions are about school and the outside world, such as getting to class on time, trying for better grades, or not teasing the neighbor's dog.

If you manage to keep these promises, it will make you feel better about yourself. So, it's important not to make wild resolutions that are too difficult to follow. Your promises to yourself should not be too hard to keep.

YOUR NEW YEAR'S RESOLUTIONS

DIRECTIONS: The box below is divided into three sections.

1. In the first section, list at least two resolutions for your *personal improvement*.

2. In the second section, list at least two resolutions that have to do with *family and friends*.

3. In the third section, list at least two resolutions about *school and the outside world*.

PERSONAL IMPROVEMENT: _____

_____

FAMILY AND FRIENDS: _____

_____

SCHOOL AND THE OUTSIDE WORLD: _____

_____

Name _____ **Date**_____

Promises! Promises!
First Draft

Nobody's perfect! The beginning of a new year seems like a good time to think about changing. That's why people make resolutions in January.

In this activity, you are going to write the first draft of an essay about your promises to yourself for the new year. The best resolutions are those that you can be pretty sure of keeping. Choose *three* of the resolutions you listed in Activity 3A—*one* about personal improvement, *one* about family and friends, and *one* about school and the outside world. Write a 5-paragraph essay about these New Year's resolutions.

Write your first paragraph here, introducing the topic.

_____

_____

Write your second paragraph here. It should describe your personal improvement promise and tell why you are making it.

_____

_____

_____

Write your third paragraph here. It should describe your family and friends resolution and tell why you are making it.

_____

_____

_____

Write your fourth paragraph here. It should describe your resolution about school and the outside world, and tell why you are making it.

_____

_____

_____

Write your fifth paragraph here. It should restate the topic and sum it up.

_____

_____

_____

Name _____ **Date** _____

Pʀᴏᴍɪsᴇs! Pʀᴏᴍɪsᴇs!
Rᴇᴠɪsɪɴɢ ᴀɴᴅ Wʀɪᴛɪɴɢ ᴀ Fɪɴᴀʟ Cᴏᴘʏ

DIRECTIONS:

1. Edit and revise the first draft of your essay about New Year's resolutions. Here are some suggestions:

> a. Does the first paragraph introduce the topic in an interesting way? Can you make it more exciting by beginning with a question or a startling statement?
>
> b. Do the next three paragraphs describe each resolution? Do you clearly explain why you are making these resolutions?
>
> c. Do you restate and sum up the topic in the last paragraph?
>
> d. Are all sentences complete? Do subjects and verbs agree?
>
> e. Is all spelling correct? Check with a dictionary.

2. Write the final copy of your essay below. Write a title on the first line. (You can use *Promises! Promises!* or any other title of your choice.) Indent at the beginning of paragraphs. Use the back of this worksheet if you need more room.

_____

_____

_____

_____

_____

_____

_____

_____

_____

Name _____ Date_____

A SCIENTIFIC LOOK
PREWRITING

"GRAVITY: The force that tends to draw all objects in the earth's sphere toward the center of the earth."

January 4, 1642 was the birth date of one of the world's greatest scientists. His name was Sir Isaac Newton, and he is credited with originating important mathematical concepts such as the binomial theorem and elements of calculus. He is best known for his discovery of the force of gravity, and a legend has grown about how he came up with this important idea. The story says that Isaac Newton was sitting under an apple tree one day when an apple fell upon his head. This led him to wonder about what force causes objects to fall to Earth.

No one knows if this tale is true, but it could have occurred that way! Many scientific discoveries arise from observing ordinary objects. Most people don't pay much attention to the things around them, but scientists don't accept the world blindly. They try to figure out how and why things are the way they are.

In this activity, *you* are going to look at some ordinary objects and try to think about them as a scientist would. No, you don't have to sit under an apple tree and wait for the fruit to bop you on the head. There are many things you see every day that can be looked at scientifically.

For example, look at a pencil. What substance enables it to make black marks on a paper? Why does an eraser wipe out these marks? Would other substances work in the same way?

Look at the person sitting next to you. What color is his or her hair? Why do some people have brown hair, while others have blonde, black, or red hair? What makes hair curly or straight?

Why do some clocks tick? Why do telephones have pushbuttons? How do voices come through an intercom? These are just a few of the things we see every day that we don't usually wonder about—*unless we are scientists*! Begin your scientific thinking by completing the brainstorming list below.

BRAINSTORMING LIST

1. Write the names of three objects you see every day that might be interesting to analyze. _____

_____

2. List *each* of these objects in the first column below. In the second column next to each one, write words or phrases that describe what it looks like. In the third column, write words or phrases about its use. In the fourth column, write words and phrases that tell how you think it works. (If you don't know how it really works, *guess!*)

OBJECT	DESCRIPTION	USES	HOW IT WORKS
1.			
2.			
3.			

Name _____ Date _____

A SCIENTIFIC LOOK
FIRST DRAFT

Did you look at the objects you listed in Activity 4A the way a scientist would? Did you think about what they look like, what makes them useful, and how they work? Now that you have done this scientific thinking, writing an essay about it will be easy.

1. The first paragraph will introduce the topic (looking at things scientifically). Capture the reader's interest by starting with a question, such as "Do you really see the everyday objects around you?" or "How would you react to being bopped on the head with an apple?" Write your first paragraph (2–4 sentences) below. (This is just a first draft!)

_____

_____

_____

2. The second paragraph will be about the first object on your brainstorming list. Describe what it looks like, how it is used, and how it works. Write your second paragraph (2–4 sentences) below.

_____

_____

_____

3. Do the same with the second object on your list. Write your third paragraph (2–4 sentences) below.

_____

_____

_____

4. Do the same with the third object on your list. Write your fourth paragraph (2–4 sentences) below.

_____

_____

_____

5. The last paragraph restates and sums up the topic. Try to connect the ending to the beginning. For example, if you asked a question in the first paragraph, refer to it, or answer it here (in 2–4 sentences).

_____

_____

Name _____ **Date** _____

A SCIENTIFIC LOOK
REVISING AND WRITING A FINAL COPY

DIRECTIONS:

1. Edit and revise the first draft of your essay about looking at things scientifically. Here are some suggestions:

a. Does your first paragraph introduce the topic? Can you change anything to make it more interesting?

b. Do each of the next three paragraphs discuss one object scientifically? Do you describe it clearly, tell what it is used for, and how it works? Is your presentation clear and interesting?

c. Does the last paragraph restate and sum up the topic? Does it refer back to what you said in the first paragraph?

d. Are your sentences complete? Do subjects and verbs agree?

e. Are any of your sentences too short and abrupt or too long and wordy? Try to use both long and short sentences.

f. Can you make your writing sharper by cutting unnecessary words?

g. Check spelling of unfamiliar words.

2. Write the final copy of your essay below. Indent at the beginning of paragraphs. (Use the back of this worksheet if you need more room.)

_____

_____

_____

_____

_____

_____

_____

_____

_____

_____

Name _____ **Date** _____

JANUARY SENTENCES

DIRECTIONS:

1. Write a sentence beginning with each of the letters in the word "January." The first one is done for you. (Don't forget to put a period, question mark, or exclamation point at the end of each sentence!)

    Jam tastes good on toast. _____

    A _____

    N _____

    U _____

    A _____

    R _____

    Y _____

2. Now, write a sentence beginning with each of the letters in "HAPPY NEW YEAR." The first one is done for you.

    How are you on this fine January day? _____

    A _____

    P _____

    P _____

    Y _____

    N _____

    E _____

    W _____

    Y _____

    E _____

    A _____

    R _____

Name _____ Date_____

CRIME BUSTERS
PREWRITING

Do you like mysteries? Most people do. They are exciting, sometimes scary, and it's always fun to try to figure out the solution.

One person, more than any other, is responsible for the kind of mysteries we read today. His name was Edgar Allan Poe. He was born on January 19, 1809, and is called the "father of the modern detective story." Poe's stories were written more than a hundred years ago, but people still like to read them. Two of his most famous mysteries are *The Gold Bug* and *Murders in the Rue Morgue*. If you haven't read any of Poe's detective stories yet, you should do so. You will surely enjoy them!

You could write a mystery story. It's not hard. All you need are:

1. a crime or mystery, such as something being stolen or someone disappearing
2. a character who solves the mystery—this detective can be an adult or a young person—it can even be you
3. some suspects—at least two or three
4. clues for the detective to discover as he or she investigates

When you complete the brainstorming list below, you will be ready to begin writing your own mystery story.

BRAINSTORMING LIST

1. Decide on a name for your main character, the detective. You can use your own name or any name you choose. Write the name below. Next to it, write words and phrases describing that person—age, appearance, personality, family, friends, interests, etc.

   MAIN CHARACTER'S NAME AND DESCRIPTION:_____

   _____

2. Describe the "crime" that must be solved. Here are some examples:
   —A teacher's record book is stolen from her desk drawer
   —A hamster disappears from its cage in the school science room
   —A Little League team can't find its new uniforms
   —A homework assignment disappears from someone's notebook

   Describe the "crime" below. Use one of the above or make up your own:

   _____

3. Make up names for two or three suspects. Next to each, write words and phrases describing that character and why he or she is a suspect:
   First suspect: _____
   Second suspect: _____
   Third suspect: _____

4. In the space below, list some *clues* the detective can find to solve the mystery:

Name _____ Date _____

CRIME BUSTERS
FIRST DRAFT

DIRECTIONS: It will be easy to write a mystery. You have already completed the hardest part by preparing a brainstorming list. Now, you just have to put the facts into story form. Here are some suggestions:

> Begin your story with the discovery of the "crime." It could be found by any character, even the detective, or by a group of people like a class.
> Tell how and why the detective decides to solve this "crime."
> Introduce the first clue quickly.
> Use a lot of dialogue, especially when the suspects are questioned.
> Show other clues as you go along, but don't make it too easy. It's best if the reader is surprised at the end.
> Be sure you clear up the mystery completely at the end.

If you are having trouble getting started, here are some possible beginning sentences:

> "Patrick was the first one in science class to notice that the hamster was not in its cage."
> "Miss Blair's face was red with anger. "Who's been at my desk drawer?' she demanded."
> "Two hours before the most important game of the season, the Red Tigers discovered that their team uniforms were missing."
> "Jennifer looked through her notebook frantically. Her homework paper had been there when she left home that morning."

Now, write a first draft of your story. Don't expect a first draft to be perfect—just concentrate on getting your thoughts down on paper. (Use the back of this worksheet if you need more room.)

_____

_____

_____

_____

_____

_____

_____

Name _____ Date_____

CRIME BUSTERS
REVISING AND WRITING A FINAL COPY

DIRECTIONS:

1. Edit and revise the first draft of your mystery story.

---

a. Is the beginning exciting? Will the reader want to go on?

b. Do you show the "crime" at the beginning? Can you make it more interesting or startling?

c. Do you describe the main character (the detective) and show what that person is like by what he or she says and does?

d. Are all characters shown clearly? Can the reader see who the suspects are and why they are suspected?

e. Do you give away the ending too soon? If so, change the story to keep the reader in suspense longer.

f. Will the reader be surprised at the end? If not, try to create more mystery.

g. Did you indent at the beginning of each paragraph? Did you indent each time a character begins to speak?

h. Use active verbs or sensory words to make the writing more vivid.

---

2. Write the final copy of your story below. Make up a title and put it on the first line. (Use the back of this worksheet if you need more room.)

_____

_____

_____

_____

_____

_____

_____

_____

_____

Name _____ **Date** _____

BLIZZARDS AND SUNSHINE

Nancy Negative thinks that January is a dreary month, filled with snow, ice, blizzards, and short dark days.

Her friend, Paul Positive, sees the bright side of January.

When Nancy says, "I can't stand all this snow and ice," Paul replies, "One sunshiny January day makes up for all the dreary ones."

Here are some of Nancy Negative's other dreary remarks. Below each one, write a cheery reply from Paul Positive. (The first one is done for you.)

1. NANCY: I hate these cold nights.

   PAUL: <u>I love winter evenings by the fire.</u> _____

2. NANCY: Icy streets are hard to walk on.

   PAUL: _____

3. NANCY: I don't like wearing boots and gloves.

   PAUL: _____

4. NANCY: The snow is too deep!

   PAUL: _____

5. NANCY: New Year's resolutions are stupid.

   PAUL: _____

6. NANCY: There are no good holidays in January.

   PAUL: _____

7. NANCY: Winter sports are boring.

   PAUL: _____

8. NANCY: It's too cold to get up in the morning.

   PAUL: _____

Name _____ **Date** _____

Pop Idols
Prewriting

Elvis Presley was born on January 8, 1935.

No matter how young you are, you have probably heard of Elvis Presley. He was the biggest pop idol of his time, perhaps of all time! Many people think he was the originator of rock-and-roll. He was called "The King" and was adored by millions of fans.

What "star" of today do you admire most? Is it a musician like Elvis? Your idol might be a TV personality, a movie star, an athlete, or a dancer. It will be fun to describe your pop idol and then share your reports and see who your classmates like best.

Your essay will be easier to write if you first prepare a brainstorming list.

BRAINSTORMING LIST

1. Write the name of your pop idol on the line below. Next to it, indicate what he or she does.

   _____

2. In the space below, write as many words or phrases as you can to describe your idol's appearance, manner, style, personality, etc.

3. In the space below, write as many words or phrases as you can to explain why you admire this person.

4. Write a beginning sentence (or sentences) for your essay on the lines below. (Example: "I like a lot of performers, but there is only one who could be called my idol.")

   _____

   _____

5. Write a concluding sentence (or sentences) for your essay below. (Example: Has there ever been such a combination of talent and personality? No wonder this is my pop idol!")

   _____

   _____

Name _____ Date _____

Pop Idols
First Draft

> It's fun and easy to write about things that really interest you, such as your favorite pop stars. It will be even more of a snap if you keep your brainstorming list in front of you while you compose this simple, 3-paragraph essay. Just follow the directions below. Remember, this is just a first draft, so don't worry too much about spelling and grammar. Just concentrate on getting your thoughts down on paper.

DIRECTIONS:

1. The first paragraph introduces the topic in a lively way. Begin with the sentence(s) from your brainstorming list, then add some interesting comments about this topic. Write your first paragraph (2–4 sentences) here:

   _____

   _____

   _____

2. The second paragraph develops the topic by describing your pop idol and why you admire him or her. Use the words and phrases you prepared in your brainstorming list. Write your second paragraph (3–7 sentences) here:

   _____

   _____

   _____

   _____

   _____

3. The final paragraph restates and sums up the topic. Use the concluding sentence(s) from your brainstorming list and build upon it. Write your final paragraph (2–4 sentences) here:

   _____

   _____

   _____

Name _____ **Date**_____

POP IDOLS
REVISING AND WRITING A FINAL COPY

DIRECTIONS:

1. Edit and revise the first draft of your essay about your pop idol. Here are some suggestions:

   a. Does the first paragraph introduce the topic? Can you use a question or startling statement to make it livelier and more interesting?

   b. Does the second paragraph accurately describe your idol and explain why you admire him or her? Can you add anything to make it clearer to the reader how your idol looks and acts, such as a description of his or her clothing, manner, or performing style? Have you clearly explained your reasons for admiring this person?

   c. Does the third paragraph restate and sum up the topic? Would it be livelier or more interesting if you worded it differently?

   d. Can you make your description more vivid with sensory language and active verbs?

   e. Are your sentences complete? Do subjects and verbs agree?

   f. Check your spelling.

2. When your essay is as perfect as you can make it, write a final copy below. Indent at the beginning of paragraphs. (Use the back of this worksheet if you need more room.)

_____

_____

_____

_____

_____

_____

_____

_____

_____

_____

Name _____ **Date** _____

WISE WORDS
PREWRITING

> "If a man could have half his wishes, he would double his troubles."
> "Half a truth is often a great lie."
> "Success has ruined many a man."
> "He that can have patience can have what he will."
> "Keep your eyes wide open before marriage and half-shut afterwards."
> "If you'd lose a troublesome visitor, lend him money."

Benjamin Franklin was born on January 17, 1706. His advice is as sound today as it was hundreds of years ago during the days of the American Revolution. He was a great American and an amazing man—printer, journalist, scientist, inventor, philosopher, statesman, and author.

Everyone knows the story of how Benjamin Franklin demonstrated his theory of electricity by flying a kite in a lightning storm. He was also the printer and author of *Poor Richard's Almanack*. This was one of the few publications in the 1700s that was read by people in all walks of life. It contains wisdom, wit, and helpful practical suggestions. Some of the comments at the top of this page were first written in *Poor Richard's Almanack*. When Benjamin Franklin died in 1790, he was mourned not only in the country he helped create, but all over the world where he was known as "the old sage."

What do you think of Benjamin Franklin's wise words? Do you think his comments about people and life are still important?

DIRECTIONS:

Choose *one* of the sayings above, and prepare to write a paragraph about it. First, complete this brainstorming list.

BRAINSTORMING LIST

1. Copy the saying you have chosen on the line below.

_____

2. In the space below, write words and phrases that could be used to describe what you think this saying means.

3. Do you think this saying is still true (*yes* or *no*)? _____

4. In the space below, write words and phrases you can use to describe the reasons for your opinion.

Name _____ Date_____

WISE WORDS
FIRST DRAFT

Here is an example of a paragraph about one of Benjamin Franklin's sayings:

> " *'Half a truth is often a great lie.'* This comment is so clever and so accurate! Sometimes people pretend to be telling the truth, but they deliberately leave out part of it. This can be worse than an outright falsehood because the listener is more easily fooled into accepting it. People have done this to me so I know how it feels. Isn't it amazing that Benjamin Franklin understood this more than two hundred years ago?"

The notes you made on your brainstorming list will make it easy for you to write a paragraph about the saying you have chosen. Here are some further suggestions:

1. State the topic in the first sentence or sentences.

2. Develop the topic in the sentences that follow, telling what you believe this saying means and whether or not you believe it is true today.

3. Include the complete quote somewhere in your paragraph.

4. Don't forget to mention the author of the paragraph.

5. Sum up the topic in the final sentence or sentences.

Write a *first draft* of your paragraph below.

_____

_____

_____

_____

_____

_____

_____

_____

_____

_____

Name _____ Date _____

Wise Words
Revising and Writing a Final Copy

DIRECTIONS:

1. Edit and revise the first draft of your paragraph about one of Benjamin Franklin's sayings. Here are some suggestions for improvement:

---

a. Can you find a more interesting way to introduce the topic in the first sentence or sentences? Some ways of doing this are using a quote, as in the example above, beginning with a question or a startling statement.

b. Do the sentences that follow make it clear to the reader what you believe the saying means and whether or not you think it is true?

c. Does your final sentence sum up the topic clearly?

d. Do you include the quote somewhere in the paragraph?

e. Do you mention the author of the saying?

f. Are all sentences complete? Do subjects and verbs agree?

g. Is your paragraph cluttered with words that are unnecessary? Take out all words that don't serve a purpose.

h. Can you make your writing sharper with active verbs and sensory words?

i. Check spelling with a dictionary.

---

2. Write the final copy of your paragraph below. Indent at the beginning of the paragraph.

_____

_____

_____

_____

_____

_____

_____

_____

_____

Name _____ **Date** _____

LOST IN A BLIZZARD
PREWRITING

DIRECTIONS: Here is the beginning of a story for you to read:

"Wow! Look at all that snow!"

Jeff Martin pulled his ski jacket hood up over his head, and gave his brother a dirty look. "It's your fault, Matt!" he said angrily. "Why did it take you half an hour to find your hat?"

Matt shrugged. "I can't help it if someone hid it on me."

The boys stood uncertainly on the school steps. No one else was around. The snow was already above their ankles. The wind was gusty and picking up speed.

"It wasn't so bad a half hour ago," Jeff muttered. "Now we'll have a messy walk home." When Matt didn't reply, he began to edge forward. "C'mon. Let's go. It's only gonna get worse."

The boys set off in the direction of their house, ten blocks away. With each step they took, the snow seemed to come down harder and harder until it was falling in blinding white sheets.

"I can't see anything," Matt complained, as the snow swirled and the wind battered against them.

Jeff blinked rapidly. It was like trying to peer through a pounding white wall. "I think it's this way," he said uncertainly. A little while later, however, it was clear that they had taken a wrong turn. The boys had no idea where they were.

CAN YOU FINISH THIS STORY? It will be easier if you first decide exactly what is going to happen to Jeff and Matt Martin. This is called the *plot*. The questions below will help you develop your plot.

1. What are some of Matt's feelings as they wander about lost in the blizzard? (You don't need sentences here—just words and phrases.)

_____

_____

2. What are some of Jeff's thoughts as they wander about in the blizzard?

_____

_____

3. List three adventures the boys will have during the blizzard. (For example, they might find a dog whimpering in the snow, or they might try to get into some houses, only to find them locked and no one answering the bell, or one of the boys could get stuck in a snowdrift.)

_____

_____

4. Will the boys arrive home safely? If so, how?

_____

_____

Name _____ **Date** _____

LOST IN A BLIZZARD
FIRST DRAFT

DIRECTIONS:

Now that you have decided on a plot, you will be able to finish the story that was begun for you in Activity 10A. Here are some suggestions:

1. Use the plot ideas you developed in Activity 10A.
2. The boys should have at least three exciting and/or scary adventures. Use a lot of active verbs to hold the reader's attention.
3. Use some dialogue (conversation) to show what is happening and what the boys are thinking and feeling.
4. Try to make the situation get worse and worse until it seems that the boys will never find their way home in the blizzard.

Write a first draft of your story. Don't be concerned about spelling and grammar now—concentrate on getting down your thoughts. You don't have to copy the beginning—continue from where it left off in Activity 10A. Indent at the beginning of each paragraph. Indent whenever someone begins to speak. Use the back of this worksheet if you need more room.

_____

_____

_____

_____

_____

_____

_____

_____

_____

_____

_____

_____

Name _____ **Date** _____

LOST IN A BLIZZARD
REVISING AND WRITING A FINAL COPY

DIRECTIONS:

1. Edit and revise the first draft of your story, as follows:

> a. A plot should have a beginning, middle, and end. The beginning of this story introduces the characters and shows them getting lost in a blizzard. Does your middle describe their adventures in an exciting and interesting way? Does the end show what finally happens to the boys?
>
> b. Do you show scary and frightening things happening to the boys?
>
> c. Do you use dialogue (conversation) to show what is happening?
>
> d. Do you use dialogue to show the boys' thoughts and feelings?
>
> e. Do you describe the blizzard vividly with active verbs and sensory language?
>
> f. Are your sentences complete? Do subjects and verbs agree?
>
> g. Check your spelling.

2. Write the final copy of the story below. Copy the beginning from Activity 10A. Then, copy your revised draft. Indent at the beginning of paragraphs and whenever someone begins to speak. Use the back of this worksheet if you need more room.

_____

_____

_____

_____

_____

_____

_____

_____

_____

_____

_____

_____

Name _____ **Date** _____

GAMES! GAMES! GAMES!
PREWRITING

Basketball is a popular game in the U.S. and in many other countries, too. Did you know that basketball has only been in existence a little more than a hundred years? It was invented by Dr. James Naismith. This game was played for the first time by students at the YMCA Training School in Springfield, Massachusetts. The date was January 20, 1892.

Don't you wish you could have been there when Dr. Naismith explained the rules of basketball for the first time? It was different from all the other games that were played at the time. Do you think the students understood it right away?

How good are you at explaining the rules of a game. In this activity, you are going to do just that. First, organize your thoughts by answering the questions below.

DIRECTIONS:

1. Choose a game. It should be a game you know well enough to show someone else how to do. You can pick any kind of game—ball game, team sport, board game, card game, party game, chess or checkers, or even a game that you have made up. Write the name of the game here: _____

2. What is the object of the game? (For example, in basketball the object is to put the ball through the basket and score more points than the other team; in Monopoly®, the purpose is to get all your opponents' money and property, etc.) Describe the object of your game here: _____

_____

3. List the rules of the game here: _____

_____

_____

4. How is the game begun? _____

_____

5. List some techniques a player can use: _____

_____

_____

6. When and how is the game over? _____

_____

7. What qualities does a player need to be good at this game? (Examples: a strong arm, muscular legs, physical speed, intelligence, cleverness, etc.)

_____

_____

Name _____ **Date**_____

GAMES! GAMES! GAMES!
FIRST DRAFT

DIRECTIONS: Write the first draft of a 4-paragraph essay explaining how to play the game of your choice. It will be easy to do if you use your answers to the questions in Activity 11A and follow these directions.

1. The first paragraph should introduce the topic by stating the name and describing the object of the game, as in this example:

> My favorite game is Monopoly®. It is played on a board. The object of the game is to get all of your opponents' money and property.

Write your first paragraph here (2–4 sentences).

_____

_____

_____

2. In the second paragraph describe the rules of the game and tell how it is begun (3–6 sentences). Write the second paragraph here. (Use your notes in Activity 11A.)

_____

_____

_____

_____

3. In the third paragraph, describe some techniques for playing this game and tell when and how the game ends (3–6 sentences). Write it here.

_____

_____

_____

_____

4. The last paragraph sums up the topic and tells why you like it, as in this example:

> A Monopoly® player needs to have luck, especially when rolling the dice and picking cards from "Chance." You should be able to count money quickly and be clever enough to decide when to buy houses and hotels. Win or lose, however, Monopoly® is lots of fun.

Write your last paragraph (2–4 sentences) below.

_____

_____

_____

_____

Name _____ **Date** _____

GAMES! GAMES! GAMES!
REVISING AND WRITING A FINAL COPY

DIRECTIONS:

1. Edit and revise the first draft of your essay explaining how to play a game. Here are some suggestions.

> a. Does the first paragraph state the name and object of the game?
>
> b. Does the second paragraph *clearly* list the rules of the game and how it is begun? Would you be able to understand these rules if you had never played the game? Can you try to express them even more clearly?
>
> c. Does the third paragraph describe techniques for playing this game? Does it clearly state how and when the game ends? Can you make it clearer?
>
> d. Does the last paragraph tell what skills a player needs and sum up your opinion of this game?
>
> e. Are all your sentences complete? Do subjects and verbs agree?
>
> f. Check spelling with a dictionary.

2. Write the final copy of your essay below. Indent at the beginning of each paragraph. Use the back of this worksheet if you need more room.

_____

_____

_____

_____

_____

_____

_____

_____

_____

_____

Name _____ Date_____

DEAR DR. KING
PREWRITING

> "Free at Last, Free at Last, Thank God Almighty, I'm Free at Last."

These words are inscribed on the tombstone of Dr. Martin Luther King, Jr. They are from an old slave song, and were used by Dr. King during his famous "I have a dream . . ." speech.

Martin Luther King, Jr. was born in Atlanta, Georgia on January 15, 1929. His birthday is celebrated on the third Monday in January. He believed that non-violent protest was the way to bring freedom and equal rights to all Americans. He inspired people of all races to join his struggle against racial discrimination, poverty, and war, and was awarded the Nobel Peace Prize in 1964.

Dr. King's "dream" was to see an America where children of all races, colors, and religions could live together in peace and love.

Martin Luther King, Jr. was murdered by an assassin's bullet in 1968. If he could see his country today, would he believe that his dream had come true? Do you think so?

In this activity, you are going to write a letter to Dr. Martin Luther King, Jr., telling him how close you think we have come to reaching his goals. First, complete the brainstorming list below.

BRAINSTORMING LIST

1. On the lines below, list ways in which there is greater equality, opportunity, and friendship among people of different races today than in Martin Luther King's day. (You don't need sentences—words and phrases are okay.)

   _____

   _____

   _____

2. On the lines below, list ways in which people still do not have equal rights.

   _____

   _____

   _____

3. On the lines below, tell what people can do now to try to make Dr. King's dream come true.

   _____

   _____

   _____

Name _____ **Date** _____

DEAR DR. KING
FIRST DRAFT

DIRECTIONS: Write a first draft of a letter to Dr. Martin Luther King, Jr. Explain how and why his "dream" has or has not come true. Use the notes on your brainstorming list. Here is one way of putting your letter together:

> In the first paragraph, introduce yourself (age, school, town, etc.), and tell whether or not you think Dr. King's dream has come true.
> In the second paragraph, describe what progress has been made.
> In the third paragraph, describe what problems remain.
> In the last paragraph, tell what people might do to reach his goals.

This is just a suggestion. Write your letter in any way you wish. Follow correct letter form as shown below. (Since Dr. King is not living, you cannot include an address.) Indent at the beginning of each paragraph.

_____
(Write your street address above)

_____
(Write your city, state, ZIP above)

_____
(Write today's date above)

Dr. Martin Luther King, Jr.

Dear Dr. King,

_____

_____

_____

_____

_____

_____

Yours truly, _____

_____
(Write your name here)

Name _____ **Date** _____

DEAR DR. KING
REVISING AND WRITING A FINAL COPY

DIRECTIONS:

1. Edit and revise the first draft of your letter to Dr. King.

> a. Did you introduce yourself and state why you are writing?
> b. Did you express your ideas in a clear and logical order? The notes on your brainstorming list can help you with this.
> c. Did you follow correct letter form as shown on the worksheet?
> d. Are your sentences complete? Do subjects and verbs agree?
> e. Check your spelling with a dictionary.

2. Write the final copy of your letter below. Use the correct form for a personal letter as shown on the first draft worksheet. (Your return address and date are in the upper right corner. Dr. King's name and the greeting begin at the margin. The greeting is followed by a comma. Indent at the beginning of paragraphs. The closing is in the lower right and is followed by a comma. Your name is under the closing.)

_____
(Write your street address above)

_____
(Your city, state, ZIP above)

_____
(Write today's date above)

Dr. Martin Luther King, Jr.

_____ (Write the greeting here, then a comma)

_____

_____

_____

_____

_____

_____

_____
(Write the closing and a comma here)

_____
(Sign your name here)

Name _____ **Date** _____

SKI THE SLOPES!

Do you like to ski? Even if you are not a skier, you will enjoy going down *these* slopes. All you need are the correct letters and words.

At the top of each ski slope below is a *two*-letter word. As it goes down, it gathers letters. Add one letter of your choice to form another word at each stopping point along the slope. By the time it reaches the bottom, it has become a *five*-letter word. (Each new letter can be added anywhere in the word.) The first one is done for you.

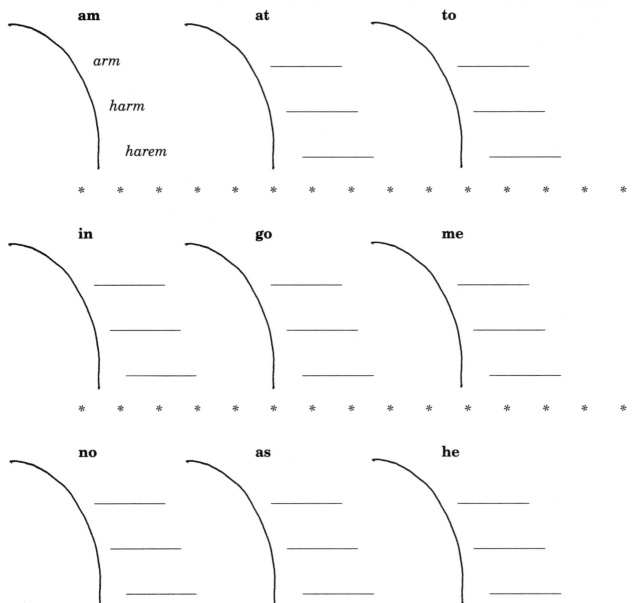

FEBRUARY

FEBRUARY

"Though February storms and blusters,
 It has the smell of summer in it."
 —old Arabic proverb

BLUSTERY FEBRUARY . . . FROSTS AND BLIZZARDS . . . GROUNDHOG DAY (FEBRUARY 2) . . . ST. VALENTINES' DAY (FEBRUARY 14) . . . GREETING CARDS AND PARTIES . . . PRESIDENTS' DAY (THIRD MONDAY) . . . BEGINNING OF LENT FOR CHRISTIANS (VARIES) . . . EXTRA DAY (FEBRUARY 29) FOR LEAP YEAR EVERY FOUR YEARS

FEBRUARY EVENTS

February 1, 1862: Julia Ward Howe's "Battle Hymn of the Republic" was published for the first time in the *Atlantic Monthly*

February 1, 1893: Thomas A. Edison finished work on the first moving-picture studio in the world in West Orange, New Jersey

February 2, 1876: Eight baseball teams organized the National League

February 4, 1861: The Confederate States of America was formed by six seceding Southern States—South Carolina, Georgia, Florida, Alabama, Mississippi, and Louisiana—in Montgomery, Alabama

February 7, 1827: The first ballet group to be formed in the U.S. performed at the Bowery Theatre in New York

February 7, 1964: The Beatles arrived at New York's Kennedy Airport to find 3,000 screaming fans waiting for them

February 8, 1910: The Boy Scouts of America was incorporated in the District of Columbia

February 20, 1792: President George Washington signed the first Postal Act, establishing the U.S. Post Office

February 20, 1962: John H. Glenn, Jr. became the first American to go into orbit

February 26, 1870: New York's first subway line was opened to the public

FEBRUARY BIRTHDAYS

February 3, 1821: Elizabeth Blackwell, first female M.D. in U.S.

February 11, 1847: Thomas Alva Edison, inventor

February 12, 1809: Abraham Lincoln, 16th president of the U.S.

February 12, 1809: Charles Darwin, British scientist, creator of the concept of evolution

February 22, 1732: George Washington, "The Father of Our Country," 1st president of the U.S.

February 22, 1892: Edna St. Vincent Millay, American poet

WRITING ACTIVITIES FOR FEBRUARY

Name _____ **Date** _____

GRUMPY GROUNDHOG
PREWRITING

Groundhogs *hibernate* (sleep) all winter. It is said that on February 2, the ground-hog comes out of his hole to see what's happening. If he sees his shadow, he goes back to sleep, and there will be six more weeks of winter. If he does not see his shadow, spring will arrive early.

What if the groundhog is grouchy? What if he doesn't want to wake up and leave his hole? That's what is going to happen in the story you are going to write.

Your story will be easy to write if you first prepare a plot summary. This is a short description of what is going to happen in the story. Preparing a plot summary will help you give the story a form and structure that works from beginning to end. Here is an example of one PLOT SUMMARY:

> Phil the Groundhog loves to sleep more than anything else in the world. Even though he has slept all winter, he still wants more. He ignores the signs that it is time for him to come out of his hole. He is awakened by the scent of February in the air. He goes back to sleep. People are waiting outside his hole, yelling that it's February 2. He groans grumpily and goes back to sleep. His sister groundhog pulls his tail. He growls at her and goes back to sleep. Finally, a rumbling in his stomach tells him he is hungry. He rouses himself and climbs out. When he sees his shadow and can go back to sleep for six weeks, he is happy.

Your story can be similar to the one above, or it can be completely different. Write a plot outline for your story below:

_____

_____

_____

_____

_____

_____

_____

_____

_____

Name _____ **Date** _____

GRUMPY GROUNDHOG
FIRST DRAFT

DIRECTIONS:

1. Writing your story will be simple if you follow the plot outline you prepared in Activity 1A. Even though you know the plot, it is sometimes hard to get started. Those first few sentences aren't always easy to come up with. Here are some examples that may help:

BEGINNING WITH CONVERSATION:
   "Wake up, Phil!"
   Groundhog Phil nestled deeper into his corner and kept his eyes tightly shut.
   "Go away," he mumbled grumpily. "I'm not getting up. Not for you. Not for anything!"

BEGINNING WITH A QUESTION:
   Was it February 2nd already? Groundhog Phil peered through half-open eyes at the calendar on the wall of his hole.

BEGINNING WITH ACTION:
   Stones tumbled through the opening in Groundhog Phil's hole. One of them struck him on the head.

---

2. Write a first draft of your story. You can copy one of the beginnings above or make up one of your own. Then, follow your plot outline for the rest of the story.

   Be sure to indent at the beginning of paragraphs and whenever someone starts to speak. Since this is a first draft, don't worry about spelling and grammar—concentrate on getting your ideas down on paper. (Use the back of this worksheet if you need more room.)

_____

_____

_____

_____

_____

_____

_____

_____

Name _____ **Date** _____

GRUMPY GROUNDHOG
REVISING AND WRITING A FINAL COPY

DIRECTIONS:

1. Edit and revise your first draft. Here are some suggestions:

a. Does the beginning spark the reader's interest? Is there any way it could be changed to be more exciting?

b. Does the story follow your plot summary?

c. Is the ending satisfying? Does it follow naturally from the action?

d Do you describe the characters and show what they are like by what they say and do?

e. Are your sentences complete? Do subjects and verbs agree?

f. Can you make your writing more vivid with active verbs and sensory words?

g. Check spelling with a dictionary.

2. Write the final copy of your story below. (Use the back of this worksheet if you need more room.)

_____

_____

_____

_____

_____

_____

_____

_____

_____

_____

_____

_____

Name _____ **Date** _____

SCRAMBLED HISTORY 1

ABRAHAM LINCOLN

The sentences below are all about Abraham Lincoln. They can be combined into a paragraph. But they are not in the correct order.

Arrange these sentences into a paragraph.

1. He was born in a log cabin in Kentucky on February 12, 1809.
2. Abraham Lincoln was the 16th president of the United States.
3. Lincoln was assassinated on April 15, 1865 when the war was almost ended.
4. Lincoln tried to hold the Union together, but the southern states seceded and the Civil War began.
5. It was a difficult time.
6. He was elected President in 1861.
7. The country was deeply divided over the issues of slavery and states' rights.

Write the paragraph below:

_____

_____

_____

_____

_____

_____

_____

_____

_____

_____

_____

Name _____ **Date** _____

SCRAMBLED HISTORY 2

GEORGE WASHINGTON

The sentences below are all about George Washington. They can be combined into a paragraph, but they are not in the correct order.

Arrange these sentences into a paragraph.

1. Washington became the general and leader of the American army.
2. In 1776, the American colonies issued a Declaration of Independence, declaring themselves independent of England.
3. He married Martha Curtis, and they lived at Mt. Vernon in Virginia.
4. This was the beginning of the American Revolution.
5. George Washington was the first president of the United States.
6. He was elected president in 1789 and served for eight years.
7. Washington is called "the father of our country."
8. He was born on February 22, 1732, in Virginia.

Write the paragraph below.

_____

_____

_____

_____

_____

_____

_____

_____

_____

_____

_____

Name _____ Date_____

IF I WERE PRESIDENT
PREWRITING

Two American presidents were born in February. For many years, they were honored on their birth dates—Abraham Lincoln on February 12 and George Washington on February 22. Later, it was decided to commemorate both presidents with one holiday. PRESIDENTS' DAY is now observed on the third Monday of February.

The president of the United States has a lot of power. He cannot, however, do whatever he likes. Only a *king* or *dictator* has complete power. The founders of the United States thought it best to have three branches of government. Do you know what these three branches are called?

If you said *executive, legislative,* and *judicial,* you are correct. The legislative branch *makes* the laws, the *executive* carries out the laws, and the *judicial* interprets the laws.

Although the president shares power with the legislative and judicial branches, he has a lot of influence over what goes on in the country.

Suppose *you* were president! What steps would you take? What would you keep the same? What would you improve? What would you change?

In this essay, you are going to describe what you would try to accomplish if you were president. First, complete this brainstorming list.

BRAINSTORMING LIST

1. What is *okay* about your country? In the first column, list *three* things that should not be changed. In the second column, tell *why* you think these things are good. (You don't need sentences here—words and phrases will do.)

2. What would you change if you were president? In the first column, list *three* things you would try to do differently. In the second column, write words and phrases that describe *why* these changes should be made.

3. On the lines below, write a beginning sentence (or sentences) for your essay that will be exciting enough to make the reader want to go on.

_____

_____

_____

Name _____ **Date** _____

IF I WERE PRESIDENT
FIRST DRAFT

DIRECTIONS: Write a 4-paragraph essay telling what you would try to do if you were the president of the country. Use the brainstorming list you prepared for Activity 3A. Here are some suggestions:

Your first paragraph should introduce the topic in an interesting way, as in this example:

> I've heard that any boy or girl can aspire to become president. I don't see any reason why it shouldn't be me! I have some great ideas that will make this a better country in which to live.

Write your first paragraph (2–4 sentences). This is just a draft, so don't worry about spelling or grammar. Just concentrate on getting down your ideas.

_____

_____

_____

Your second paragraph can describe three things you *would not* change and tell why you think these things are good (3–7 sentences).

_____

_____

_____

_____

Your third paragraph can describe three things you *would* change, and why (3–7 sentences).

_____

_____

_____

_____

Your fourth paragraph should restate and sum up the topic. Example:

> This is a wonderful country, but it could be even better. If I were president, I would make this the greatest country in the world.

Write your last paragraph (2–4 sentences).

_____

_____

_____

© 1997 by The Center for Applied Research in Education

Name _____ **Date**_____

If I Were President
Revising and Writing a Final Copy

DIRECTIONS:

1. Edit and revise the draft of your essay.

a. Does the first paragraph introduce the topic clearly? Would a question or startling statement make it more exciting?

b. Does the second paragraph describe three things you think are good and explain why you would not change them?

c. Does the third paragraph describe things you would change?

d. Does the last paragraph restate and sum up the topic?

e. Are your sentences complete? Do subjects and verbs agree?

f. Check spelling with the dictionary.

2. Write the final copy of your essay below. Indent at the beginning of each paragraph. (Use the back of this worksheet if you need more room.)

_____

_____

_____

_____

_____

_____

_____

_____

_____

_____

_____

_____

Name _____ Date _____

A FAMOUS FIRST
PREWRITING

Elizabeth Blackwell, who was born on February 3, 1821, was the first female doctor in the U.S. When she decided at the age of 23 that she wanted to be a physician, she was ridiculed and no medical school would admit her. She persisted in the face of jeers and criticism, and was finally allowed to study medicine at the Geneva Medical School in New York State, where she graduated at the top of her class.

All through her career, Dr. Blackwell met with prejudice and intolerance, but her courage and determination opened the door for other women to become doctors.

It's not easy to be the *first* in anything. Do you think you would be brave enough? In this essay, you are going to imagine what it would be like to be the first. Here are some possibilities:

❑ the first human to set foot on Mars
❑ the first woman president of the United States
❑ the first person under 18 to become a school principal
❑ the first person to be frozen and awakened in a thousand years
❑ the first kid to live on a space station
❑ the first traveler in a time machine
❑ the first person under 14 to star in a World Series
❑ the first _____

Check one of the boxes above, or *check* the last box and fill in your own *"first"* idea. Then complete the BRAINSTORMING LIST below.

BRAINSTORMING LIST

1. In the box below, write words and phrases to describe the *"first"* you have decided to write about, and why you have chosen it.

2. In the box below, list difficulties and problems you might encounter.

3. In the box below, list the personal qualities you will need to accomplish this and how it will make you feel.

4. On the lines below, write an interesting first sentence for your essay. (Examples: "For centuries, people have wondered what it would be like to explore another planet." "Is this country ready to elect a woman president?")

_____

_____

_____

© 1997 by The Center for Applied Research in Education

Name _____ Date_____

A Famous First
First Draft

Pretending to be a *"famous first"* should be fun. Your essay will be easy to write if you use the notes on your brainstorming list and follow these directions. (This is a first draft, so don't be concerned about spelling and grammar. Concentrate on getting down your ideas.)

1. The first paragraph introduces the topic in a lively way. Use the beginning sentence from your brainstorming list and add one to three additional sentences that expand on that idea. Write your first paragraph here.

_____

_____

_____

2. In the second paragraph, describe the problems and difficulties you may encounter, such as prejudice, ridicule, failed attempts, etc. Write your second paragraph here (2–5 sentences).

_____

_____

_____

_____

_____

3. In the third paragraph, describe the qualities you will need to accomplish this "first," such as intelligence, perseverance, athletic ability, scientific knowledge, etc. Write your third paragraph here (2–5 sentences).

_____

_____

_____

_____

4. In the last paragraph, restate and sum up the topic, as in this example: "A lot of obstacles will be placed in the path of the first woman president of the U.S. I know I can overcome all of these obstacles and open a door for others to follow." Write your last paragraph here (2–4 sentences).

_____

_____

_____

_____

Name _____ Date _____

A FAMOUS FIRST
REVISING AND WRITING A FINAL COPY

DIRECTIONS:

1. Edit and revise the first draft of your essay. Here are some suggestions:

> a. Can you capture the reader's attention in the first paragraph by starting with a question or a startling statement?
>
> b. In the second paragraph, do you discuss all the difficulties that will be encountered by the "first?" Can you make these stronger with active verbs and vivid language?
>
> c. In the third paragraph, do you discuss the personal qualities that will help you succeed? Do you explain why these are important?
>
> d. In the last paragraph, do you restate and sum up the topic?
>
> e. Are your sentences complete? Do subjects and verbs agree?
>
> f. Check spelling with a dictionary.

2. Write your essay below. Indent at the beginning of each paragraph. Use the back of this worksheet if you need more room. (Make up a title for your essay and write it on the first line.)

_____

_____

_____

_____

_____

_____

_____

_____

_____

_____

_____

Name _____ Date_____

HEARTFELT GREETING
FIRST DRAFT

   Valentine's Day is a time to think about the people who are important to us. It's the perfect occasion to let these special folks know how we feel.

   Write a letter to someone you like a lot (or even *love*). It can be one of your friends, or a person in your class (student or teacher), or a member of your family, or a neighbor, or anyone else you may admire.
   Tell this person how you feel and *why* you like, love, or admire him or her.

   Write your letter in the heart below. Put today's date on the first line. This is just a DRAFT so you can scratch out or make changes anytime you wish.

Dear _____,   _____

_____

_____

_____

_____

_____

_____

_____

                    Love,

                    _____
                    (Write your name here)

Name _____ Date _____

HEARTFELT GREETING
REVISING AND WRITING A FINAL COPY

1. Read the first draft of your Valentine letter and make any needed changes:

> a. Did you tell the person you admire how you feel?
> b. Did you describe what it is that you admire about that person?
> c. Are your sentences complete? Do subjects and verbs agree?
> d. Are you sure all words are spelled correctly? Check with a dictionary.

2. Write the final copy of your letter below. Put today's date on the first line. Sign your name on the last line.

   (When you finish the letter, you can cut out the heart and give the letter to your "Valentine," if you wish.)

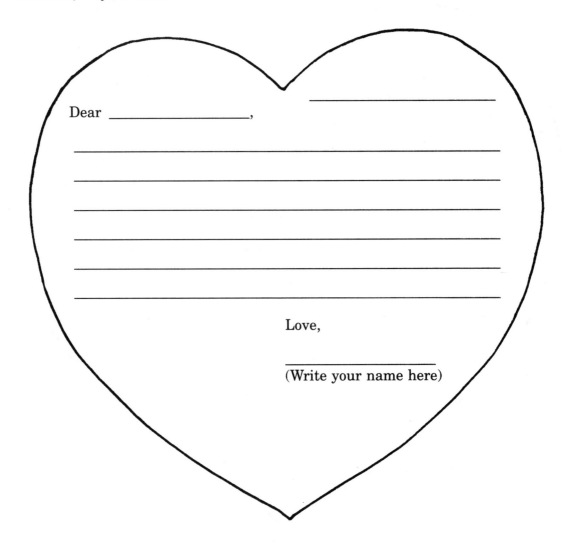

Dear _____,

_____

Love,

_____
(Write your name here)

Name _____ Date_____

PARTY TALK
PREWRITING

Most people enjoy reading stories or books that have a lot of conversation. This is called *dialogue*. Do you use dialogue in the stories you write?

In this activity, you are going to write a story about a Valentine party. But you are *not* going to write the *whole* story. You will write just one scene—a scene with lots of dialogue, as in this example:

> Patrick picked up the phone on the first ring. "Hello?"
> "Hi, Pat!" It was his friend, Luke.
> "Hi." Patrick plopped onto his bed. "What's up?"
> "You goin' to the party?"
> Patrick frowned. It was the first he'd heard about a party. "What are you talking about?"
> "Cindy Freeman's Valentine party. Aren't you going?" Luke's voice had a husky quality that made it sound as though he always had a cold.
> "Um . . .", Patrick hesitated. He didn't want to let on that he hadn't been invited. "Uh . . . I dunno."
> "You don't know?" Luke sounded annoyed. "Do you want to be the only kid in the whole class who's not there?"
> Patrick couldn't answer. He felt as though he'd been kicked in the stomach.

This dialogue works well because:

1. It is always clear who is speaking.

2. There is action and description that helps the reader to see the people who are talking and what is happening.

> In the above scene, *underline* the phrases and sentences that show action. Then, *underline* the phrases and sentences that show description. Are there any sentences that show someone's thoughts? *Underline* these, too.

Now go to Activity 6B to see if you did this correctly.

Name _____ Date _____

PARTY TALK
MORE PREWRITING

Look at the dialogue scene in Activity 6A. Did you *underline* all the phrases and sentences that show action, description, or someone's thoughts? This is what it should look like:

Patrick picked up the phone on the first ring. "Hello?"

"Hi, Pat!" It was his friend, Luke.

"Hi." Patrick plopped onto his bed. "What's up?"

"You goin' to the party?"

Patrick frowned. It was the first he'd heard about a party. "What are you talking about?"

"Cindy Freeman's Valentine party. Aren't you going?" Luke's voice had a husky quality that made it sound as though he always had a cold.

"Um . . . ," Patrick hesitated. He didn't want to let on that he hadn't been invited. "Uh . . . I dunno."

"You don't know?" Luke sounded annoyed. "Do you want to be the only kid in the whole class who's not there?"

Patrick couldn't answer. He felt as though he'd been kicked in the stomach.

If you missed any of these, *underline* them now and think about how they show action, description, or someone's thoughts.

Here is another scene with dialogue from the same story:

"Why aren't you eating, Pat?" asked his mom.

"I'm not hungry."

"Are you sick?"

"No."

"Then, what's the matter?"

"I'm just not hungry!"

"Well, there must be some reason why you're not hungry."

"I guess I'm upset."

"What are you upset about?"

"It's this dumb Valentine party. Everyone's invited but me."

There are several things wrong with this scene. First, it's not always clear who's speaking. Second, there is no action or description, so the reader can't really *see* the scene. The scene would also be improved if it showed someone's thoughts.

Can you fix up this scene so it comes alive for the reader? Rewrite this scene on a separate sheet of paper. The conversation can be the same. All you have to do is add the following:

ACTION
DESCRIPTION
SOMEONE'S THOUGHTS

Name _____ Date_____

Party Talk
First Draft

Did you complete the first two parts of this activity? If you did, you are now ready to write exciting dialogue scenes!

DIRECTIONS: Write a scene with lots of dialogue for a story about a Valentine party. Here are some suggestions:

1. Someone goes to a Valentine party and finds he has arrived on the wrong day at the wrong time.
2. Two boys at a Valentine party get into a fight over who is the stronger.
3. Two girls at a Valentine party get into a fight because they are wearing the same dress.
4. Someone meets a stranger at a Valentine party, and discovers that they are cousins who have never met before.

Choose one of these situations or make up one of your own. Write a scene with lots of *dialogue*. Be sure to also show *action* and *description*, and possibly, someone's *thoughts*.

Write the first draft below. Indent at the beginning of paragraphs. Also indent each time someone begins to speak.

_____

_____

_____

_____

_____

_____

_____

_____

_____

_____

_____

_____

Name _____ Date _____

PARTY TALK
REVISING AND WRITING A FINAL COPY

DIRECTIONS:

1. Edit and revise your dialogue scene, as follows:

> a. Is it always clear who is speaking? If not, add something to make it clearer.
>
> b. Can you add more *action* to make the scene vivid?
>
> c. Can you add more *description* to make the scene vivid?
>
> d. Would it be helpful to add *someone's thoughts* anywhere in the scene?
>
> e. Do you indent each time someone begins to speak?
>
> f. Do you put "quotation marks" around each speech?
>
> g. Are your sentences complete? Do subjects and verbs agree?
>
> h. Do you need to check the spelling of any words in a dictionary?

2. Write the final copy of your dialogue scene below. (Use the back of this worksheet if you need more room.)

_____

_____

_____

_____

_____

_____

_____

_____

_____

_____

_____

© 1997 by The Center for Applied Research in Education

Name _____ Date_____

Underground Journey
Prewriting

On February 26, 1870, New York City's first subway line was opened to the public.

Have you ever been on a subway train? If you have, you know what it is like to travel underground. If you have never ridden on a subway, you can use your imagination to write a story about an "Underground Journey."

PLOT: First, you need to decide upon the plot, which is what occurs from beginning to end. A plot summary tells this briefly, leaving out details. Here is one possible plot summary for a story about an "Underground Journey."

The Murdoch family takes a trip to New York City. It is their first visit there. They go down to the subway. 12-year-old Matthew and his 10-year-old sister Polly are so amazed by the tunnels and train tracks and crowds of people that they get separated from their parents. They board the next train that comes along. They ride around for hours, getting off at some stations and boarding other trains. Some of the people they meet are scary. Some try to help them. After many adventures underground, they seek out a transit police officer and are reunited with their parents.

Write a plot summary for your "Underground Journey" story below.

_____

_____

_____

_____

_____

_____

MAIN CHARACTER: A story usually works best if it is told through the eyes of one *main character*. Decide upon a main character for your story. Write the main character's name and description below.

Name: _____ Description: _____

_____

Now, list some other characters who will be in your story. Next to each name, tell who that person is and give a short description.

_____

_____

_____

_____

Name _____ **Date** _____

UNDERGROUND JOURNEY
FIRST DRAFT

DIRECTIONS: Write a first draft of your story, "Underground Journey." Here are some suggestions:

1. Begin with an exciting scene, such as a frightening sight or a shocking conversation.
2. Use dialogue (conversation).
3. Build up the suspense as the story goes along. The reader should not know how things turn out until the end.
4. Use active verbs such as *jump, scream, smash, rush, hustle, leap.*
5. Use sensory works (referring to taste, touch, sound, sight, smell).

This is a first draft. Don't be concerned with spelling or grammar. Just concentrate on getting your thoughts down on paper. Use the back of this worksheet if you need more room. If you are having trouble getting started, here are some beginning sentences you can borrow:

"The subway station was the scariest place Shari had ever seen."
" 'Mom! Dad! Where are you?' Jimmy's parents were nowhere to be seen."
"The crowd was jostling and pushing Amy away from her family."

Name _____ **Date** _____

Underground Journey
Revising and Writing a Final Copy

DIRECTIONS:

1. Edit and revise your draft, as follows:

> a. Is the beginning interesting enough to make the reader continue? Can you make it even more exciting?
>
> b. Is the story seen through the eyes of your main character?
>
> c. Can you describe all the characters more clearly so the reader can picture them?
>
> d. Take out all unnecessary words that slow down the action.
>
> e. Do you keep up the suspense until the end of the story?
>
> f. Do you use dialogue? Is it the way people really talk? Do you indent each time someone begins to speak?
>
> g. Are your sentences complete? Do subjects and verbs agree?
>
> h. Check spelling with a dictionary.

2. Write the final copy of your story below. Indent at the beginning of paragraphs and whenever someone begins to speak. Use the back of this worksheet if you need more room.

_____

_____

_____

_____

_____

_____

_____

_____

_____

_____

_____

Name _____ Date _____

A Lovely Light
Prewriting

> "My candle burns at both ends;
> It will not last the night;
> But ah, my foes, and oh, my friends
> It gives a lovely light"

These lines were written by a famous American poet. Her name was Edna St. Vincent Millay. She was born on February 22, 1892 in Maine. As a child, she wrote verses, songs, and plays. When she was 14, she sent a poem to *St. Nicholas* magazine and it won their "gold badge" award. At 20, she published a wonderful long poem called "Renascence," which received nation-wide attention.

Most people are not aware that Millay's first ambition was to become a pianist. She worked and studied hard for many years. But when she was a teenager, she discovered that her hands were too small for her ever to have a career as a concert pianist. Her dreams were dashed. In her misery, she turned to writing, which had always been a useful form of expression. She found she was able to pour all her passion and love of life into poetry.

Not everyone can be a great poet like Edna St. Vincent Millay, but language can be a useful tool for anyone to express thoughts and feelings.

> Can you come up with language that expresses feelings? Next to each feeling below, write as many words or phrases as you can think of that have something to do with that feeling. (The first one is begun for you.)

SADNESS: _____ mopey, down-in-the-dumps, tears, _____

_____

HAPPINESS: _____

_____

ANGER: _____

_____

SURPRISE: _____

_____

LOVE: _____

_____

HATE: _____

_____

Name _____ **Date** _____

A LOVELY LIGHT
FIRST DRAFT

> "Stranger, pause and look;
>   From the dust of ages
> Lift this little book,
>   Turn the tattered pages,
> Read me, do not let me die!
>   Search the fading letters, finding
> Steadfast in the broken binding
>   All that once was I!"

In this poem, Edna St. Vincent Millay hopes that people will know all about her thoughts and feelings by reading what she has written.

Sometimes, it's hard to tell others about your true, deep feelings. But you can do it with poetry!

Write a first draft of a poem about feelings. Here are suggestions:

1. How you felt when you did poorly on a test
2. How you felt when your team won an important game
3. How you felt when your parents surprised you on your birthday with something you had dreamed of having for a long time
4. How you felt when your best friend moved away
5. How you felt when a group of kids made fun of you
6. How you felt when your brother was sick and was taken to the hospital
7. How you feel when someone tells you that you're great
8. How you feel when you get the highest mark in the class
9. How you feel on the first day of summer vacation

You can use any of these suggestions or any other strong feelings that you remember. Write a poem about it. Use the list of "feelings" words and phrases from Activity 8A.

Write the first draft of your poem. It should have *at least* four lines. Write about one feeling or several feelings in one poem. (Or, you can write several poems about different feelings.) It doesn't have to rhyme unless that is what you want. (Use the back of this worksheet if you need more room.)

_____

_____

_____

_____

_____

Name _____ **Date** _____

A LOVELY LIGHT
REVISING AND WRITING A FINAL COPY

> "I cannot but remember
>   When the year grows old—
> October—November—
>   How she disliked the cold!"

These lines are so simple. It seems as though Edna St. Vincent Millay must have just dashed them off.

Perhaps she did, but it's not likely. Poets usually edit and revise their work many times before it is as perfect as the stanza above. Poetry is shorter than other kinds of writing, so each word and each phrase must be the absolutely BEST ONE!

Think about this when you edit and revise your own poem about feelings. Here are some specific suggestions:

1. Is each word perfect for that particular spot? Can you think of a word or phrase that would work better?
2. Are your feelings clear to the reader? Can you add anything to make it even clearer?
3. Did you use vivid language such as sensory words or active verbs?
4. Did you leave out anything important? Would your poem be stronger if you added several lines?

Write the final copy of your poem below. Make up a title and put it on the first line. You can draw illustrations in the side and bottom margins.

_____

_____

_____

_____

_____

_____

_____

_____

_____

Name _____ Date _____

THE SMELL OF SUMMER
PREWRITING

> "Though February storms and blusters,
> It has the smell of summer in it."

1. Read the old Arabic proverb above. What does it mean? On the lines below, write down what you think these lines mean.

_____

_____

2. Did this proverb suggest to you that even though icy storms still rage in February, it is getting closer to the end of winter? That is why February has "the smell of summer in it."

Here is a paragraph about February. Fill in the missing words.

> The last few _____ of February are here. It has been a long _____. There have been many _____ days and _____ storms. The weather outside is still _____. Sometimes, it seems as though _____ will never end. But we are not fooled by the _____ days of February. _____ will not last forever. _____ will soon be here, then summer. That is why February has the smell of _____ in it.

(See activity 9B for one possible way to complete this paragraph.)

3. In the box below, make two lists of words and phrases that have something to do with the month of February. In the first column, write words and phrases that describe February as it is *now*. In the second column, write words and phrases that describe what you can *look forward to in future months*.

FEBRUARY NOW	*FUTURE MONTHS*

Name _____ **Date** _____

The Smell of Summer
First Draft

1. Here is one possible solution to the incomplete paragraph in Activity 9A:

> The last few *days* of February are here. It has been a long *winter*. There have been many *cold* days and *blustery* storms. The weather outside is still *freezing*. Sometimes, it seems as though *winter* will never end. But we are not fooled by the *frigid* days of February. *Winter* will not last forever. *Spring* will soon be here, then summer. That is why February has the smell of *summer* in it.

2. Now you are going to compose your own paragraph about February and why it has the "smell of summer in it." It will be easy if you use the list of words and phrases you wrote for Activity 9A.

   Describe what February is like *now*. Then tell what you are looking forward to *in the coming months*.

   This is just a first draft. Don't worry about spelling and grammar. Concentrate on getting down your thoughts. Write your paragraph below.

_____

_____

_____

_____

_____

_____

_____

_____

_____

_____

Name _____ Date_____

THE SMELL OF SUMMER
REVISING AND WRITING A FINAL COPY

DIRECTIONS:

1. Edit and revise the draft of your paragraph. Here are some suggestions:

<table>
<tr><td>a.</td><td>Does your first sentence introduce the topic of the paragraph?</td></tr>
<tr><td>b.</td><td>Do you describe how February feels now?</td></tr>
<tr><td>c.</td><td>Do you describe what you are looking forward to?</td></tr>
<tr><td>d.</td><td>Does your last sentence restate or sum up the topic?</td></tr>
<tr><td>e.</td><td>Do you use sensory words like freezing, icy, snowy, warmer, spring fragrances?</td></tr>
<tr><td>f.</td><td>Can you make your writing more exciting with active verbs such as blow, bluster, skid?</td></tr>
<tr><td>g.</td><td>Are your sentences complete? Do subjects and verbs agree?</td></tr>
<tr><td>h.</td><td>Check spelling with a dictionary.</td></tr>
</table>

2. Write the final copy of your paragraph below. If you wish, you can draw illustrations on the side and bottom margins.

_____

_____

_____

_____

_____

_____

_____

_____

_____

_____

Name _____ **Date** _____

FEBRUARY SENTENCES 1

DIRECTIONS: The letters below spell out FEBRUARY. For each letter, write a sentence in which all or most of the words begin with that letter. (The first one is done for you.)

When you finish all the sentences, draw February illustrations in the side and bottom margins.

F Friendly folk fry fatty food in February. _____

_____

E _____

_____

B _____

_____

R _____

_____

U _____

_____

A _____

_____

R _____

_____

Y _____

_____

Name _____ **Date** _____

FEBRUARY SENTENCES 2

DIRECTIONS: The letters below spell out GROUNDHOG DAY.

For each letter, write a sentence in which all or most of the words begin with that letter. (The first one is done for you.)

When you finish your sentences, draw illustrations in the side and bottom margins.

G Gophers and guppies giggle at groundhogs. _____

_____

R _____

_____

O _____

_____

U _____

_____

N _____

_____

D _____

_____

H _____

_____

O _____

_____

G _____

_____

D _____

_____

A _____

_____

Y _____

_____

Name _____ Date _____

BE A MOVIE CRITIC
PREWRITING

Something amazing happened on February 1, 1893. It was on that date that Thomas A. Edison finished building the first moving-picture studio in the world. It was located in West Orange, New Jersey, and it cost the inventor $637. It's hard to believe there was a time when there were no movies for people to see. Thanks to Thomas Edison, America's greatest inventor, the age of movie-making began on that winter day in 1893. Now, there are many movie studios all over the world. Most of them are in Hollywood, California. They cost a lot more than $637 to build. They turn out hundreds of films every year. The popularity of movies has created a new profession—movie critic.

Do you ever read the movie reviews in newspapers and magazines? Mostly, each review is just one person's opinion about a film. It's a lot like writing a book review (or book report). In this activity, you are going to be a movie critic. It will be easy if you first complete this brainstorming list.

BRAINSTORMING LIST

1. Choose a movie (or a video) to review. It can be one you have seen recently or something from a long time ago. It can even be a movie or video you like to watch over and over again. Write the title on the line below:

_____

2. If you know the names of any of the actors, write them below:

_____

3. Write a short (one- or two-sentence) summary telling what the movie is about:

_____
_____

4. Name two or three characters in the movie. Next to each name, write a list of words and phrases that describe that character:

NAME	DESCRIPTION

5. What was good about this film? (You don't need sentences—just words and phrases describing good things about the movie.)

_____

6. What was bad about this film? (words and phrases)

_____

7. Would you recommend this movie? (yes or no) _____

Name _____ **Date** _____

BE A MOVIE CRITIC
FIRST DRAFT

Many people decide whether or not to see a film after they read the review. Remember this when you write the first draft of your movie or video review. Use your brainstorming list and follow these directions.

1. The first paragraph should introduce the film in an interesting way. Example:

> "If you have pets, stay away from 'The Denville Dogs.' The animals in this film are so unpleasant, they could turn the most devoted animal-lover into one who hates all canines."

Write your first paragraph (2–4 sentences) below:

_____

_____

_____

2. Your second paragraph should describe the main characters and the story. If you know the actors' names, mention them here (4–7 sentences).

_____

_____

_____

_____

_____

3. Your third paragraph should list both the good and bad things about the film (3–6 sentences).

_____

_____

_____

_____

_____

4. Your last paragraph should sum up your feelings about this movie, and tell whether or not you recommend it, as in this example:

> " 'The Denville Dogs' is so poorly made that even the hectic action and gross happenings aren't enough to keep most viewers awake. If you want to nap, stay home and save your money."

Write your last paragraph (2–4 sentences) below. (If you wish, you can rate it on a scale of no stars to four stars.)

_____

_____

_____

Name _____ **Date** _____

BE A MOVIE CRITIC
REVISING AND WRITING A FINAL COPY

1. Edit and revise the first draft of your movie review. Here are some suggestions:

a. Does your first paragraph name the movie and introduce it in an interesting way? Can you make it more exciting with some startling statements, questions, or comparisons?

b. Does your second paragraph describe the story and characters so that the reader can clearly understand who the characters are and what the story is about? Can you take out any unnecessary details that just confuse?

c. Does the third paragraph tell the *good* and *bad* points of the film? Is your opinion of this movie clear to the reader?

d. Does the last paragraph sum up your opinion of this film?

e. Can you make your writing more exciting by using vivid language, such as sensory words, active verbs, or similes?

f. Humor can often be used to make a review interesting. Can you add any humor to your review?

g. Are your sentences complete? Do subjects and verbs agree?

h. Check spelling.

2. Write the final copy of your movie review below. Indent at the beginning of paragraphs. (Use the back of this worksheet if you need more room.)

_____

_____

_____

_____

_____

_____

_____

_____

_____

Name _____ Date _____

Extra! Extra!

February is the shortest month of the year. It usually has 28 days. But every four years, an extra day is added, to make 29 days. That is called *leap year*.

Extras are usually nice to have. An extra point to help your team win is good. An extra portion of dessert is usually yummy. An extra guest at a party could be fun.

Here are some *language extras* for you to have fun with.

PART ONE: Change the words below into other words with different meanings by *adding* one extra letter *anywhere* in the word. (The first two are done for you.)

car	cart	one	
pen	open	bar	
ear		ant	
rat		man	
net		say	
ark		hat	

PART TWO: The sentences below make no sense. That is because one word is missing in each sentence. Copy each sentence and add an extra word to make that sentence complete. (The first one is done for you.)

1. February a short, cold month.

   February is a short, cold month.

2. Did you see the groundhog come of his hole?

3. February has 29 days every four.

4. Abraham Lincoln was in February.

5. Do you send on Valentine's Day?

Name _____ **Date** _____

Bundle Up!
Prewriting

February is a cold month, especially in northern climates. Can you remember a time when you were very, *very* COLD? Or, can you imagine what it might be like to be very, *very* COLD?

There are a lot of words in the English language that can be used to describe the feeling of cold. In the box below, list as many words as you can think of that describe some kind of cold and how it feels. (The list is begun for you. Can you add *at least six more words*?)

nipping, chilly,

Sometimes, one word isn't enough to show how cold feels. How many phrases can you think of to describe cold? List them in the box below. (The list is begun for you. Can you add *at least three more phrases*?)

chattering of teeth, cold as marble,

Have you remembered a time when you were very, *very* cold? If you can't think of one, use your imagination and make one up. Here are some situations you might use:

It's the coldest day of the year. You are waiting outside school to be picked up by your mom, but her car is stuck in the snow and you have to wait *two hours*!

The power goes out during a blizzard and your house becomes as cold as a refrigerator.

You go skiing. The temperature at the top of the mountain is below zero.

Choose one of these subjects or one of your own to write about in a short, 3-paragraph essay. On the lines below, write one sentence that briefly describes the situation you have chosen:

_____

_____

_____

_____

_____

Name _____ Date_____

BUNDLE UP!
FIRST DRAFT

Did you get goosebumps when you wrote your list of words and phrases about cold? Did it help you to remember a time when you felt that way?

These lists will help you write a 3-paragraph essay about that time.

> Write about a real incident that happened to you; **OR**
> Write about an imaginary adventure in the cold; **OR**
> Write about ONE of the subjects suggested in Activity 13A.

In the first paragraph, tell WHERE this incident took place, WHEN it happened, and WHO was there. Begin with a sentence that captures the reader's interest, such as, "I thought I was a goner that day!" or "'Won't this cold ever end?' my sister whined."

In the second paragraph, describe what happened and how it felt. Use your lists of cold words and phrases to bring the scene to life.

In the last paragraph restate the topic and sum it up, as in this example: "I'll never forget how it felt to be waiting and wondering if I would ever get picked up on that frigid afternoon. Those were the two longest and coldest hours of my life."

> Write a first draft of your essay below. Indent at the beginning of each paragraph. Remember, this is just a draft, so don't worry about spelling or grammar. Just concentrate on getting down your thoughts. (Use the back of this worksheet if you need more room.)

_____

_____

_____

_____

_____

_____

_____

_____

_____

Name _____ **Date** _____

BUNDLE UP!
REVISING AND WRITING A FINAL COPY

DIRECTIONS:

1. Edit and revise your first draft, as follows:

---

a. Does your first paragraph introduce the topic? Can you make it more exciting so the reader will want to continue?

b. Does your second paragraph give all the details about what happened? Does it describe WHAT happened? WHERE it occurred, and WHO was there?

c. Does the last paragraph restate and sum up the topic?

d. Does the language you use really describe what it was like and how it felt? Can you think of any words and phrases that would be even better?

e. Are your sentences clearly written and to the point? Are there any unnecessary words that you can cut?

f. Are your sentences complete? Do subjects and verbs agree?

g. Check spelling with a dictionary.

---

2. Write the final copy of your essay below. Indent at the beginning of each paragraph. (Use the back of this worksheet if you need more room.)

_____

_____

_____

_____

_____

_____

_____

_____

_____

_____

MARCH

MARCH

"How the March sun feels like May!"
—Robert Browning

MONTH OF MARS, GOD OF WAR . . . CHANGEABLE WEATHER ("IN LIKE A LION, OUT LIKE A LAMB") . . . MARCH MADNESS ("MAD AS A MARCH HARE") . . . THE WEARING OF THE GREEN ON ST. PATRICK'S DAY (MARCH 17) . . . VERNAL EQUINOX (SPRING) . . . "BEWARE THE IDES OF MARCH" . . . (MARCH 15) . . . NATIONAL LETTER-WRITING WEEK (THIRD WEEK)

MARCH EVENTS

March 1, 1781: American colonies adopted the Articles of Confederation

March 1, 1961: President John F. Kennedy established the Peace Corps

March 3, 1931: "Star-Spangled Banner" became national anthem of U.S.

March 5, 1770: British troops fired on civilians in Boston, angering colonists who called it the "Boston Massacre"

March 8, 1917: Russian Revolution began with riots in St. Petersburg

March 8, 1954: RCA manufactured first color television

March 10, 1876: Alexander Graham Bell transmitted the first clear telephone message in Boston

March 11, 1888: The Blizzard of '88 raged along the Atlantic Coast, crippling New York City

March 20, 1852: Uncle Tom's Cabin, Harriet Beecher Stowe's story of slavery, was published in book form

March 21, 1965: Reverend Martin Luther King, Jr. led a march of civil rights demonstrators from Selma to Montgomery, Alabama

March 26, 1953: Dr. Jonas Salk announced the discovery of a vaccine against polio

March 30, 1858: The first pencil with an eraser was patented by Hyman L. Lipman of Philadelphia

March 30, 1867: U.S. purchased Alaska for $7,200,000 (known as Seward's Folly)

March 30, 1870: 15th Amendment passed guaranteeing vote to all races

March 30, 1932: Amelia Earhart was first woman to fly solo across Atlantic Ocean

MARCH BIRTHDAYS

March 3, 1847: Alexander Graham Bell, inventor of the telephone

March 6, 1475: Michelangelo Buonarroti, Italian painter and sculptor

March 21, 1685: Johann Sebastian Bach, German composer and musician

March 26, 1875: Robert Frost, American poet

Name _____ **Date** _____

MARS' MONTH
PREWRITING

Did you know that the month of March was named after Mars, the Roman god of war? To modern eyes, it may not seem nice to name a month after a war god, but in ancient times, war was important. A country's survival could depend upon being able to defeat one's enemies. Romans depended on Mars to help them. Besides, Mars was not only the god of war. He was also in charge of crops and vegetation. And what could be more important than food?

The Romans had a whole pantheon of gods from which to choose when naming the months of the year. Nowadays, we prefer to look upon humans as our heroes.

What if we could rename all the months of the year after our current heroes? Which ones would you choose? In this essay, you are going to choose *two* candidates for this honor and tell why each one deserves to have a month named after him or her. First, complete the brainstorming list below.

BRAINSTORMING LIST

1. On the lines below, list two people (living or dead) for whom you would like to name a month:

_____

_____

2. In the box below, write as many words and phrases you can think of that describe the first person on your list and why you have chosen him or her:

3. In the box below, write as many words and phrases you can think of that describe the second person on your list and why you have chosen him or her:

4. Write a beginning sentence (or sentences) for your essay that introduces the topic in an interesting way. (Example: "Why are months named after ancient Roman gods? They are no longer important!") Write your introductory sentence or sentences below:

_____

_____

_____

Name _____ **Date** _____

MARS' MONTH
FIRST DRAFT

> *DIRECTIONS*: Write a first draft of a 4-paragraph essay telling which present-day heroes you would choose to name a month for. Use the information you organized on your brainstorming list. (This is just a draft, so don't worry about grammar or spelling—concentrate on getting your thoughts on paper.

1. The first paragraph introduces the topic in an interesting way. (See the example on your brainstorming list.) Write *your* first paragraph here (2–4 sentences):

_____

_____

_____

2. In the second paragraph, tell the name of your hero, describe him or her, and tell why a month should be named after this person. Write your second paragraph here (4–7 sentences):

_____

_____

_____

_____

_____

3. In the third paragraph, tell the name of your second hero, describe him or her, and tell why a month should be named after this person. Write your third paragraph here (4–7 sentences):

_____

_____

_____

_____

4. The last paragraph should restate and sum up the topic in an interesting way, as in this example:

> I don't see why we should keep calling months like March or January after ancient Romans. Modern months should be named after modern heroes.

Write your last paragraph here (2–4 sentences):

_____

_____

_____

Name _____ **Date** _____

MARS' MONTH
REVISING AND WRITING A FINAL COPY

DIRECTIONS:

1. Edit and revise the first draft of your essay, as follows:

> a. Does your first paragraph introduce the topic in an interesting way? Can you make it even more exciting so the reader will want to continue? Sometimes beginning with a question or a startling statement will help.
>
> b. Does the second paragraph describe your first hero in detail? Can you add anything to convince the reader that this person should have a month named after him or her?
>
> c. Does the third paragraph describe your second hero in detail? Can you add anything to convince the reader that this person should have a month named after him or her?
>
> d. Does the last paragraph restate and sum up the topic? Would it be stronger if you used humor or irony?
>
> e. Have you used vivid language, such as sensory words and active verbs, to make your points?
>
> f. Can you make your writing stronger by cutting unnecessary words?
>
> g. Check spelling with a dictionary.

2. Write the final copy of your essay below. Indent at the beginning of paragraphs. (Use the back of this worksheet if you need more room.)

_____

_____

_____

_____

_____

_____

_____

_____

Name _____ Date_____

MARCH WINDS
PREWRITING

> "March winds and April showers
> Are sure to bring May flowers." —Old Proverb

March is known as a windy month! Have you ever been out on a very windy day? What was it like? Did you have to hold on to your hat to keep it from blowing away? Did you have to struggle to walk into the wind? If the wind was blowing from behind, did you feel as though it was pushing you along?

Here is what one person wrote about such a day:

> I felt the sharp bite of the wind as soon as I walked down the steps in front of the school. It caught my hat and whipped it right off my head. I had to run a long way before I could catch my hat as it kept dancing away from me. Sharp blasts lashed me from behind and pushed me along the street. I was thankful when those icy gusts finally blew me right to my front door.

DIRECTIONS:

1. Underline the vivid words and phrases in the paragraph above that make the scene come strongly to life.

2. Did you underline the following words and phrases?

   sharp bite, whipped it right off my head, dancing away from me, sharp blasts, lashed me, icy gusts, blew me

3. In the box below, write as many words and phrases as you can think of that describe a strong March wind.

4. In the box below, write as many words and phrases as you can think of that describe what a strong March wind can do to people and things.

Name _____ **Date** _____

MARCH WINDS
FIRST DRAFT

In Activity 2A, you read a paragraph that described what happened to one student on a windy March day. Now, you are going to write a paragraph, telling about a time when you were out on such a day. Here are some suggestions that will help you.

1. Reread the example in Activity 2A.
2. Use the lists of words and phrases you prepared in Activity 2A to make your paragraph exciting and realistic.
3. If you cannot remember an actual time when you were out on a windy day, make one up.

Write a first draft of your paragraph below. This is just a draft, so don't be concerned about spelling and grammar. Concentrate on getting your thoughts down on paper.

_____

_____

_____

_____

_____

_____

_____

_____

_____

_____

_____

_____

_____

_____

Name _____ Date _____

MARCH WINDS
REVISING AND WRITING A FINAL COPY

DIRECTIONS:

1. Edit and review the first draft of your paragraph about a windy March day. Here are some ideas:

   a. Does the first sentence tell what the paragraph is about? Can you make it more interesting or exciting so the reader will want to go on?

   b. Do you use a lot of vivid words and phrases like those in the example to help the reader *see* and *feel* exactly what you *saw* and *felt*?

   c. Can you remember any details that would make your description more exciting?

   d. Does the last sentence end the paragraph in a way that will satisfy the reader?

   e. Are your sentences complete? Do subjects and verbs agree?

   f. Check spelling with a dictionary.

2. Write the final copy of your paragraph below. If you wish, you can draw illustrations in the side and bottom margins.

_____

_____

_____

_____

_____

_____

_____

_____

_____

_____

Name _____ **Date** _____

MIGHTIER THAN THE SWORD
PREWRITING

> The pen is mightier than the sword.

1. What does this saying mean? Write your explanation here:

_____

_____

2. There have been many times when the power of a writer's words have brought about great changes.

On March 20, 1852, a book was published that had more influence on American history than any book ever written. The book was *Uncle Tom's Cabin*. The author was Harriet Beecher Stowe. Harriet Beecher Stowe was terribly disturbed by the evil of slavery. She wrote *Uncle Tom's Cabin* to show how black men, women, and children suffered under the cruelty of slavery. The book was an instant success. It sold 3 million copies before the start of the American Civil War, and was translated into more than 20 languages. It is commonly believed that Stowe's book awakened many to the horrors of slavery and provided inspiration to fight for its end.

Uncle Tom's Cabin is proof that "the pen *is* mightier than the sword."

3. Let's see how powerful *your* pen can be! What is wrong or unfair in your family, school, town, or country? Can you make up a story like Harriet Beecher Stowe did to show why there should be a change? It will be easier if you first answer the questions below.

a. What would you like to see changed, and why? _____

_____

_____

b. Make up some fictional people (kids or adults or both), and a scene that shows this problem. Make up names for three characters and list them below. Next to each name, describe that character and how he or she is connected to the others. (You don't need sentences here—words and phrases are enough.)

NAME	DESCRIPTION

c. Now, put these characters into a situation or scene that shows the problem you think should be changed. Describe this scene briefly below:

_____

_____

Name _____ **Date** _____

MIGHTIER THAN THE SWORD
FIRST DRAFT

Will your pen (or typewriter or computer) be mightier than a sword? Can you write something strong and truthful that will make people want to change something that is wrong or unfair?

Write a first draft of your story below. Use the characters and situation you described in Activity 3A. You can write a complete story with lots of different things happening, or you can write just one exciting scene that shows the problem clearly.

For example, perhaps your school has a dress code that you think is wrong and unfair to some students. You might show a scene between the principal and the family of a student who cannot afford to purchase the required clothes.

Write your story or scene here. This is a draft, so don't be concerned about spelling or grammar. Concentrate on getting down your ideas. (Use the back of this worksheet if you need more room.)

_____

_____

_____

_____

_____

_____

_____

_____

_____

_____

_____

_____

_____

Name _____ **Date** _____

Mightier Than The Sword
Revising and Writing a Final Copy

DIRECTIONS:

1. Edit and revise your first draft. Here are some suggestions for making your story stronger and more convincing:

---

a. Do you begin the scene with action or conversation that is exciting and introduces the problem? Can you make it more exciting?

b. Does each character serve a purpose in the story? Do you describe each character clearly? Do their actions show who and what they are?

c. Is there enough action or conversation to hold the reader's attention? If there are any boring moments, cut them out.

d. At the end of the story or scene, will a reader be convinced that there is a problem that should be changed? Can you think of any way to make it more convincing, such as showing how one of the characters is hurt by it?

e. Do you use strong action verbs and sensory language?

f. Are your sentences complete? Do subjects and verbs agree?

g. Do you use quotation marks (" ") each time someone begins and ends a speech?

---

2. Write the final copy of your story below. Indent at the beginning of each paragraph. (Use the back of this worksheet if you need more room.)

_____

_____

_____

_____

_____

_____

_____

_____

_____

Name _____ **Date** _____

MARCH IN MARCH 1

Will you march in the St. Patrick's Day parade in March?

The word MARCH appears twice in the above sentence. Each march sounds alike but has a different meaning.

Words that sound alike but have different meanings are called *homonyms*.

Sometimes *homonyms* are spelled differently as in:
   pair, meaning two
         and
   pear, meaning a fruit

Sometimes *homonyms* are spelled the same as in:
   fly, meaning something done by a bird or airplane
         and
   fly, meaning a common insect

In this activity, all the homonyms will have the same spelling!

DIRECTIONS: One word is underlined in each of the sentences below. That word has a homonym that is spelled the same and sounds the same, but has a different meaning. Write another sentence below using this homonym. (The first one is done for you.)

1. The weatherman predicted a fair day ahead.

   The student didn't think his mark was fair. _____

   _____

2. Soldiers use arms such as guns and rifles.

   _____

3. When the ceiling is too low, you must duck your head.

   _____

4. The two-act play was performed on the stage.

   _____

5. Cinderella danced at the ball.

   _____

6. Park the car in the garage.

   _____

7. Fall is my favorite season of the year.

   _____

Name _____ **Date** _____

MARCH IN MARCH 2

Homonyms are words that sound alike, but have different meanings.

In Activity 4A, you used homonyms that sound alike and are also spelled the same.

In this activity, you will use homonyms that sound alike, but are *spelled differently*, as in this example:

> *stair*, meaning a flight of steps
>   and
> *stare*, meaning to look at closely

DIRECTIONS: One word is underlined in each of these sentences. That word has a homonym that sounds alike, but is spelled differently and has a different meaning. Write a sentence below using the homonym for that word. (The first one is done for you.)

1. The eagle <u>soars</u> through the air.

   The sores on his leg were painful.

2. <u>Weigh</u> the box on the scale.

   _____

3. The ship sailed upon the <u>sea</u>.

   _____

4. It is hard to drive a car through the <u>mist</u>.

   _____

5. The department store is having a big <u>sale</u>.

   _____

6. The scale tells how much you <u>weigh</u>.

   _____

7. There is a <u>grate</u> in the fireplace.

   _____

8. A <u>male</u> horse is called a stallion.

   _____

9. A tug can <u>tow</u> other boats through the harbor.

   _____

Name _____   Date_____

THE MARCH HARE
PREWRITING

The March Hare is a character in *Alice's Adventures in Wonderland* by Lewis Carroll. The author does not describe this strange rabbit, except to say that he is "mad," but there is a description of the March Hare's house:

"The chimneys were shaped like ears and the roof was thatched with fur."

Why is this unusual creature called the *March* hare? Why is he mad? Is there something weird about the month of March?

We can only guess at the answers to these questions. In this activity, you are going to create your own extraordinary March animal and write a story about it. It might be a MARCH LION, or a MARCH DOLPHIN, or a MARCH DINOSAUR, or a MARCH FROG, or a . . . well, you get the idea! Before writing a story about your one-of-a-kind March creature, complete this brainstorming list.

BRAINSTORMING LIST

1. Decide upon a March creature and write its name below:

   The March _____

2. In the box below, write as many words and phrases as you can think of to describe the appearance of your March creature (what it looks like). You can make it as weird as you wish. (You don't need sentences here—words and phrases are enough.)

3. In the box below, write words and phrases to describe where your March creature lives.

4. In the box below, write words and phrases that describe how your March creature speaks, what it says, and how it acts.

5. On the lines below, list the names of at least two other characters who will appear in this story.

   _____

   _____

Name _____ Date _____

THE MARCH HARE
FIRST DRAFT

What kind of March creature are you going to write about? Is it wild? Is it weird? Is it funny or scary? Is it huge or tiny? How many ears does it have? Does it have a tail or wings?

Write a story about your March creature. Your story can be as short or long as you wish. Use the information you prepared on your brainstorming list to show what this creature is like. Use the other characters you listed, too.

This is just a first draft, so don't be concerned about spelling or grammar—just concentrate on getting your thoughts down on the paper. (Use the back of this worksheet if you need more room.)

Write the creature's name on the title line.

THE MARCH _____

_____

_____

_____

_____

_____

_____

_____

_____

_____

_____

_____

_____

_____

_____

Name _____ Date_____

THE MARCH HARE
REVISING AND WRITING A FINAL COPY

Did you have fun writing the first draft of your story abut a March creature? Did you make the creature really weird and unusual? Did it do strange and fantastic things?

1. Here are directions for revising and editing your story:

a. Do you describe your March creature so vividly that the reader can make it? Can you add any *sensory words* or *strong, active verbs* to make it more real?

b. Do you show how your March creature acts with the other characters? Can you add more action to make the story exciting?

c. Add some conversation to show how your characters speak to each other.

d. Are your sentences complete? Do subjects and verbs agree?

e. Check your spelling with the dictionary.

2. Write the final copy of your story below. Put the title on the first line. Indent at the beginning of paragraphs and whenever someone begins to speak. Use the back of this worksheet if you need more room. (If you wish, you can draw illustrations in the margins and at the end of the story.)

_____

_____

_____

_____

_____

_____

_____

_____

_____

Name _____ **Date** _____

BEWARE THE IDES OF MARCH!
PREWRITING

Have you ever heard the expression "Beware the ides of March!"? Do you know what it means? In the ancient Roman calendar, "ides" referred to a day in the middle of a month. In March, the ides fell on March 15.

Why should anyone be afraid of March 15? It's because of something that happened on that date over 2,000 years ago. On that day, Julius Caesar was assassinated. Julius Caesar was Rome's greatest general and statesman. Rome was a republic then—similar to the United States and other countries of today. Some people were afraid that Caesar wanted to become king. They plotted to murder him, even though they pretended to be his friends. He did not suspect anything. It is said that he was warned by a soothsayer (someone who can see into the future) to "beware the ides of March." Caesar paid no attention to the warning. He was stabbed to death on the steps of the Capitol on the ides of March. Shortly after, the Roman republic ended anyway, and Rome was ruled by an emperor.

Julius Caesar's assassination was such an important event in world history that even now, so many years later, people still write and talk about it. In this activity, you are going to write a story about a warning that is ignored. First, complete the brainstorming list below.

BRAINSTORMING LIST

1. Here are some suggestions for a story about a warning that was ignored:

    ❏ A student is warned that she won't pass if her term paper is not turned in on time.
    ❏ Someone is warned that it's not safe to go into the empty old house down the block.
    ❏ A boy wants to go to a party without his twin brother, so he warns the brother not to show up there.
    ❏ A school bully warns a smaller child that he'll get beaten up if he doesn't give money to the bully regularly.

Check one of the above, or write your own story idea here:

_____

2. Write a plot summary of your story. Tell who the characters are, describe the problem, tell the main things that happen along the way, and how it all turns out at the end. Don't write the whole story here. A plot summary is just a short description of what happens. Try to use no more than five or six sentences.

_____

_____

_____

_____

Name _____ Date _____

BEWARE THE IDES OF MARCH
FIRST DRAFT

DIRECTIONS: The plot summary you prepared in Activity 6A will help you write a story about a warning that was ignored. Here are more suggestions that may help:

BEGINNING—Begin in a way that makes the reader want to continue. Starting with dialogue or an exciting or scary scene are often effective.

CHARACTERS—Tell the story through the eyes of the main character. Don't have too many other characters in a short story—that can be confusing to the reader; it's best to have just two or three others, certainly not more than four. The actions of the characters should show what they are like.

LANGUAGE—Use lots of active verbs (like *speed* instead of *go*, *mumble* instead of *say*, etc.). Use sensory words that appeal to the five senses (touch, smell, sight, sound, taste).

Write a first draft of your story below. Since this is just a draft, don't worry about spelling or grammar—just concentrate on getting your story down on paper. Decide on a title and put it on the first line. (Use the back of this worksheet if you need more room.)

_____

_____

_____

_____

_____

_____

_____

_____

_____

_____

_____

_____

Name _____ Date _____

BEWARE THE IDES OF MARCH
REVISING AND WRITING A FINAL COPY

DIRECTIONS:

1. Edit and revise the first draft of your story, as follows:

---

a. Is the beginning interesting enough? Can you make it more exciting with dialogue or a startling scene?

b. Is the story told through the eyes of the main character. Do this person's thoughts and actions show what he or she is like?

c. Do the other characters serve a purpose in the story? If you took one out, would it make a difference? If not, remove that character from the story.

d. Are the characters different enough so the reader won't confuse them with one another? Can you make each character more unique by showing how they walk and talk and do things?

e. Is the warning clear? Does the reader see what could happen if the main character ignores it? Can you build more suspense here?

f. Is the ending satisfying? Does it solve the problem?

g. Are sentences complete? Do subjects and verbs agree?

h. Check spelling with a dictionary.

---

2. Write the final copy of your story below. Put the title on the first line. Indent at the beginning of paragraphs. (Use the back of this worksheet if you need more room.)

_____

_____

_____

_____

_____

_____

_____

_____

_____

Name _____ Date_____

SPRING FLING
PREWRITING

Spring begins on March 20! People are usually happy to welcome the "vernal equinox." (That means the beginning of spring!) Those who live in northern climates are especially glad to see the end of icy, freezing, blizzardy winters.

Writers and poets are often inspired by this season. Here are what some poets have written about spring:

> "Spring, the sweet Spring, is the year's pleasant king;
>   Then blooms each thing, then maids dance in a ring"
>   —Thomas Nashe

> "I dreamed that as I wandered by the way,
>   Bare Winter suddenly was changed to Spring"
>   —P.B. Shelley

> "Buttercups and daisies,
> Oh, the pretty flowers;
> Coming ere the Springtime
> To tell of sunny hours."
>   —Mary Howitt

> "Their smiles,
> Wan as primroses gathered at midnight
> By chilly-fingered Spring."
>   —John Keats

> "When the hounds of spring are on winter's traces,
>   The mother of months in meadow or plain
> Fills the shadows and windy places
>   With lisp of leaves and ripple of rain."
>   —A.C. Swinburne

You, too, can write poems about spring. It's fun to do! First, complete this brainstorming list.

1. In the space below, write words and phrases that describe things you see in nature at the beginning of spring:

2. In the space below, name events that happen in your home, town, country, or world in spring:

3. In the space below, write words and phrases that describe feelings you have at the beginning of spring:

4. In the space below, write pairs of rhyming spring words (examples: *spring, fling; flower, power*):

Name _____ **Date** _____

SPRING FLING
WRITING A POEM

DIRECTIONS:

1. Read the poems in Activity 7A aloud. Can you *feel* their rhythm and beat?

2. Look at your brainstorming list of spring words and phrases. Can you think of any more to add?

3. Here is a simple, 2-line rhyming verse about spring:

> Spring appears as Winter closes,
> Tulips, followed soon by roses.

4. Use the words and rhymes in your brainstorming list to write a simple, 2-line rhyming verse about spring below.

_____

_____

5. Here is a longer poem about spring:

> My heart was icy, cold and grey
>   Within the winter's long, dark night,
> Then Spring appeared and blew away
>   The darkness with its blessed light.

6. Write a poem about spring. It should have at least four lines, but can be longer. The example above uses rhyme, but poems don't have to rhyme. You may choose to rhyme or not in your poem. Use words and phrases from your brainstorming list. (If you wish, you may draw illustrations at the bottom and in the side margins.)

_____

_____

_____

_____

_____

_____

© 1997 by The Center for Applied Research in Education

Name _____ Date_____

WRITE NOW!
PREWRITING

Did you know that the third week in March is *National Card and Letter-Writing Week?*

Even in today's high-tech world with phones, faxes, and e-mail, people communicate with cards and letters. Many business executives still prefer the personal touch given by a letter. Lots of people have gotten to know each other well through letters. When you write a letter, you have the time to plan and think about what you want to say. It's easier to share one's truest feelings in a letter.

Is there someone with whom you would like to become better acquainted—someone you wish knew more about you? A letter is a great way to start such a special friendship.

In this activity, you are going to write a letter to someone you don't know well, but wish you knew better. It can be a boy or girl in your class, a neighbor, a family member, a person on your basketball team. Anyone! (You don't have to mail this letter unless you want to. Perhaps you'll end up writing such a good letter that you'll just *have* to mail it!) First, organize your ideas in the brainstorming list below.

BRAINSTORMING LIST

1. On the line below, write the name of the person to whom you are writing, and a phrase telling who he or she is. (Example: *Luke, a boy in my music class*)

_____

2. In the box below, write words and phrases that describe things you have noticed about this person that make you want to know him or her better.

3. In the box below, list things about yourself you would like this person to know. In the first column, write words and phrases that describe your interests, such as reading, sports, etc. In the second column, write words and phrases that describe your feelings and wishes, such as goals and dreams, fears, etc.

INTERESTS	FEELINGS AND WISHES

Name _____ Date _____

WRITE NOW!
FIRST DRAFT

DIRECTIONS: Use the information in your brainstorming list in Activity 8A to write the first draft of a letter to someone you would like to get to know better. Here is one *suggestion* for organizing your letter:

In the first paragraph, tell who you are and why you would like to know this person better.

In the second paragraph, tell about your interests.

In the third paragraph, tell about your feelings and goals.

In the fourth paragraph, describe what you hope this person will tell you about himself or herself.

Write your letter below, following the guides for correct form for a personal letter. (Indent at the beginning of paragraphs.)

_____
(Write your street address here)

_____
(Write your city, state, ZIP here)

_____
(Write today's date here)

Dr. _____,

_____

_____

_____

_____

_____

_____
(Write closing such as Your friend, Yours truly,)

_____
(Sign your name here)

Name _____ **Date** _____

WRITE NOW!
REVISING AND WRITING A FINAL COPY

DIRECTIONS:

1. Edit and revise the first draft of your letter:
   a. Have you introduced yourself?
   b. Do you describe your interests, feelings, and goals?
   c. Do you tell why you would like to get better acquainted?
   d. Do you indent at the beginning of each paragraph?
   e. Are your sentences complete? Do subjects and verbs agree?

2. When your letter is as perfect as you can make it, write your final copy below, following correct letter form as shown in Activity 8B. (If you plan to mail your letter, you can detach it at the dotted line or write it on a separate sheet of paper.)

— —

                         _____

                         _____

                         _____

_____ ,

_____

_____

_____

_____

_____

_____

                         _____

                         _____

Name _____ **Date** _____

MR. WATSON, COME HERE!
PREWRITING

"Mr. Watson, come here; I want you." These historic words were spoken by Alexander Graham Bell to his assistant—the first words ever to be transmitted through a telephone!

Great inventors often change the lives of everyone. Can you imagine a world without telephones? Our Earth was such a world until Alexander Graham Bell came along. He was born on March 3, 1847. Despite his great invention, Bell never considered himself primarily an inventor. Most of his life was dedicated to teaching and helping the deaf. The telephone grew out of his experiments with devices to help hearing-impaired people. Bell's invention, however, affected not only the deaf, but everyone else as well.

Today, it is hard to picture a world without telephones. How would we contact a doctor in a medical emergency, or get help from the police if we saw a crime being committed? If you got sick at school, how would the teacher get in touch with your parents? What would you do if you needed to call a classmate one evening to get a homework assignment? There are so many ways the telephone is essential to us that we just take it for granted.

In this activity, you are going to describe what it might have been like to live in a world without telephones. First, complete the brainstorming list below.

BRAINSTORMING LIST

1. On the lines below, list as many things you can think of for which you and your family use the telephone.

_____

_____

_____

2. On the lines below, list uses the telephone has for businesses, schools, and others.

_____

_____

_____

3. On the lines below, list methods of communication that people and businesses would have to use if there were no telephones.

_____

_____

_____

© 1997 by The Center for Applied Research in Education

Name _____ Date _____

MR. WATSON, COME HERE!
FIRST DRAFT

DIRECTIONS: Can you describe what the world would be like if Alexander Graham Bell had never invented the telephone? The brainstorming list in Activity 9A and the directions below will help you organize your ideas.

1. The first paragraph will introduce the topic in an interesting way, as in this example: *Everyone depends on the telephone in today's world. It seems impossible to picture a world without phones, but suppose this important tool had never been invented. Many things would be very different.*

    Write your first paragraph below (2–4 sentences). This is just a first draft, so don't be concerned about spelling or grammar. Just concentrate on getting your thoughts down on paper.

    _____

    _____

    _____

    _____

2. The second paragraph can tell how things would be different for you and your family. Use your brainstorming list for ideas, and write your second paragraph below (3–5 sentences).

    _____

    _____

    _____

    _____

3. Your third paragraph (3–5 sentences) can tell how businesses, schools, etc., would communicate without telephones.

    _____

    _____

    _____

    _____

4. The last paragraph should restate and sum up the topic, as in this example: *Communication would be a lot slower and harder without telephones. This would surely be a different world if Alexander Graham Bell had never lived.*

    Write your last paragraph (2–4 sentences) below.

    _____

    _____

    _____

Name _____ **Date** _____

MR. WATSON, COME HERE!
REVISING AND WRITING A FINAL COPY

DIRECTIONS: Edit and revise the first draft of your essay about a world without telephones, as follows:

1. Does the first paragraph introduce the topic in an interesting way? Can you make it more interesting by beginning with a question or a startling statement?
2. Does the second paragraph show how things would be different in your home without telephones? Did you leave out anything important?
3. Does the third paragraph describe how businesses and schools around the world would communicate without telephones?
4. Does the last paragraph restate and sum up the topic clearly?
5. Are your sentences complete? Do subjects and verbs agree?
6. Can you cut out unnecessary words such as *very, however, then, so,* etc., to make the writing stronger and clearer?
7. Are all words spelled correctly? Check with a dictionary.

Write the final copy of your essay below. Indent at the beginning of paragraphs. Use the back of this worksheet if you need more room.

_____

_____

_____

_____

_____

_____

_____

_____

_____

_____

_____

_____

Name _____   Date_____

SHAMROCKS AND LEPRECHAUNS 1

> St. Patrick's Day is observed on March 17 in honor of the patron saint of Ireland. But not only Irish people celebrate St. Patrick's Day. Many others join in as well with parades and parties.
>
> Here is a word game for St. Patrick's Day.

DIRECTIONS: These sentences are incomplete. There is one word missing in each sentence. Choose a word from the list at the bottom of the page and rewrite the sentence, making it complete. The first one is done for you.

1. There are St. Patrick's Day in many cities on March 17.

   There are St. Patrick's Day parades in many cities on March 17. _____

2. Grow in Ireland.

   _____

3. Cute little are Irish elves.

   _____

4. Did you ever swing a?

   _____

5. The color is often worn on St. Patrick's Day.

   _____

6. Can you sing "When Eyes Are Smiling?"

   _____

7. Many restaurants serve corned beef and on St. Patrick's Day.

   _____

8. An Irish dance is called a.

   _____

shamrocks   cabbage
leprechauns green
parades   jig

Irish
shillelagh

Name _____ **Date** _____

SHAMROCKS AND LEPRECHAUNS 2

DIRECTIONS:

Here are six sentences about St. Patrick's Day. Can you rearrange them in the proper order for a clearly-written paragraph? Write the paragraph on the lines below.

1. He founded many churches and was a great religious leader.
2. His name was St. Patrick, and he came to Ireland in the fifth century.
3. Even in America, there are parties and parades on St. Patrick's Day.
4. March 17 is a special day for the people of Ireland.
5. March 17, the anniversary of his death, is celebrated with parades and religious ceremonies.
6. It is when they celebrate the life of their patron saint.

Write your paragraph on the lines below. If you wish, you can illustrate it in the space at the bottom of the page.

_____

_____

_____

_____

_____

_____

_____

_____

_____

Name _____ Date_____

SHAMROCKS AND LEPRECHAUNS 3

DIRECTIONS: Here are some more sentences about St. Patrick for you to arrange into a paragraph. Can you put the sentences in the proper order? Write the paragraph on the lines below.

1. St. Patrick fearlessly drove all the snakes out of Ireland into the ocean.
2. One of them is about St. Patrick and the snakes.
3. This is just a legend, but it could have happened that way.
4. The snakes were vicious and caused trouble for the people.
5. There are many stories about St. Patrick.
6. It is said that there was a large number of snakes in Ireland when St. Patrick arrived there.

Write your paragraph below. If you wish, you may illustrate it in the space at the bottom of the page.

_____

_____

_____

_____

_____

_____

_____

_____

_____

Name _____ **Date** _____

ADVENTURE AND SERVICE
PREWRITING

On March 1, 1961, President John F. Kennedy established the Peace Corps. This volunteer organization has grown through the years into an opportunity for people of all ages to seek adventure and gain experience while at the same time helping others.

The purpose of the Peace Corps is to promote the spread of democracy throughout the world by helping other countries to develop their people and resources. Peace Corps volunteers from all over the United States travel abroad to serve as teachers, nurses, technicians, artisans, and willing workers. Many young people see it as an opportunity to enrich their lives through travel and adventure. It is also a chance to experience the satisfaction of helping others.

What do you think of the Peace Corps? Is it a good idea? Do you think it works? Would you like to be part of it some day if you could? In what areas might you enjoy serving?

Before writing an essay stating your thoughts about the Peace Corps, first complete the brainstorming list below.

BRAINSTORMING LIST

1. In the box below, write words and phrases that tell what might be good about being a Peace Corps volunteer.

2. In the box below, list words and phrases that tell what might be bad about being a Peace Corps volunteer.

3. In the box below, list some jobs you might like to perform in the Peace Corps.

4. On the lines below, list at least three places in the world where you would like to travel. Next to each name, state why you want to go there.

_____

_____

_____

_____

Name _____ **Date** _____

ADVENTURE AND SERVICE
FIRST DRAFT

DIRECTIONS: Write an essay telling what you think of the Peace Corps and whether or not you would like to be a Peace Corps volunteer. Use your brainstorming list and follow the suggestions below. (This is just a first draft, so don't be concerned about spelling or grammar—concentrate on getting your ideas on paper.)

1. The first paragraph should introduce the topic and state your general opinion of the Peace Corps, as in this example: *Ever since it was founded, the Peace Corps and its volunteer workers have been a shining example of the advantages of democracy. I hope that some day I may be able to be part of this exciting program.* Write your first paragraph (2–4 sentences) below:

_____

_____

_____

2. In the second paragraph, state what is good and bad about the Peace Corps, or list the advantages and disadvantages of becoming a volunteer. Write your second paragraph (3–5 sentences) below:

_____

_____

_____

3. The third paragraph can list the places in the world you might like to serve (and why) and the job or jobs you could perform. Write your third paragraph (3–5 sentences) below:

_____

_____

_____

4. The last paragraph should restate and sum up the topic, as in this example: *I can't imagine anything more exciting than serving as a Peace Corps volunteer. It would be a thrilling adventure and a chance to really make a difference in the world.* Write your last paragraph (2–4 sentences) below:

_____

_____

_____

Name _____ Date _____

ADVENTURE AND SERVICE
REVISING AND WRITING A FINAL COPY

DIRECTIONS:

1. Edit and revise the first draft of your essay about the Peace Corps. Here are some suggestions:

   a. Does the first paragraph introduce the topic in an interesting way? Can you make it more striking with words like *exciting, thrilling, dangerous, travel, unpredictable, far-off*?

   b. Does the second paragraph contrast the good and bad things about the Peace Corps?

   c. Does the third paragraph name places you would like to go and jobs you might do? Do you give reasons for these choices?

   d. Does the last paragraph restate and sum up the topic?

   e. Are your sentences complete? Do subjects and verbs agree?

   f. Check spelling wherever you are unsure.

2. Write your final copy below. Indent at the beginning of paragraphs. Use the back of this worksheet if you need more room.

_____

_____

_____

_____

_____

_____

_____

_____

_____

_____

_____

_____

Name _____ Date_____

OUT LIKE A LAMB 1

There is an old saying:

"March comes in like a lion, and goes out like a lamb."

It's fun to think of the cold, blustery start of March as a *lion*, and the spring-like end of the month as a *lamb*.

This kind of comparison is called a *simile*. Similes usually use the word *like*, as in the example above, or *as*, as in, "I felt as peaceful as a baby that has just been fed." The use of similes can make your writing much more striking and unique. It can be challenging to think up new and unusual similes.

DIRECTIONS: Complete each sentence below with a simile. Try to make your similes as original as possible.

1. Her hair was like _____

2. He was as cold as _____

3. The room was dark, like _____

4. His eyes were as black as _____

5. The hot sand felt like _____

6. Paul ran as fast as _____

7. The visitor felt as comfortable as _____

8. The new town was as strange to him as _____

9. Mr. Maxwell was as strong as _____

10. His expression was icy, like _____

11. I am as happy as _____

12. She is as sad as _____

13. She looked at me kindly, like _____

14. This activity is as easy as _____

15. My day has been like _____

Name _____ **Date** _____

OUT LIKE A LAMB 2

Similes can make your writing more striking. Some similes have been used so often that they can be boring, such as "as good as gold," or "as green as grass." You can create your own similes, however, that are original and unique. These can make even everyday occurrences come to life, as in the following paragraph about one boy's ordinary morning:

> The shriek of my alarm was as jolting as an air raid siren. I stared at the clock. It was seven o'clock, time to rise and face the day. I yawned, feeling my jaw stretching taut like the muscles of an athlete. I sat up and swung my feet to the floor. The tiles were as cold as a mountaintop in winter. I shivered and forced myself to get up.

There are three similes in this paragraph. Can you find and underline them?

It's easy to write about simple, ordinary occurrences. On the lines below, write a paragraph about something out of your own life. Make your writing exciting by including at least three similes. Here are some suggestions:

> getting up in the morning (like the paragraph above)
> riding a school bus
> getting dressed
> a family meal
> a class lesson
> hanging out with your friends
> a baseball game

Write a paragraph describing one of these scenes, or any other you wish. Use at least three similes. Try to make them as original as you can!

_____

_____

_____

_____

_____

_____

_____

_____

Name _____ **Date**_____

A Dreaded Disease
Prewriting

On March 26, 1953, an important event occurred in the history of health and medicine. Dr. Jonas Salk announced the discovery of a vaccine to prevent polio.

For many years, polio was one of the most dreaded diseases to attack young people. Parents and physicians were helpless against the epidemics of infantile paralysis, as it was then called, that occurred regularly. They could only watch in despair as their children died or suffered permanent, lifelong paralysis.

Today, thanks to Dr. Jonas Salk, polio is practically unknown. This did not come about easily. Dr. Salk had to study and work for many years as a doctor and researcher before he was successful in developing an effective vaccine. Now, the world is safer for children because Dr. Salk dedicated his life to wiping out this terrible disease.

Now, other dedicated scientists are struggling to find ways to cure or prevent dreaded illnesses, such as AIDS, cancer, heart disease, and many others. In this activity, you are going to tell which of these you would find a cure for, if you could, and how you might go about accomplishing this. This essay will be easy to write if you first prepare a brainstorming list.

BRAINSTORMING LIST

1. In the box below, write the name of the disease you would like to cure. Then make a list of words and phrases that describe why you have chosen this particular illness.

> Name of Disease: _____

2. In the box below, write a list of words and phrases that describe how you would prepare yourself to do this (education, training, work experience, abilities to develop, attitudes, etc.).

3. In the box below, write as many words and phrases as you can think of to describe how people's lives would be better when this cure is discovered.

Name _____ **Date** _____

A DREADED DISEASE
FIRST DRAFT

DIRECTIONS: Write the first draft of a 3-paragraph essay about a disease for which you would like to find a cure. Since this is just a draft, don't be concerned about spelling or grammar—concentrate on getting your thoughts down on paper. This will be easy to do if you keep your brainstorming list handy.

The first paragraph should tell about the disease and why you want to find a cure for it, as in this example:

How would you feel if you received a death sentence? That is what it is like for people who are diagnosed with AIDS. This dreadful disease is spreading with frightening speed. The greatest thing I could do in life would be to find a cure for AIDS.

Write your first paragraph (2–4 sentences) here:

_____

_____

_____

The second paragraph should describe how you would prepare to do this work (schools, subjects, abilities, attitude, jobs, etc.). Write your second paragraph (3–7 sentences) below:

_____

_____

_____

_____

_____

_____

The last paragraph should restate the topic and describe how people's lives would be changed by your discovery. Write your last paragraph (2–4 sentences) below:

_____

_____

_____

Name _____ **Date**_____

A Dreaded Disease
Revising and Writing a Final Copy

DIRECTIONS:

1. Edit and revise the draft of your essay about finding a cure for a dreaded disease, as follows:

> a. Does your first paragraph introduce the topic in an interesting way? Could you make it more exciting by beginning with a question, a quotation, or a startling statement?
>
> b. Does the second paragraph give a clear, detailed discussion of the subject? Does it include a description of how you would prepare yourself to do this task, and what steps you would take to accomplish it?
>
> c. Does the last paragraph restate and sum up the topic?
>
> d. Is your writing clear and easy to understand Have you used any awkward phrasing that could be made smoother and clearer?
>
> e. Are your sentences complete? Do subjects and verbs agree?
>
> f. Is the spelling correct? Check with a dictionary.

2. Write the final copy of your essay below. Indent at the beginning of paragraphs. (Use the back of this worksheet if you need more room.)

_____

_____

_____

_____

_____

_____

_____

_____

_____

_____

_____

APRIL

APRIL

"Blossoming boughs of April in laughter shake."
—Robert Bridges

SPRING BUDS, TULIPS AND DAFFODILS ... APRIL FOOLS' DAY ...
EASTER AND PASSOVER ... EARTH DAY (APRIL 21) ... BASEBALL
SEASON OPENS ... DAYLIGHT SAVINGS TIME ("SPRING FORWARD") ...
PATRIOTS' DAY (APRIL 19)

APRIL EVENTS

April 3, 1910: Mt. McKinley, highest mountain in North America, was scaled

April 8, 1513: Ponce de Leon landed in Florida (near what is now St. Augustine) seeking the Fountain of Youth

April 9, 1833: The first public library in the U.S. was opened in Peterborough, New Hampshire

April 9, 1865: General Lee surrendered to General Grant at Appomattox Court House, Virginia, ending the Civil War

April 11, 1947: Jackie Robinson joined the Brooklyn Dodgers, becoming the first African-American in major league baseball

April 12, 1861: The Civil War began when Confederate troops fired upon Fort Sumpter in Charleston, South Carolina

April 15, 1865: Abraham Lincoln, 16th president of the U.S., died after being shot by John Wilkes Booth at Ford's Theater in Washington, D.C.

April 15, 1912: The luxury liner, *Titanic*, sank after striking an iceberg, with a loss of 1,517 lives

April 19, 1775: British soldiers fired upon Minute Men in Lexington, Massachusetts ("the shot heard round the world")

April 29, 1913: The zipper was patented by Gideon Sundback of New Jersey

April 30, 1803: The U.S. doubled in size with the Louisiana Purchase

April 30, 1975: U.S. forces evacuated Vietnam; Saigon surrendered

APRIL BIRTHDAYS

April 2, 1805: Hans Christian Andersen, Danish writer of fairy tales

April 3, 1783: Washington Irving, American writer ("Rip Van Winkle")

April 7, 1770: William Wordsworth, English poet

April 12, 1916: Beverly Cleary, popular writer of children's books

April 13, 1743: Thomas Jefferson, 3rd president of the U.S.

April 21, 1926: Queen Elizabeth II of Great Britain

April 23, 1564: William Shakespeare, English dramatist and poet

WRITING ACTIVITIES FOR APRIL

Name _____ **Date** _____

APRIL FOOL 1

April 1 is sometimes called April Fools' Day. Do you ever try to fool people on that day? Here is an April Fool activity.

The following sentences are trying to trick you. Each contains at least one error. Write each sentence *correctly* on the line below.

1. Do you no what happens on April 1?

_____

2. Did you sea the trick that Alan played on Greg?

_____

3. Alan held out a coin and said, "Here's twenty-five sense."

_____

4. Greg said, "Thanks," but it was not a reel quarter.

_____

5. Alan laughed so hard he almost fell down the stares.

_____

> Did you find all the misspelled homonyms in these sentences? Homonyms are words that sound alike but have different meanings. Sometimes homonyms can even be spelled the same, as in *state*, meaning "to say," and *state*, meaning part of a country. The homonyms in the sentences above are spelled differently. Did you find them all? They were: *no* for *know*, *sea* for *see*, *sense* for *cents*, *reel* for *real*, and *stares* for *stairs*.

Here are more sentences with the wrong homonyms. Write the sentences correctly below. (*Note:* Some sentences have more than one wrong homonym.)

1. Their are April raindrops on the window pain.

_____

2. It is not write to play cruel April Fool jokes.

_____

3. Did you here about the funny knew April Fool trick?

_____

4. Wood you like to learn a good trick?

_____

Name _____ Date_____

APRIL FOOL 2

DIRECTIONS: April Fools' Day tricks can be fun! The paragraph below is an April Fool joke. It has *ten* mistakes. Some of these are wrong homonyms and some are misspellings.

You won't become an April Fool if you are a good proofreader.

First, circle all the words that are spelled wrong.

Then, copy the paragraph correctly on the lines below.

As soon as I woke up in the mourning, I new that this was a special day. I looked at the calendar. I was write! It was the first day of a knew month. IT WAS APRIL FOOLS' DAY! I got dressed quickly and ran down the stares. I told my sister that their was a bug on her hare. She screamed and grabbed her head. I said, "April Fool!" Then I told my Mom there was smoke in the kichen. She just smiled and said, "I know. April Fool." The truble was, there realy was smoke. Luckily, Dad saw the smoke and took out the burnt toast.

Did you find all ten misspelled words? You did? Then, you are no April Fool!

Now, write the paragraph correctly on the lines below:

_____

_____

_____

_____

_____

_____

_____

_____

_____

_____

_____

_____

_____

Name _____ **Date** _____

APRIL SHOWERS
PREWRITING

> "March winds and April showers
> Are sure to bring May flowers."

Everyone knows this folk saying. The same theme is used in an old song:

> "Though April showers may come your way
> They bring the flowers that bloom in May."

The month of April seems to inspire poetry. Here are more lines of poetry that have been written about April:

> ". . . it comes from the west lands, the old brown hills,
> And April's in the west wind, and daffodils."
> —John Masefield
>
> "Proud-pied April, dressed in all his trim
> Hath put a spirit of youth on everything."
> —William Shakespeare

People seem to think happy thoughts about April. Perhaps that is because it is the first full month of spring. It's easy to write poetry about a month as nice as April. Before you write your April poem, first prepare a brainstorming list of April words and phrases.

BRAINSTORMING LIST

1. In the box below, write all the *nouns* you can think of that remind you of April. The list is begun for you. You should add *at least* six more.

Easter, rain,

2. In the box below, write *adjectives* that describe April. Add *at least* six more to the list.

showery, yellow

3. In the box below, write *verbs* that remind you of April. Add *at least* six more to the list.

stroll, play

4. In the box below, write some *rhyming words* that could be used in a poem about April, such as bunny/funny, flower/tower.

Name _____ **Date**_____

APRIL SHOWERS
FIRST DRAFT

1. The easiest kind of poem to write is a *couplet*. It has just two lines with the same beat and rhyme. Here are some examples of couplets about April that were written by students:

> "April comes in like a jewel,
> Though the first is just a fool."
>
> "April pours its waters on the ground
> Giving birth to flowers all around."

On the lines below, write the first draft of a couplet about April. You can use the rhyming words from your brainstorming list.

_____

_____

2. The second poem you are going to write is even easier than a couplet because it doesn't have to rhyme or have any set rhythm. It's a poem where the first letter of each line spells out the subject of the poem. Here is an example of this kind of poem that was written about the month of March:

> **M**arch blows and throws its weight
> **A**bout; it huffs and puffs and
> **R**oars a
> **C**old and windy
> **H**owl.

Write a first draft of a poem like this about April. The first letter of each line is written out for you.

A_____

P_____

R_____

I _____

L_____

Name _____ Date _____

April Showers
Revising and Writing a Final Copy

DIRECTIONS: The first draft of a poem is not usually the final one. A writer can always think of better words and phrases to express thoughts and descriptions.

Examine the first draft of the two poems you wrote for Activity 2B. They are both short, so each word is even more important than it would be in a longer piece of writing. Ask yourself the following questions, and make the necessary corrections on your first draft:

1. Are there words in the brainstorming list that would be better than the ones you used?
2. Would another rhyme work better than the one you used in the couplet?
3. Do your poems show something about the *essence* of April? Are there other words and phrases that would do this better?

When your two poems are as perfect as you can make them, write the final copy of each one below. Write the couplet first. Below it, write the poem where each line begins with a letter in APRIL. (If you wish, you can draw illustrations in the margins around each poem.)

A _____

P _____

R _____

I _____

L _____

© 1997 by The Center for Applied Research in Education

Name _____ **Date**_____

SAVE OUR EARTH!
PREWRITING

Did you know that the first Earth Day was celebrated on April 22, 1970? It was the idea of Gaylord Nelson, a senator from Wisconsin.

Since that time, more and more people have become concerned about the environment, pollution, and misuse of the world's resources. There are serious problems with the air we breathe, the water we drink, and the food we eat. Earth Day is a time to pay attention to our beautiful Earth and try to learn how to preserve a healthy, safe environment for future generations.

Have you ever thought about what you might to do help in this campaign? Everybody can do something, such as taking part in community trash cleanups, reusing paper bags, and helping to sort items that can be recycled.

You are going to write an essay about Earth Day and how ordinary people can help preserve the environment. First, complete the brainstorming list below.

BRAINSTORMING LIST

1. In the box below, write all the words and phrases you can think of that describe the kind of environment human beings need, such as pure water, healthy food, etc.

2. In the box below, write all the words and phrases you can think of that describe dangers to the environment, such as nuclear accidents, poisoned fish, etc.

3. In the box below, write words and phrases that describe ways of preserving the environment, such as recycling, planting trees, etc.

4. On the lines below, write a beginning (one or two sentences) for an essay about Earth Day. (Example: "Will our children and grandchildren be able to breathe air that is not polluted or eat food that is not contaminated? Earth Day reminds us that we are the ones who must preserve the environment.")

_____

_____

_____

Name _____ **Date** _____

SAVE OUR EARTH!
FIRST DRAFT

> *DIRECTIONS:* Write a first draft for a 5-paragraph essay about Earth Day and what it means to you. Use the brainstorming list you prepared for Activity 3A and follow the guidelines below. (*Remember:* This is just a first draft!)

1. The first paragraph should introduce the topic in an interesting way as in this example: "Will our children and grandchildren be able to breathe air that is not polluted or eat food that is not contaminated? Earth Day reminds us that we are the ones who must preserve the environment."

   Write your first paragraph (2–4 sentences) here:

   _____
   _____
   _____

2. Your second paragraph should describe the resources of the Earth that are necessary for human survival, such as clean air, unpolluted rivers, etc. Write your second paragraph (3–5 sentences) here:

   _____
   _____
   _____
   _____

3. Your third paragraph should describe dangers to the environment, such as oil spills, etc. Write your third paragraph (3–5 sentences) here:

   _____
   _____
   _____
   _____

4. Your fourth paragraph should describe ways in which you can help preserve the environment, such as recycling, planting trees, etc. Write your fourth paragraph (3–5 sentences) here:

   _____
   _____
   _____
   _____

5. Your last paragraph should restate and sum up the topic, as in this example: "We should all get out there on Earth Day and show our support for the environment. But that is not enough. We must do things every day of the year to preserve the good things of this Earth." Write your last paragraph (2–4 sentences) here:

   _____
   _____
   _____

Name _____ **Date** _____

SAVE OUR EARTH!
REVISING AND WRITING A FINAL COPY

DIRECTIONS:

1. Edit and revise your first draft as follows:

a. Does the first paragraph introduce the topic in an interesting way? Can you make it more interesting with a question or a startling statement?

b. Does the second paragraph describe the Earth's resources that are necessary for human survival? Can you think of anything else important to add?

c. Does the third paragraph describe dangers to the environment? Do you make it clear why these things are bad? Can you add any more?

d. Does the fourth paragraph describe things you can do to help preserve the environment? Are there enough details so the reader can see how these things will help? Can you add anything more?

e. Does the last paragraph restate and sum up the topic?

f. Can you substitute active verbs, such as *build*, *run*, or *demand*, for passive verbs like *make* or *go*?

g. Do you have any unnecessary words? If so, cutting them out will usually make your writing clearer and stronger.

h. Are your sentences complete? Do subjects and verbs agree?

i. Check spelling with a dictionary.

2. Write the final copy of your essay below. Indent at the beginning of paragraphs. (Use the back of this worksheet if you need more room.)

Name _____ **Date** _____

FRACTURED FAIRY TALES
PREWRITING

"They knock at my forehead and say, 'Here I am!'" This is how Hans Christian Andersen described the way he wrote his stories for children.

The Ugly Duckling, The Red Shoes, The Princess and the Pea, The Little Mermaid. These are just a few of the 168 immortal fairy tales that "knocked on the forehead" of Hans Christian Andersen.

Hans was born in Denmark on April 2, 1805. His father died when Hans was 11. His family was poor and hardworking. Hans was apprenticed to a weaver, then to a tobacconist, then to a tailor. Poor Hans was a failure in all these things. His only interests were books, stories, and the theater. His early life was filled with poverty and suffering, but little by little, the news of his magical tales spread. Eventually, he became famous and wealthy, but he always thought of himself as the boy who loved to tell stories.

Most people could never match the genius of Hans Christian Andersen as a storyteller. Anyone, however, can have fun retelling his familiar tales in new and unusual ways. Have you ever written a "fractured fairy tale"? Here are some examples.

Goldilocks and the Three Bears: Goldilocks breaks into the house of the three bears. She eats up all their food and trashes all their furniture. When the bears come home, Goldilocks chases them away, and they rush off, never again to return to that house.

Little Red Riding Hood: Red's mother gives her a basket of food to bring to her grandmother. Red eats up all the food. She knows her grandmother will be angry, so she goes to her friend, the wolf. She asks him to frighten her grandmother, then let himself be chased away by Red. That way, the grandmother will be too grateful to care about the food. The wolf falls along the way and sprains his leg so he never gets to Grandma's house. When Red arrives, she thinks the wolf is in Grandma's bed. She says, "What big eyes you have, what big ears you have," etc. Grandma jumps out of bed and demands her food.

These are just summaries of fractured fairy tales. The complete story will be told with lots of action, description, and dialogue. Before writing your fractured fairy tale, first complete the brainstorming list below.

BRAINSTORMING LIST

1. Write the name of the fairy tale you have chosen to "fracture" below:

_____

2. Write a summary of your fractured fairy tale as in the examples above.

_____

_____

_____

_____

Name _____ Date_____

FRACTURED FAIRY TALES
FIRST DRAFT

DIRECTIONS: It's fun to write a fractured fairy tale. You don't have to dream up a whole new story, because it's already there! You just have to change it around a bit. You can be as silly as you wish. Your characters don't have to act the same as in the original. Here are some helpful suggestions:

---

1. PLOT: The plot is basically what you wrote in your summary in Activity 4A. It can be similar to the original plot with just a few changes or it can be very different. The plot should hold the reader's interest and be convincing. The plot must hold together and make sense, even if the events themselves are ridiculous. There should be a beginning where you introduce the setting (where the story takes place) and the main character or characters. Then the plot should be developed with several exciting scenes that lead to the conclusion.

2. CHARACTERS: Describe your characters so the reader can see them. Show their character traits and personalities by what they *do* and *say*.

3. DIALOGUE: There should be some dialogue at several points in the story. Be sure the reader knows who is talking at any time. Make the scene come to life by showing what they are *doing* during the dialogue.

Now, write a first draft of your story below. Don't be concerned about spelling and grammar at this point. Just concentrate on getting your ideas on paper. Follow the suggestions above, and use your summary as a guide.

Indent at the beginning of each paragraph, and whenever a character begins to speak. (Use the back of this worksheet if you need more room.)

_____

_____

_____

_____

_____

_____

_____

_____

Name _____ Date _____

FRACTURED FAIRY TALES
REVISING AND WRITING A FINAL COPY

DIRECTIONS:

1. Revise and edit the first draft of your fractured fairy tale as follows:

> a. Do you introduce the setting and main characters at the beginning?
>
> b. Do you develop the plot with action and dialogue? Can you think of ways to make the action more exciting? Are any parts confusing? If so, make these scenes clearer to the reader.
>
> c. Do you have several scenes with dialogue? Should any of the dialogue be changed to better show the personalities of these characters? Would the scene come to life more if you put in a few phrases showing what the characters are doing while they speak? Does the reader always know which character is speaking?
>
> d. Can you describe the characters more sharply, with striking phrases that show their appearance, their clothing, the way they walk, how they speak, etc.?
>
> e. Does your conclusion bring the story to an end? Is this clear to the reader?
>
> f. Can you make the writing more interesting by using words and phrases that appeal to the five senses (sight, hearing, smell, touch, and taste)?
>
> g. Can you make your writing more exciting by changing passive verbs to active ones? For example, instead of *go*, use *race* or *saunter*; instead of *see*, use *stare* or *peer*, etc.

2. When your fractured fairy tale is as good as you can make it, write your final copy below. Indent at the beginning of paragraphs and whenever anyone begins to speak. Use the back of this worksheet if you need more room. (Write the title on the first line.)

Name _____ Date_____

THE APRIL WAR
PREWRITING

Did you know that three of the most important events of the American Civil War happened during the month of April? On *April 12, 1861*, Confederate troops fired on Fort Sumpter in Charleston, South Carolina. This marked the beginning of the Civil War. On *April 9, 1865*, General Robert E. Lee surrendered to General Ulysses S. Grant at Appomattox Court House in Virginia, ending this War Between the States. Then, on *April 15, 1865*, President Abraham Lincoln died after being shot by John Wilkes Booth at Ford's Theater in Washington, D.C.

The Civil War was a major event in American history. As a result, the Union was preserved so that today the United States is one country, extending from ocean to ocean, and from Canada to the north to Mexico to the south.

What would have happened if the South had won the war, or if the southern states had been permitted to secede? There could have been two countries instead of one—the United States of America and the Confederate States of America.

What would it be like to have two American nations, and perhaps even more, on this continent? Can you write a description of a boy or girl just like yourself living in one of these nations? How would life be the same? How would it be different? The brainstorming list below will help you get ideas.

BRAINSTORMING LIST

1. Would things be better or worse if the Confederacy had won the war? In what ways? (You don't need sentences here—words and phrases are enough.)

_____

_____

2. What happened to all the western territories? Did they become part of the Confederacy or the Union, or did they form their own nation or nations? Write a few sentences below telling what you think these states would have done.

_____

_____

3. Write a few sentences telling how your city and state might be different and why.

_____

_____

4. What about advances in science and industry and new inventions, such as automobiles, airplanes, electric power, computers, etc.? Write a few sentences telling how these would be the same or different, and why.

_____

_____

Name _____ **Date** _____

THE APRIL WAR
FIRST DRAFT

DIRECTIONS: Write the first draft of an essay about what your life might be like if the South had won the Civil War. Use your brainstorming list, and follow the suggestions below. (This is just a draft, so don't be concerned with spelling or grammar; concentrate on getting down your thoughts.)

1. The first paragraph should introduce the topic, as in this example: "The U.S.A. is not perfect, but it would be a lot worse if it had been divided after the Civil War. I hate to imagine what my life would be like if I had to live in that kind of country." Write your first paragraph (2–4 sentences) here:

_____

_____

_____

2. Develop the theme in the second paragraph by describing the state and country in which you might be living, such as the Confederate States of America, the United States of America, or some other. Describe the size, government, laws, people, schools, business, etc. Write the second paragraph (3–5 sentences) here:

_____

_____

_____

_____

3. Develop the theme further in the third paragraph by describing the history of your "country" since the Civil War and how this has affected advances in science, medicine, technology, social changes, etc. Write the third paragraph (3–5 sentences) here:

_____

_____

_____

_____

4. The last paragraph should restate and sum up the theme, as in this example: "It makes me shudder to picture what my state and country would be like if the Civil War had turned out differently. I'm thankful and happy to live in a strong, powerful, advanced nation." Write your last paragraph (2–4 sentences) here:

_____

_____

_____

Name _____ **Date**_____

THE APRIL WAR
REVISING AND WRITING A FINAL COPY

DIRECTIONS:

1. Edit and revise your draft of an essay describing what the U.S.A. would be like if the Confederacy had won the Civil War, as follows:

> a. Does the first paragraph clearly state the topic? Can you make it more interesting with a question or a startling statement?
>
> b. Does the second paragraph develop the theme by describing life in your state and country as it would be if the South had won the Civil War? Can you add more details? Can you make the descriptions of your town, family, and school more vivid?
>
> c. Does the third paragraph develop the topic further by describing the history of the separate nations on this continent? Can you add more details about their governments, their laws, their scientific and technical accomplishments, etc.?
>
> d. Does the last paragraph restate and sum up the topic? Can you think of a way to say it more interestingly?
>
> e. Is your writing too wordy? Can you make it sharper and clearer by cutting out unnecessary words?
>
> f. Can you add sensory language and active verbs to make the writing more vivid?
>
> g. Are your sentences complete? Do subjects and verbs agree?
>
> h. Check spelling.

2. Write the final copy of your essay below. Indent at the beginning of paragraphs. (Use the back of this worksheet if you need more room.)

_____

_____

_____

_____

_____

_____

_____

_____

Name _____ **Date** _____

MY CAPTAIN!
PREWRITING

On April 15, 1865, one of the saddest events in American history occurred. President Abraham Lincoln died after being shot by John Wilkes Booth while attending a performance at Ford's Theater in Washington, D.C.

The country was shocked and saddened. People wept on the streets. Walt Whitman expressed the pain that everyone felt in his poem, "Oh, Captain! My Captain!" Here are some lines from this poem:

> "O Captain! my Captain! our fearful trip is done,
> The ship has weather'd every rack, the prize we sought is won,
> The port is near, the bells I hear, the people all exulting,
> While follow eyes the steady keel, the vessel grim and daring;
>   But O heart! heart! heart!
>   O the bleeding drops of red,
>   Where on the deck my Captain lies,
>   Fallen cold and dead."

Whitman uses *metaphor* in this poem. The *ship* is a metaphor for the *nation*. The *captain* is the *president*. Imagine how readers of the time responded. But you don't have to know that the poem is about the death of Lincoln to be touched by it. Anyone who has ever lost someone or something dear can identify with the grief this poem expresses so vividly.

What loss in your own life does this poem remind you of? It might be the death of a grandparent or a kind neighbor, or even someone you never met such as a singer or actor whom you admired. The death of a pet can also cause great emotional pain. There are other losses besides death that are difficult, such as the loss of a close friend who moves away or who ignores you after a fight. Or, perhaps you once moved a long distance and lost contact with friends who were important to you. Such a loss can be as painful as a death.

Writing about a loss isn't always easy, but it can often help deal with these big and unpleasant feelings. Decide what loss in your own life you are going to write about, and tell what it is on the line below:

_____

You can write about this loss in any form that seems most comfortable—a *poem*, a *paragraph*, an *essay*, or a *story*. Put a circle around the one you have chosen.

Before beginning to compose your piece, first build a vocabulary for it by preparing two lists, as follows:

1. In the box below, write as many words and phrases as you can think of to describe the person or thing you lost and how the loss occurred.

>

2. In the box below, write as many words and phrases as you can think of that describe your feelings about this loss. (You can "borrow" words from Whitman's poem.)

>

© 1997 by The Center for Applied Research in Education

Name _____ Date _____

MY CAPTAIN!
FIRST DRAFT

> "O Captain! my Captain! rise up and hear the bells;
> Rise up—for you the flag is flung—for you the bugle trills,
> For you bouquets and ribbon'd wreaths—for you the shores a'crowding,
> For you they call, the swaying mass, their eager faces turning;
>   Here Captain, dear father!
>   This arm beneath your head!
>   It is some dream that on the deck,
>   You've fallen cold and dead."

Many poems, stories, and essays were written upon the death of Abraham Lincoln. It was one way of expressing grief. The same thing happened when President John F. Kennedy was assassinated in 1963. People felt these deaths as a personal loss.

When writing about your own personal loss (in a poem, paragraph, story, or essay), keep three things in mind:

1. First, remember that your reader may not know the person or thing you are mourning. You must paint a *word picture* of this subject. Include appearance, character, personality, interests. Also give examples of things you did together, if possible. Use the words and phrases you prepared for Activity 6A to make this person or thing seem real and important.

2. Tell how the loss occurred with as much detail as possible.

3. Describe your feelings and actions at the time. What are your emotions now when remembering the event? (Use the list of words you prepared for Activity 6A.)

Write a first draft of a poem, paragraph, essay, or story about a personal loss. This is just a rough copy, so don't be concerned about spelling or grammar. Concentrate on getting your thoughts down on paper. (Use the back of this worksheet if you need more room.)

_____

_____

_____

_____

_____

_____

Name _____ **Date** _____

My Captain!
Revising and Writing a Final Copy

> "My Captain does not answer, his lips are pale and still,
> My father does not feel my arm, he has no pulse nor will,
> The ship is anchor'd safe and sound, its voyage closed and done,
> From fearful trip the victor ship comes in with object won;
>   Exult O shores, and ring O bells!
>   But I with mournful tread,
>   Walk the deck my Captain lies,
>   Fallen cold and dead."

DIRECTIONS:

1. Edit and revise the first draft of the poem, paragraph, essay, or story you wrote about loss. Here are some suggestions:

   a. Do you describe the subject in details that will make this person or thing real to the reader? Do you show some actions or events, particularly those that affected you? Did you leave out anything important?

   b. Do you tell how the loss occurred? Can you add any details or phrases to make it more vivid to the reader?

   c. Do you describe your emotions? Can you make them more vivid with metaphors or similes, such as "I felt like someone who has been transported to an empty world"? Try to include at least one simile or metaphor.

   d. Reread the lines from "Oh Captain! My Captain!" Notice the details and vivid words and phrases that touch the reader's emotions. Can you add some of these to your own work?

2. When your poem, paragraph, essay, or story is as perfect as you can make it, write your final copy below. (Use the back of this worksheet if you need more room.)

_____

_____

_____

_____

_____

_____

Name _____ Date_____

A WORLD OF BOOKS
PREWRITING

> "Oh for a book and a shady nook, either indoor or out;
> With the green leaves whispering overhead or the street cries all about.
> Where I may read all at my ease, both of the new and old;
> For a jolly good book whereon to look is better to me than gold."
> —John Wilson

Do you use your school and public libraries? Libraries are part of our lives. We take them for granted and think they have always been around.

Not so! The first public library in the United States opened in Peterborough, New Hampshire in 1833. It was not until many years later that most U.S. cities and towns had public libraries. Even today, there are many places around the world where no public libraries are available.

Public libraries make books available to everyone—even to those who cannot afford to buy books of their own. Often men and women who have not been able to attend college have educated themselves at public libraries.

Books teach us about the world. They help us understand science, history, other people, even our own selves. They take us on fantastic journeys. Best of all, books can offer hours of adventure and entertainment.

What is the best book you ever read? Is it one that taught you something or changed you in some way or just entertained you? It will be easier to write about this book if you first complete a brainstorming list.

BRAINSTORMING LIST

1. Write the name of your favorite book here. Put down the author's name, too, if you know it.

_____

2. Tell what the book is about in one or two sentences.

_____

_____

3. Write a list of words and phrases that describe *places* in the book.

_____

4. Write a list of names, words, and phrases that describe *people* (real or fictional) in the book.

_____

5. Write a list of words and phrases that describe *events* in the book.

_____

6. Write a list of words and phrases that describe your *feelings and thoughts* while reading this book.

_____

Name _____ **Date** _____

A WORLD OF BOOKS
FIRST DRAFT

> "A good book is the best of friends, the same today and forever."
> —Martin Tupper

DIRECTIONS: Write a first draft for a 4-paragraph essay about your favorite book. Use your brainstorming list and the suggestions below. (Since this is just a first draft, don't be concerned about spelling or grammar. Just concentrate on getting your thoughts down on paper.)

1. The first paragraph should state the topic in an interesting way, as in this example: "Did you ever get so lost in a book that hours passed when you forget who and where you really were? That's what happened to me when I read *Kidnapped*, by Robert Louis Stevenson." Write your first paragraph (2–4 sentences) below.

_____

_____

_____

2. In the second paragraph, tell what the book is about and briefly describe the people, places, and events in it (3–7 sentences).

_____

_____

_____

_____

3. In the third paragraph, describe your thoughts and feelings while reading this book, and the effect the book had upon you (2–5 sentences).

_____

_____

_____

4. The last paragraph should restate and sum up the topic, as in this example: "Reading *Kidnapped* was like taking part in a great adventure. Any time I want to experience this thrill again, I just have to open the pages of this book." Write your last paragraph (2–4 sentences) below.

_____

_____

_____

Name _____ Date_____

A World of Books
Revising and Writing a Final Copy

> "Books . . . are a substantial world, both pure and good.
> Round these with tendrils strong as flesh and blood,
> Our pastimes and our happiness will grow."   —William Wordsworth

DIRECTIONS:

1. Edit and revise the first draft of your essay about a favorite book. Here are some suggestions:

a. Does the first paragraph introduce the topic? Could you make it more interesting by beginning with a question or a startling statement?

b. Does the second paragraph tell what the book is about? Did you omit any important details? Can you use stronger, more active verbs and more vivid language to describe the people, places, or events?

c. Does the third paragraph describe your thoughts and feelings? Can you find better ways to describe the strength of these feelings?

d. Does the last paragraph restate and sum up the topic?

e. Are your sentences complete? Do subjects and verbs agree?

f. Are you sure all words are spelled correctly?

2. Write the final copy of your essay below. Indent at the beginning of each paragraph. (Use the back of this worksheet if you need more room.)

_____

_____

_____

_____

_____

_____

_____

_____

_____

Name _____ **Date** _____

HOLIDAY HUNT
SENTENCES

The Christian celebration of Easter and the Jewish festival of Passover usually occur in April. Both holidays include treasure hunts. Brightly colored eggs are hunted at Easter. At Passover, the children search for a hidden piece of matzo called the *afikomen*.

It's fun to go on treasure hunts, whether for Easter eggs, for matzos, or even for words, as in this activity.

DIRECTIONS: There is one misspelled word in each of the sentences below. Circle the word that is spelled wrong. Then write the complete sentence correctly on the line below. (The first one is done for you.)

1. Many pet shops sell (rabits) at Easter.

   Many pet shops sell rabbits at Easter.

2. Easter and Passover are springtime hollidays.

   _____

3. Peeple wear their new spring clothes on Easter and Passover.

   _____

4. Evry year, there is an Easter Parade in New York City.

   _____

5. The Easter celebration is allways on a Sunday.

   _____

6. Passover comes on a diferent day of the week each year.

   _____

7. Somtimes, people send out greeting cards on Easter and Passover.

   _____

(See Activity 8B for answers.)

© 1997 by The Center for Applied Research in Education

Name _____ Date_____

Holiday Hunt
Paragraph

Did you find the misspelled word in each sentence in Activity 8A. Here they are, spelled correctly:

1. rabbits	5. always
2. holidays	6. different
3. People	7. Sometimes
4. Every	

Did you get them all right? If so, you are an excellent speller and a great proof-reader! Now you are ready for a more difficult challenge. This time, you must find all the misspelled words in a paragraph.

DIRECTIONS: Circle the words that are spelled wrong in the following paragraph. Then, copy the entire paragraph correctly on the lines below. (**Hint:** There are thirteen (13) misspelled words in this paragraph.)

Many people say that spring is their favrite season. Hear are some of the reasons they give. Frist of all, they are happy to sea the end of winter and to say good-bye to ice and snow. In the springtime, it seams as thogh the earth is being reborn. Trees begin to budd, pretty flowers spring up from the grond, and the days grow wormer. Their are great holidays like Passover and Easter. Best of all, for some folks, spring marks the begining of the basball season.

Did you find all 13 incorrectly spelled words? If you did, you are a *great* proof-reader! Now, write the paragraph correctly below:

_____

_____

_____

_____

_____

_____

_____

Name _____ **Date** _____

Baseball Mania
Prewriting

April is an important month for sports fans. It marks the beginning of the base-ball season.

Baseball is often called America's national game. Everyone plays it—little kids, teenagers, men, women, professionals, and amateurs. All over America baseball diamonds become as busy as beehives in April. It is an exciting time for both players and fans.

An important event in the history of this sport occurred on April 11, 1947. Jackie Robinson joined the Brooklyn Dodgers. He was the first African-American in major league baseball. There had been many fine African-American baseball players before then, but they had not been allowed on major league teams. Jackie Robinson led the way, both as a great player and as a man who fought prejudice and won.

There are many times in athletic competition when players have to face difficult challenges. These are not usually so great as the prejudice and unfairness that Jackie Robinson had to overcome, but they can be hard for the person involved.

Can you think of a situation where someone has to overcome a hurdle during a baseball game? Perhaps there is a kid whom no one wants on the team because he seems clumsy and weak. Or maybe a star player injures her batting arm just before coming up to bat at a crucial time. Maybe there is an umpire who is prejudiced in favor of one team and makes unfair calls all through the game.

You are going to take one of these situations, or any other, and make up a story about it. First, complete the brainstorming list below.

BRAINSTORMING LIST

1. Describe the situation you are going to write about in one or two sentences.

   _____

   _____

   _____

2. Name at least three characters who will be in your story. Next to each name, write a list of words and phrases describing that character. (Put the main character first.)

   _____ : _____

   _____ : _____

   _____ : _____

3. Write two or three beginning sentences. Catch the reader's interest right away by using dialogue (conversation) or exciting action.

   _____

   _____

Name _____ **Date** _____

BASEBALL MANIA
FIRST DRAFT

Are you ready to write a first draft of your story about a difficult situation during a baseball game? Here are some guidelines.

1. Look over the brainstorming list you prepared for Activity 9A. It will help you get started.
2. Begin the story with some exciting action or interesting dialogue, as in this example:

"Time to choose up sides," ordered Mr. Furillo in his commanding gym-teacher voice. "Red team first."

Big Mike Ince, the sandy-haired captain of the red team, grinned. He could pick the best player now. "Rob Levine," he said.

Rob strode up confidently. His arm was killing him, but he managed to hide his pain. He knew everyone would expect him to spark his team. He wouldn't let them down.

---

3. Show the characters clearly—how they look, how they sound, how they act. Keep in mind each character's importance to the story.
4. Show the feelings and emotions of the main character; this will help the reader understand how he or she feels.

Write your baseball story below. Remember, this is just a draft, so don't be concerned about spelling or grammar.

Decide upon a title and write it on the first line.

Use the back of this worksheet if you need more room.

_____

_____

_____

_____

_____

_____

_____

_____

Name _____ **Date** _____

BASEBALL MANIA
REVISING AND WRITING A FINAL COPY

DIRECTIONS:

1. Edit and revise the first draft of your baseball story, as follows:

> a. Can you make the beginning more interesting or exciting so the reader will want to continue?
>
> b. Do you describe each character? Can you make them more real to the reader by showing how they talk and act?
>
> c. Is the main character vivid and interesting? Can you include more phrases or sentences that show what this character is thinking and feeling?
>
> d. Do you include some dialogue? Does this dialogue show something about the characters?
>
> e. Can you use more active verbs like *slam, smash, leap, slide, shout*?
>
> f. Check spelling with a dictionary.

2. Write the final copy of your story below. Write the title on the first line. Indent at the beginning of paragraphs and wherever someone begins to speak. (Use the back of this worksheet if you need more room.) If you wish, you may illustrate your story on the back.

_____

_____

_____

_____

_____

_____

_____

_____

_____

Name _____ Date_____

THE WORLD'S A STAGE
PREWRITING

William Shakespeare was born on April 23, 1564 in Stratford-upon-Avon, England. He is considered by many to be the greatest writer of all time. Many of the lines he wrote for his plays are familiar to everyone. Here are some:

> "All the world's a stage,
> And all the men and women merely players;
> They have their exits and entrances;
> And one man in his time plays many parts."
>
> "O Romeo, Romeo! wherefore art thou Romeo?"
>
> "What's in a name? that which we call a rose
> By any other name would smell as sweet."
>
> "Lord, what fools these mortals be!"
>
> "The quality of mercy is not strained,
> It droppeth as the gentle rain from heaven
> Upon the place beneath; it is twice blessed;
> It blesseth him that gives and him that takes."
>
> "Friends, Romans, countrymen, lend me your ears;
> I come to bury Caesar, not to praise him.
> The evil that men do lives after them,
> The good is oft interred with their bones."
>
> "Neither a borrower nor a lender be;
> For loan oft loses both itself and friend."
>
> "This above all; to thine own self be true,
> And it must follow, as the night the day,
> Thou canst not then be false to any man."

These are only a few of the many familiar lines from Shakespeare's plays. Can you figure out what they mean?

In this activity, you are going to choose one of these quotations and write a paragraph explaining what it means.

DIRECTIONS:

1. Read the quotations again. Then, *circle* the one you have chosen to write about.

2. On the lines below, write a topic (beginning) sentence for your paragraph, as in this example: *"Does the speaker of the line, 'Friends, Romans, countrymen, lend me your ears,' really expect people to cut off their ears and hand them over?"* Write your beginning sentence below:

_____

_____

_____

Name _____ **Date** _____

THE WORLD'S A STAGE
FIRST DRAFT

DIRECTIONS:

1. Copy below the lines from Shakespeare you have chosen to write about:

_____

_____

_____

_____

2. Write a paragraph explaining what you think these lines mean. Use the topic sentence you prepared for Activity 10A. Your paragraph should have *at least* five sentences. (A topic sentence, at least three sentences that develop your idea, and a concluding sentence that sums up the topic.)

   This is just a draft, so don't be concerned about spelling or grammar. Concentrate on getting your ideas down.

_____

_____

_____

_____

_____

_____

_____

_____

_____

Name _____ Date_____

THE WORLD'S A STAGE
REVISING AND WRITING A FINAL COPY

DIRECTIONS:

1. Edit and revise the first draft of your paragraph about a quotation from Shakespeare, as follows:

a. Does the beginning sentence state the topic clearly?

b. Do the sentences that follow develop the theme of the paragraph?

c. Can you include some words or phrases from the quotation in your paragraph?

d. Does the last sentence sum up the topic?

e. Are your sentences complete? Do subjects and verbs agree?

f. Check spelling with a dictionary.

2. Write the final copy of your paragraph below. Indent at the beginning.

_____

_____

_____

_____

_____

_____

_____

_____

_____

_____

_____

_____

_____

Name _____ **Date** _____

Spring Things 1

> *DIRECTIONS:* Next to each number are three words that have something to do with the spring season. Write a sentence containing all three words. (The first one is done for you.)

1. robin, rain, nest
   The baby robin was sheltered from the rain in its nest. _____
   _____

2. April, Easter, Passover
   _____
   _____

3. showers, sprinkle, grass
   _____
   _____

4. baseball, team, fun
   _____
   _____

5. tulips, daffodils, lilies
   _____
   _____

6. first, fool, tricks
   _____
   _____

7. coats, sweaters, warm
   _____
   _____

8. buds, trees, green
   _____
   _____

9. yellow, pink, white
   _____
   _____

Name _____ **Date** _____

Spring Things 2

DIRECTIONS:

1. Here is a list of words that have something to do with the month of April or the season of spring.

April Fool	Earth Day	Easter
Passover	matzos	eggs
rabbit	flowers	lilies
daffodils	tulips	buds
leaves	trees	rain
showers	grow	grass
birds	robins	nest
walk	outdoors	play
baseball	bike	sports

2. Can you write a paragraph about April, or spring, or both, that contains *all* of the words in the above list? Is that too hard? Can you write a paragraph containing *most* of the words in the list? Okay—just write a paragraph containing *as many* of these words as you can!

   Write your paragraph below. When you finish, compare it with your classmates' paragraphs and see how you rate. (If you wish, you can draw illustrations in the side and bottom margins.)

_____

_____

_____

_____

_____

_____

Name _____ Date _____

A SPRING PLACE
PREWRITING

DIRECTIONS:

1. Read the following description of a special place in April:

> You will never find this special place unless I choose to guide you there. It is well hidden, like a great, mythical treasure. First, the seeker must climb over steep hills covered with thick carpets of bright golden daffodils. Beyond waits a small patch of deep, dark woods where the air feels cool and moist. Your feet sink into the soft, wet ground. Ahead, you glimpse shafts of sunshine reaching down like fingers of light. Past a stand of bent, gnarled trees, you step out into a bright, open clearing. It is a circle of magic, protected by woods all around, as peaceful and silent as a churchyard.

2. The reader is able to picture this scene because of the vivid language used to describe it. The writer has used:

   a. ACTIVE VERBS—Instead of passive verbs such as *go* or *is*, the writer has used the active verbs *guide* and *waits*. On the lines below, list all the active verbs you can find in the paragraph above.

   _____

   _____

   b. SENSORY WORDS—Words that appeal to the five senses (touch, sight, hearing, taste, and smell) make a description more vivid. Many adjectives do this, such as *dark* (sense of sight) and *moist* (sense of touch). On the line below, list all the sensory words you can find in the paragraph above.

   _____

   _____

   c. SIMILES AND METAPHORS—Similes are comparisons that use *like* or *as*. Metaphors are more direct comparisons that do not use these words. Examples: "He is as sly as a fox." (*simile*); "He is a real fox." (*metaphor*)
   On the lines below, list the similes and metaphors in the paragraph above.

   _____

   _____

3. Choose a place to describe. It can be as ordinary as a room in your house or your backyard, or it can be an unusual place that you have seen.

   a. In the space below, write a list of *sensory* words and phrases that could be used to describe this place.

   b. In the space below, write at least three *similes* and *metaphors* that could be used to describe this place.

   c. In the space below, write a list of *active verbs* that could be used in a description of this place.

Name _____ **Date** _____

A SPRING PLACE
FIRST DRAFT

DIRECTIONS: Write a first draft of a description of "A Spring Place." Use the lists you prepared in Activity 12A to make your description come alive by using:

SENSORY WORDS
SIMILES AND METAPHORS
ACTIVE VERBS

This is just a draft, so don't be concerned about spelling or grammar. Concentrate on getting your thoughts down on paper.

A SPRING PLACE

_____

_____

_____

_____

_____

_____

_____

_____

_____

_____

_____

_____

_____

_____

Name _____ **Date** _____

A Spring Place
Revising and Writing a Final Copy

DIRECTIONS:

1. Edit and revise the first draft of your description of "A Spring Place" as follows:

---

a. Does the first sentence introduce the topic in an interesting way?

b. Have you used active verbs? Can you use more active verbs to make the writing livelier?

c. Have you used sensory words? Can you find places to insert additional sensory words?

d. Do you use one or two exciting similes or metaphors? Can you add more?

e. Are your sentences complete? Do subjects and verbs agree?

f. Check spelling with a dictionary.

---

2. Write the final copy of your description below. Write the title on the first line (You can use "A Spring Place" or any other appropriate title.)

   If you wish, you can illustrate your description on the back of this worksheet.

_____

_____

_____

_____

_____

_____

_____

_____

_____

_____

MAY

MAY

"All in the merry month of May.
When green buds they were swelling." —Barbara Allen (Ballad)

MONTH OF MAIA (GODDESS OF SPRING) . . . BRILLIANTLY COLORED AZA-
LEAS, MAGNOLIAS, AND DOGWOOD . . . MAY DAY AND MAYPOLE DANC-
ING . . . CINCO DE MAYO . . . MOTHER'S DAY . . . MEMORIAL DAY . . . ARBOR
DAY AND TREE PLANTING

MAY EVENTS

May 5, 1862: Mexican soldiers drove out French troops (Cinco de Mayo)

May 5, 1961: Alan B. Shepard, Jr. rocketed 115 miles into space from Cape Canaveral,
becoming America's first space explorer

May 7, 1945: Germany surrendered, ending World War II in Europe

May 9, 1926: U.S. Navy Commander Richard E. Byrd became first person to fly over
the North Pole

May 10, 1869: First transcontinental railway in U.S. was completed

May 11, 1928: First regularly-scheduled television programs began at station WGY,
Schenectady, New York

May 14, 1948: The birth of the state of Israel was proclaimed

May 20, 1927: Charles A. Lindberg began the first solo nonstop flight across the
Atlantic

May 21, 1881: The American Red Cross was founded by Clara Barton

May 24, 1883: The Brooklyn Bridge, a miracle of design by John Roebling, was opened
to traffic

May 25, 1940: A "Crypt of Civilization" containing thousands of objects of daily life in
the twentieth century was sealed at Oglethorpe University in Georgia, to be opened
in the year 8113

May 27, 1937: The Golden Gate Bridge opened in San Francisco

May 28, 1934: The first quintuplets to survive infancy were born in Canada to Mrs.
Oliva Dionne

MAY BIRTHDAYS

May 6, 1856: Sigmund Freud, "father of psychoanalysis"

May 7, 1840: Peter Ilyich Tchaikovsky, Russian composer

May 12, 1820: Florence Nightingale, English nurse

May 25, 1803: Ralph Waldo Emerson, American poet, essayist, and philosopher

May 29, 1917: John Fitzgerald Kennedy, 35th president of U.S.

May 31, 1819: Walt Whitman, American poet

WRITING ACTIVITIES FOR MAY

Name _____ **Date** _____

FINISH THE THOUGHT—MAY

DIRECTIONS: All the sentence beginnings below have something to do with the month of May. Finish each sentence.

(Don't forget to put a period, question mark, or exclamation point at the end of each sentence.)

---

1. On May 1, _____

   _____

2. The best thing about May is _____

   _____

3. On an afternoon in May, I like to _____

   _____

4. On weekends in May, I sometimes _____

   _____

5. May weather is _____

   _____

6. May is _____

   _____

7. The flowers that bloom in May _____

   _____

8. I like May because _____

   _____

9. A holiday in May is _____

   _____

10. This year in May, I want to _____

    _____

11. At the beginning of May, _____

    _____

12. At the end of May, _____

    _____

13. My favorite May activity is _____

    _____

Name _____ **Date** _____

FINISH THE THOUGHT—MOTHER'S DAY

DIRECTIONS: All the sentence beginnings below have something to do with mothers or Mother's Day. Complete each sentence.

(Don't forget to put a period, question mark, or exclamation point at the end of each sentence.)

1. My mom is _____
_____

2. My mom likes to _____
_____

3. A mom should _____
_____

4. Some moms can _____
_____

5. On Mother's Day, my family _____
_____

6. Last Mother's day, my mom _____
_____

7. Moms don't like it when _____
_____

8. My mom is happy when _____
_____

9. I wish my mom _____
_____

10. On Mother's Day, I will _____
_____

11. I wish I could give my mom _____
_____

12. A Mother's Day card _____
_____

13. My mother never _____
_____

Name _____ **Date** _____

A SURPRISE FOR MOM
PREWRITING

Everybody likes surprises—even moms. Here is a story about one mom's unexpected Mother's Day.

> Matt and Caitlin were so excited, they couldn't even finish their dinner. It was hard to keep the secret. Every time they looked at Mom, they wanted to blurt it out. But they managed to stay quiet.
>
> After dinner, they said they were going to their rooms to do homework. Instead, they sneaked down to the basement. That's where their costumes were hidden. They put on their costumes, and rehearsed one last time. When they were ready, they called to their mother and asked her to come downstairs.
>
> As soon as she saw them, Mom began to laugh. Both Matt and Caitlin were dressed like babies. They wore bibs and bonnets, and were sucking lollipops. They told Mom to sit on a comfortable chair. Then they acted out the play they had written for her. They pretended to cry. They pretended to be hungry. They pretended to scream for toys. They pretended to have tantrums. Each time, they showed how their wonderful Mom had known just what to do to make them feel better. At the end, they both shouted, "Happy Mother's Day!"
>
> Mom said it was the biggest surprise and the best Mother's Day she had ever had.

DIRECTIONS: In this activity, you are going to make up a story about a Mother's Day surprise. It will be easy if you first prepare a brainstorming list below.

BRAINSTORMING LIST

1. Decide what the surprise in your story will be, and describe it briefly: _____

_____

2. List the names of each character in your story. Next to each name, tell who that character is and give a brief description. (You don't need sentences here—just words and phrases. (Use the back of this worksheet if you need room for additional characters.)

_____

_____

_____

3. Write a brief summary of your plot in the box below. Use three or four sentences to describe what happens.

© 1997 by The Center for Applied Research in Education

Name _____ **Date**_____

A SURPRISE FOR MOM
FIRST DRAFT

DIRECTIONS: Write a first draft of a story about a Mother's Day surprise. Use the brainstorming list you prepared in Activity 2A.

Try to begin your story in an interesting manner so the reader will want to continue. One way of doing this is to present a mystery or puzzle, as in the example in Activity 2A. Other good beginnings use dialogue or exciting action.

This is just a draft, so don't be concerned about spelling or grammar. Just concentrate on getting your story down on paper.

Write the title on the first line. Indent at the beginning of paragraphs and whenever a character begins to speak. (Use the back of this worksheet if you need more room.)

Name _____ **Date** _____

A Surprise For Mom
Revising and Writing a Final Copy

DIRECTIONS:

1. Revise and edit the first draft of your story, as follows:

> a. Is the beginning interesting enough? Can you make it more exciting with dialogue or action?
>
> b. Do you always show which character is speaking or doing something? If not, make this clear to the reader.
>
> c. Can you add active verbs or sensory language to make the writing more vivid?
>
> d. Are your sentences complete? Do subjects and verbs agree?
>
> e. Check your spelling with a dictionary.

2. Write the final copy of your story below. Put the title on the first line. Indent at the beginning of paragraphs and whenever someone begins to speak. (Use the back of the worksheet if you need more room.)

_____

_____

_____

_____

_____

_____

_____

_____

_____

_____

Name _____ **Date** _____

Whose Day?
Prewriting

We all remember our moms on Mother's Day. Did you know that Mother's Day did not become official until 1914? In that year, President Woodrow Wilson designated the second Sunday in May as a day to honor the nation's mothers.

Mother's Day actually got started back in 1907, thanks to Anna Jarvis. She campaigned to set aside a day to recognize mothers. Anna Jarvis believed that mothers deserved this honor, and fought to make her dream become real. Now, Mother's Day is an accepted custom.

One person can make a difference. Anna Jarvis worked hard to convince people of the rightness of her cause. All mothers have benefited from her vision.

There are many people whose importance is not always recognized. Can you think of someone or some group of people who should have a day set aside in their honor? Can you write an essay to convince readers that this is a good idea? Before you write your essay, prepare a brainstorming list below.

BRAINSTORMING LIST

1. Write the name of a person (a neighbor, someone in your community, etc.) or a group of people (firefighters, teachers, aunts, mailcarriers, dentists, etc.) who you would like to honor with a day of their own:

   _____

2. Choose a date for this celebration. It can be a number date, such as "October 15," or a time-of-month date, such as "the third Sunday in July." Write the date here: _____

3. In the box below, make a list of words and phrases that can be used to describe what this person or group does to be worthy of this honor. Write as many positive and interesting words and phrases as you can:

4. Write a beginning sentence (or sentences) for your essay. It should introduce the topic in an interesting way that will make the reader want to continue. Here are some examples:

   "My neighborhood would be a poorer and sadder place if Mr. Ron Alderman did not live in it."

   "Don't you feel safer knowing that firefighters are working all the time to keep you safe?"

   Write your beginning below:

   _____

   _____

Name _____ **Date** _____

WHOSE DAY?
FIRST DRAFT

DIRECTIONS: Are you ready to propose a special day to honor a worthy person or group? You are going to write the first draft of a simple, 3-paragraph essay about this. Your essay will be a snap to write if you keep your brainstorming list in front of you, and follow these directions. (This is just a first draft, so don't be concerned about spelling or grammar—just get your thoughts down.)

---

1. The first paragraph should introduce the topic in an interesting way. Use the sentences you prepared at the bottom of the brainstorming list to begin. Add some details such as a proposed date and the general purpose of this honor. Write your first paragraph (2–4 sentences) here:

   _____

   _____

   _____

2. The second paragraph should list at least three reasons to support your proposal. Use the words and phrases in the box of your brainstorming list. Use one or two sentences for each reason. Write your second paragraph (3–6 sentences) here:

   _____

   _____

   _____

3. The last paragraph should restate and sum up the topic. It should also try to convince the reader that this is a worthwhile idea, as in this example:

   "It is clear that Ron Alderman is one in a million. Many people are indebted to him in so many ways. Mr. Alderman himself has no interest in being rewarded for his good works, but don't you agree that he deserves a special day in his honor?"

   Write your last paragraph (3–5 sentences) here:

   _____

   _____

   _____

Name _____ **Date** _____

WHOSE DAY?
REVISING AND WRITING A FINAL COPY

DIRECTIONS:

1. Edit and revise your essay, as follows:

> a. Is your beginning catchy and interesting? Would it be more exciting if you began with a question or a startling statement?
>
> b. Is your second paragraph convincing? Do you list at least three reasons for your proposal? Is there anything you can add to make your suggestion stronger?
>
> c. Does your last paragraph restate and sum up the topic? Can you think of a more dynamic ending that would influence the reader?
>
> d. Is your language persuasive? Can you put in some strong, active verbs to be more convincing?
>
> e. Are your sentences complete? Do subjects and verbs agree?
>
> f. Check spelling with a dictionary.

2. Write the final copy of your essay below. Indent at the beginning of paragraphs. (Use the back of this worksheet if you need more room.)

_____

_____

_____

_____

_____

_____

_____

_____

_____

_____

Name _____ Date _____

OLÉ, CINCO DE MAYO!
PREWRITING

> Cinco de Mayo means the Fifth of May. It is an important holiday for Mexicans and people of Mexican descent, like our Independence Day.
>
> In 1861, French troops invaded Mexico. The Mexicans fought bravely for their freedom. On May 5, 1862, an army of Mexican Indians under General Ignacio Zaragoza repelled the French invaders at the "Batalla de Puebla," a battle near the town of Puebla.
>
> The French later defeated the Mexicans and ruled over Mexico until 1867. Inspired by their great victory on "Cinco de Mayo," the Mexican people, led by Benito Juarez, once again won their freedom.
>
> Cinco de Mayo is celebrated with parades, dancing, and music.

Most of us take our freedom for granted, but sometimes it is necessary to fight for that independence. In this activity, you are going to imagine that your town is being invaded. Can you write a story describing how the people in your community manage to drive off the invaders? The brainstorming list below will help you plan this story.

BRAINSTORMING LIST

First, decide upon answers to these questions:

> a. Describe the invaders. Are they aliens from another galaxy, or soldiers from another nation on Earth, or an army of robots (or anything else you can imagine)? Name the invaders and make a list of words and phrases that describe them.

NAME OF INVADERS: _____

DESCRIPTIVE WORDS AND PHRASES: _____

_____

> b. Describe the community that is being invaded.

NAME OF COMMUNITY: _____

WORDS AND PHRASES YOU CAN USE TO DESCRIBE COMMUNITY AND THE PEOPLE WHO LIVE IN IT: _____

_____

> c. Every story needs heroes and heroines. Make up names for two main characters ("good guys"). Next to each name, make a list of words and phrases that describe that person.

NAME OF FIRST MAIN CHARACTER: _____

DESCRIPTIVE WORDS AND PHRASES: _____

NAME OF SECOND MAIN CHARACTER: _____

DESCRIPTIVE WORDS AND PHRASES: _____

Name _____ **Date**_____

OLÉ, CINCO DE MAYO
FIRST DRAFT

DIRECTIONS:

1. Write a first draft of a story about a town or country threatened with invasion, as Mexico was on May 5, 1862. Keep your brainstorming list handy as you create your story.

2. BEGINNINGS: Sometimes, the hardest part of a story is knowing how to get started. Here are some possible beginnings for this story:

"The stillness of the cold December morning was shattered by the sound of a violent explosion. People ran to look out the windows. Breakfasts were left half-eaten as families rushed out of their homes. They stared in confusion and horror at the clouds of fire and black smoke that were spreading nearby. This is it, Chris thought, they've come at last."

*   *   *   *   *   *   *

"The townspeople gathered in the courthouse and turned to their grim-faced mayor.

'The invaders are only a hundred miles away.' Mayor Dickenson's voice was hollow. 'They're moving quickly. No one can stop them. We must be prepared to surrender.'

'Never!' roared a voice from the back of the room. 'We will never surrender!' Mike Friedman jumped up. 'I have a plan!'"

You can use one of these beginnings or think up your own. This is only a first draft, so don't be concerned about spelling or grammar. Concentrate on getting down your story. (Make up a title and write it on the first line. Use the back of this worksheet if you need more room.)

_____

© 1997 by The Center for Applied Research in Education

Name _____ Date _____

OLÉ, CINCO DE MAYO
REVISING AND WRITING A FINAL COPY

DIRECTIONS:

1. Edit and revise the first draft of your story about invaders, as follows:

---

a. Does your beginning introduce the plot and at least one main character in a suspenseful way? Can you make it more exciting by using dialogue or thrilling action?

b. Is it clear right away who the main characters are? Do you show what they are like by what they *do* and *say*? Can you add any action or dialogue that brings them more to life?

c. When writing dialogue, each time someone speaks, do you enclose it in "quotation marks"?

d. Change passive verbs, such as *go* or *see*, to active ones like *leap* or *glare*.

e. Do you show the setting (where the action is taking place) so that the reader can picture it?

f. Are your sentences complete? Do subjects and verbs agree?

g. Check spelling with a dictionary.

---

2. Write the final copy of your story below. Put the title on the first line. Indent at the beginning of paragraphs and every time someone begins to speak. (Use the back of this worksheet if you need more room.)

_____

_____

_____

_____

_____

_____

_____

_____

Name _____ Date_____

MERRY MONTH OF MAY
PREWRITING

"There are twelve months in all the year,
   As I hear many men say,
But the merriest month in all the year
   Is the merry month of May."

These lines are from an old English ballad. Poets have always enjoyed writing about the month of May. It is such a beautiful, happy time. The weather is pleasant, trees and flowers are in bloom, and people can be outdoors having fun.

Here is another poem about May. This one is by Ben Johnson.

"A lily of a day,
Is fairer far in May."

See how easy it is? You, too, can write a poem about May. But, first, complete the brainstorming list below.

BRAINSTORMING LIST

1. In the box below, write down as many words and phrases as you can think of that have anything to do with the month of May. (You may include names of people, events, and holidays.) The list is started for you. Add *at least* 10 words and phrases.

buds, green, picnics,

2. In the box below, write as many words as you can think of that *rhyme* with May. The list is started for you. Add *at least* 10 rhyming words.

yesterday, display, clay,

3. Here is a list of words that could be used in a poem about May. Next to each word, write another that rhymes with it. (The first one is done for you.)

leaf	belief _____	green	_____
tree	_____	warm	_____
bird	_____	bud	_____
song	_____	play	_____
flower	_____	breeze	_____

Name _____ **Date** _____

MERRY MONTH OF MAY
FIRST DRAFT

> "And it fell upon a day.
> In the merry month of May,
> Sitting in a pleasant shade
> Which a grove of myrtles made."
> —Richard Barnfield

A poem does not have to rhyme, but it is fun to try to work with rhyming lines. The month of May is a good subject for this kind of poem because there are so many words about May that can be easily rhymed.

DIRECTIONS:

1. Look at the rhyming words at the bottom of your brainstorming list. Can you use some of these in a 4-line poem like the one above where the first two lines rhyme with each other and the last two lines rhyme? (*Day* rhymes with May; *shade* rhymes with *made*.) Here is another example:

> "A mild and gentle breeze
> Moves softly through the trees,
> Upon this golden day
> In the bright month of May.

What are the two rhyming words in lines 1 and 2? Write them here: _____

_____

What are the two rhyming words in lines 3 and 4? Write them here: _____

_____

> Did you write *breeze* and *trees*? *day* and *May*?

2. Write a first draft of your own 4-line poem here:

_____

_____

_____

_____

3. Write another poem about May in the box below. You can rhyme or not rhyme, and you can have as many lines as you wish. (This is also a first draft.)

© 1997 by The Center for Applied Research in Education

Name _____ **Date** _____

MERRY MONTH OF MAY
REVISING AND WRITING A FINAL COPY

> "All in the merry month of May,
> When green buds they were swelling."
> —"Barbara Allen" (*old ballad*)

DIRECTIONS:

1. Edit and revise your two poems, as follows:

a. Since poems are short, every word is important. Is every word in your poem as effective as it can be? Would the poem be better if you changed some words?
b. Can you use sensory words (taste, touch, smell, sound, sight) to make your poem stronger?
c. Do the lines in your poem have a regular beat? Try saying them aloud to get a better idea of the smoothness of the rhythm. Make any changes that are necessary.

2. When your poems are as perfect as you can make them, write each poem in one of the boxes below. If you wish, you can also illustrate each poem in the margins.

Name _____ **Date** _____

INTO THE FUTURE
PREWRITING

> Think about the year 8113! That is far, far in the future. No one knows what Earth will be like then. But whoever is living in that distant time may know a lot about twentieth-century Earth.
>
> On May 25, 1940, a box was buried and sealed at Oglethorpe University in Georgia. It is called the "Crypt of Civilization" and contains thousands of objects of daily life in the twentieth century, as well as directions for opening in 8113.
>
> Who, or what, will be here then? What will they think of the artifacts they have uncovered? What will our century seem like to these Earth dwellers of the future?
>
> Suppose you could deposit a letter in such a "Crypt of Civilization"? What would you like to tell the people of that far-off time about you and about the world of your time?
>
> In this activity, you are going to write a letter to be opened in 8113. It will be easy if you first complete this brainstorming list.

BRAINSTORMING LIST

1. In the box below, make a list of words and phrases that describe you personally—your physical appearance, your personality, your character, hobbies, etc.

2. In the box below, make a list of words and phrases that describe your family.

3. In the box below, make a list of words and phrases that describe your school, your friends, and your town.

4. In the box below, make a list of words and phrases to describe important things about your country and the world.

5. In the box below, make a list of words and phrases to describe the world you hope will exist in 8113.

© 1997 by The Center for Applied Research in Education

Name _____ **Date** _____

INTO THE FUTURE
FIRST DRAFT

DIRECTIONS: Write a first draft of a letter to be opened in 8113. Use your brainstorming list, and follow these directions:

1. In the first paragraph, tell about yourself and your family.
2. Describe your school and friends in the second paragraph.
3. In the last paragraph, tell about your country and the world today. Finish with your hopes for the world of 8113.

Follow correct letter form as shown below. This is just a first draft, so don't be concerned about spelling or grammar. Concentrate on organizing the thoughts on your brainstorming list into a letter.

_____
(Write your street address above)

_____
(Your city, state, ZIP here)

_____
(Write today's date above)

My Unknown Friend
Year 8113
The Earth

_____
(Write a greeting here, such as <u>Dear Unknown Friend</u>,)

_____
_____
_____
_____
_____
_____
_____

_____
(Write a closing, such as "Your friend," here)

_____
(Sign your name here)

Name _____ Date _____

INTO THE FUTURE
REVISING AND WRITING A FINAL COPY

DIRECTIONS: Edit and revise your letter to the year 8113, as follows:

1. Have you left out anything important about yourself or your world?
2. Is your language clear and understandable? Will your descriptions be clear to someone who has never seen your world?
3. Are your sentences complete? Do subjects and verbs agree?
4. Did you indent at the beginning of each paragraph?
5. Check spelling with a dictionary.

Write the final copy of your letter below. Use correct letter form as shown in Activity 6B.

Name _____ **Date** _____

PARADES AND BARBECUES 1

Many people think of Memorial Day as a time for parades and barbecues. It means much more than that!

The five sentences below tell about Memorial Day. Can you rearrange them in the proper order for a clearly-written paragraph?

Write the paragraph on the lines at the bottom of the page.

1. Now it is called Memorial Day, and honors all war dead.
2. Memorial Day is celebrated at the end of May.
3. People fly flags on this day, and there are parades in many cities and towns.
4. It was established in 1868 in memory of the soldiers who were killed in the Civil War.
5. For many years, this holiday was known as Decoration Day.

Write the paragraph on the lines below. If you wish, you can illustrate it in the space at the bottom of the page.

_____

_____

_____

_____

_____

_____

_____

_____

Name _____ **Date** _____

PARADES AND BARBECUES 2

DIRECTIONS: Here are more sentences about Memorial Day for you to arrange into a paragraph. Can you put the sentences in the proper order? Write the paragraph below.

---

1. These parades often have stirring bands and colorful floats.
2. It is traditional for many people to have a barbecue for family and friends.
3. The Memorial Day weekend is often considered the beginning of the summer season, even though summer does not start officially until late in June.
4. People celebrate the holiday in different ways.
5. These things are fun, but we should never forget the true meaning of this day.
6. They fly flags and march in parades.

Write the paragraph below. If you wish, you may illustrate it in the space at the bottom of the page.

_____

_____

_____

_____

_____

_____

_____

_____

_____

Name _____ Date_____

LIGHT A LAMP
PREWRITING

When we think of *nurses*, one name that immediately comes to mind is Florence Nightingale, who led a movement to improve hospital conditions in nineteenth-century England.

Florence Nightingale was born in Florence, Italy on May 12, 1820, to a wealthy English family. While growing up in England, she felt isolated and different from her sisters and mother. She did not share their interest in clothes and jewels. She did not care about fitting into upper-class society. She preferred tending sick pets, and dreamed of some day serving a useful purpose in the world. At an early age, she decided to study nursing, over the objections of her family. She was shocked at the unsanitary conditions in hospitals and at the limited training that most nurses received.

In the early 1850s she served at military hospitals in the Crimean War. More soldiers were dying from fever and infection than from wounds. She cleaned up these hospitals. With her own money, she bought clothing, healthful food, and sanitary bed linens, and was able to reduce the death rate from 45% to 2%. Patients began to look eagerly for the "lady with the lamp" who would ease their suffering.

She became world-famous, and used her fame to campaign for hospital reforms and to set high standards for the training of nurses.

Florence Nightingale found that one person could make a difference. In her time, there was an urgent need for improvement in hospitals and nursing care. She worked hard to bring about change.

You, too, might be able to "light a lamp." What would you improve if you could? Would you like to feed starving families? Perhaps you could do something to improve race relations in our country. Would you like to save species of animals or plants that are becoming extinct? Your dream might be simple, such as taking care of abandoned pets in your community, or providing every student in your school with a computer. A brainstorming list will help you organize your thoughts.

BRAINSTORMING LIST

1. *What* would you like to change? You can choose one of the suggestions above, or list your own idea. (You don't need sentences here—words and phrases are enough.)

_____

2. *Why* is this change necessary? (List *at least* two reasons.)

_____

3. What preparation or training will you need to accomplish this?

_____

4. How would you make this change? (List *at least* two steps.)

_____

Name _____ **Date** _____

Light A Lamp
First Draft

DIRECTIONS: Write a first draft of an essay telling how you would "light a lamp," as Florence Nightingale did for hospital and nursing care in nineteenth-century England. Use your brainstorming list. (This is a first draft, so don't be concerned about spelling and grammar.)

---

1. The first paragraph introduces the topic in an interesting way as in this example: "Muffy was run over by a car last month. She was an adorable black-and-white kitten who had been abandoned by her family when they moved away. I want to establish shelters for animals like Muffy." Write your first paragraph (2–4 sentences) here:

   _____

   _____

   _____

2. The second paragraph can tell *why* a change is needed. Write your second paragraph (3–5 sentences) here:

   _____

   _____

   _____

   _____

3. In the third paragraph tell what training you will need, and what steps you will take to make this change. Write your third paragraph (3–5 sentences) here:

   _____

   _____

   _____

4. The last paragraph should restate and sum up the topic, as in this example: "Abandoned pets like Muffy should not have to die. In my shelter, these animals would receive love and care and be offered for adoption to families who want them." Write your last paragraph (2–4 sentences) here:

   _____

   _____

   _____

Name _____ **Date** _____

LIGHT A LAMP
REVISING AND WRITING A FINAL COPY

DIRECTIONS:

1. Edit and revise your first draft of an essay about "lighting a lamp," as follows:

a. Does the first paragraph state the topic clearly? Can you make it more interesting with a question, quotation, or startling statement?

b. Does the second paragraph explain why this change is needed? Can you add anything to make it more convincing?

c. Does the third paragraph describe the steps you would take to become trained and then accomplish this work? Did you leave out anything important you might need to know and do?

d. Does the last paragraph restate and sum up the topic?

e. Are your sentences complete? Do subjects and verbs agree?

f. Check your spelling with a dictionary.

2. Write the final copy of your essay below. Put a title on the first line. (You can use the title "Light a Lamp," or any other title you choose.) Indent at the beginning of paragraphs. (Use the back of this worksheet if you need more room.)

_____

_____

_____

_____

_____

_____

_____

_____

_____

_____

_____

Name _____ **Date** _____

SONG OF YOURSELF
PREWRITING

"I celebrate myself and sing myself."

May 31 marks the birthday of Walt Whitman. He is considered by many to be the greatest American poet. Whitman was born in Long Island, New York in 1819. He was one of six children, and his father was a carpenter. Walt Whitman was poor for most of his life except for the richness of his work.

Walt Whitman had a great love for his country. Much of his writing is about America and its people. He saw beauty and grandeur in each person and in each blade of grass—in the smallest things, such as:

"I believe a leaf of grass is no less than the journeywork of the stars,
And the pismire is equally perfect, and a grain of sand, and the eggs of the wren,
And the tree toad is a chef-d'oeuvre for the highest,
And the running blackberry would adorn the parlors of heaven."

During the Civil War, Whitman served as a nurse and tended the wounded. He was saddened by the fighting and had a vision of a more perfect country:

"I dream'd in a dream I saw a city invincible to the
    attacks of the whole of the rest of the earth,
I dream'd that was the new city of Friends."

Can you look at the small things around you—in your home, your neighborhood, your school, your town—and try to see them as Walt Whitman might have done? Choose one or several things to write about (it might be a park, or children in a playground, or the intensity of a ball game, or your pet cat, or an afternoon at the beach, or a snowy morning in winter, or any other object or scene). You can write a poem about it as Walt Whitman might have done, or you can describe it in prose (paragraph writing). Before you begin, it will help to organize your ideas in a brainstorming list.

BRAINSTORMING LIST

DIRECTIONS: List the parts of the scene or object you are writing about in the first column. Next to each listing, write words and phrases that could be used to describe it. (Example: "daffodils: yellow as the sun, tangled together, reaching toward the sky.")

_____ : _____

_____ : _____

_____ : _____

_____ : _____

_____ : _____

Name _____ Date_____

Song of Yourself
First Draft

"In the faces of men and women, I see God."

Walt Whitman was able to see the beauty and uniqueness of ordinary things, ordinary places, and ordinary people. His love for America and its people comes across clearly in his writing.

Think about the object or place you have chosen to describe, and try to see it as Walt Whitman might have done. Here are some more lines by Whitman to put you in the mood:

> "I think I could turn and live with animals, they are so placid and self-
>   contain'd,
> I stand and look at them long and long.
> They do not sweat and whine about their condition,
> They do not lie awake in the dark and weep for their sins . . .
> Not one is respectable or unhappy over the whole earth."

> "A child said, *What is the grass*? fetching it to one with full hands; . . .
> I guess it is the handkerchief of the Lord,
> A scented gift and remembrancer . . ."

> "I am he that walks with the tender and growing night,
> I call to the earth and see half-held by the night."

DIRECTIONS: Write the first draft of a paragraph, essay, poem, or story about the specialness of something ordinary. Use the brainstorming list you prepared for Activity 9A. Make your description vivid by using active verbs (such as *sweat* or *whine*), similes or metaphors (such as *handkerchief of the Lord*), and vivid phrases (such as *the tender and growing night*). This is just a first draft, so don't try for perfection—concentrate on getting your ideas down on paper. Use the back of this worksheet if you need more room.

_____

_____

_____

_____

_____

_____

_____

Name _____ Date _____

SONG OF YOURSELF
REVISING AND WRITING A FINAL COPY

> "Give me the splendid silent sun with all his beams full-dazzling." —Walt Whitman

DIRECTIONS:

1. Edit and revise the first draft of your poem, paragraph, essay, or story describing the specialness of something ordinary, as follows:

   a. Did you omit anything that helps show the uniqueness or beauty of this ordinary thing? Can you find the best place to add it?

   b. Can you make your writing more vivid with sensory words and phrases such as "splendid, silent sun" or "beams full-dazzling"? Change any dull words to richer, more exciting ones.

   c. Can you add comparisons such as similes or metaphors to make your writing more exciting?

   d. Is each word and phrase the best one for that thought or description?

2. Write the final copy of your poem, story, paragraph, or essay that celebrates something ordinary. Decide on a title and put it on the first line. If you wish, you can illustrate it in the side and bottom margins. (Use the back of this worksheet if you need more room.)

_____

_____

_____

_____

_____

_____

Name _____ Date_____

MAY TIME 1

Fragment means a piece of something. Sentence fragments are pieces of sentences. The use of incomplete sentences is a common error in writing. Here are some examples of sentence fragments:

1. When we go on picnics.
2. At least once during the month of May.
3. Laugh and shout and run across the grass.

A sentence must express a complete thought. The above examples are fragments of sentences because they do not express complete thoughts. Here is what each one might look like as a complete sentence:

1. When we go on picnics, we always take our dog, Max.
2. Our family has a picnic at least once during the month of May.
3. In the park, we love to laugh and shout and run across the grass.

DIRECTIONS: The sentences below are all about the month of May. They are not correct. They are not complete sentences. They are only fragments. Rewrite each one on the lines below, making it into a sentence by expressing a complete thought.

1. The flowers that bloom in May.

_____

_____

2. My Little League team each Saturday in the spring.

_____

_____

3. The expression on my mom's face when she sees her Mother's Day Card.

_____

_____

4. Leading the big parade on Memorial Day.

_____

_____

5. The last field trip our class took.

_____

_____

6. Enjoying some of the best days of the year.

_____

_____

Name _____ **Date** _____

MAY TIME 2

In Activity 10A, you worked with sentence fragments. Another common writing error is run-on sentences.

A run-on sentence is like a train that doesn't stop at the station. It keeps on going past the point where it is supposed to stop, as in these examples:

---

1. We take trips to Lakeside Park in May it is a great place for a picnic.

2. Sometimes it is sunny and warm then we go swimming.

3. My little brother has to wear a tube he can't swim yet.

These are all run-on sentences because they go past the point of expressing a complete thought. Here is how they might be fixed:

---

1. We take trips to Lakeside Park in May. It is a great place for a picnic.

2. Sometimes we go swimming when it is sunny and warm.

3. My little brother has to wear a tube because he can't swim yet.

DIRECTIONS: All the sentences below are about the month of May. They are also incorrect because they are run-on sentences. Write each sentence correctly on the lines below.

1. I see my friends after school we like to ride our bikes.

_____

_____

2. I love going to a parade the music is great.

_____

_____

3. Our high school band wears white uniforms my brother plays the clarinet.

_____

_____

4. I always have trouble choosing a Mother's Day card my sister helps me.

_____

_____

5. In the morning, we put breakfast on a tray Mom is still in bed.

_____

_____

© 1997 by The Center for Applied Research in Education

Name _____ **Date** _____

MAY TIME 3

DIRECTIONS:

1. Read the following paragraph. *Underline* the sentence fragments and run-on sentences. Then, rewrite the paragraph correctly on the lines below.

May is my favorite month of the year there are lots of reasons for this. It is sometimes cool. But not too cold. Many days are warm. But not hot. Every week new flowers bloom in the garden. Lilies, tulips, and hyacinths. After school, my friends and I can play outdoors it's better than being stuck in the house. May has some great holidays, too. Mother's Day and Memorial Day. Every month of the year has its good and bad points everything about May is good.

---

2. Did you find all the sentence fragments and run-on sentences? Now, rewrite the paragraph correctly below:

_____

_____

_____

_____

_____

_____

_____

_____

_____

_____

_____

_____

_____

_____

Name _____ **Date** _____

News Flash
Prewriting

On May 24, 1883, the Brooklyn Bridge was opened for traffic. This was one of the major events of the 19th century. Newspapers all over the world featured front-page stories about this amazing achievement.

You are going to pretend you are a newspaper reporter in 1883. You are going to write a news article about the opening of the Brooklyn Bridge. Here are some details you need to know:

1. The Brooklyn Bridge spans the East River in New York City.

2. It connects Manhattan and Brooklyn.

3. It was originally called the "East River Bridge."

4. It was the first cable-wire steel suspension bridge in the world.

5. The Brooklyn Bridge is 1,595 feet long.

6. It was considered a miracle of design.

7. The bridge was designed by John Augustus Roebling.

8. Roebling died in an accident early in construction.

9. After Roebling's death, his son, Washington Roebling, supervised construction.

10. Construction was begun in 1869, but was not completed until 1883.

11. There were many mishaps and accidents that slowed construction.

Now you have enough facts to write your news article. When writing a news article, the first sentence or two (called the *lead*) must sum up the event briefly. The lead must answer these questions: WHO? WHAT? WHEN? WHERE? In addition to summing up these facts, the lead must also catch the reader's interest. One way of doing this is with a quotation, such as " 'I never thought I'd live to see anything like this,' said 80-year-old Jonathan Blackman. Blackman was one of the hundreds of people in the crowd attending the long-awaited opening today of the Brooklyn Bridge connecting Brooklyn with Manhattan in New York City."

On the lines below, write *two* possible leads for this story.

1. _____

_____

2. _____

_____

Name _____ **Date** _____

NEWS FLASH
FIRST DRAFT

DIRECTIONS: Write a first draft of your news article about the opening of the Brooklyn Bridge, as follows:

1. Write the news story as though you are reporting on May 24, 1883.

2. Write a headline for your news story on the first line. (A headline is like a title, but it usually contains at least one action verb, as in "BROOKLYN BRIDGE OPENS" or "THOUSANDS ATTEND BRIDGE OPENING.") You may use one of these headlines, or any other you choose.

3. Choose *one* of the leads you wrote for Activity 11A.

4. After the lead, the facts of the story are related in order of their importance. The most important facts should follow the lead. The least important facts should be at the end. That way, if a reader does not read the whole article, that reader will still know the most important facts. All the facts listed in Activity 11A are true. Do not change any of them.

5. If your activity needs information that is not listed in Activity 11A to make a better news story, you can make up additional details, such as number of people present, names and positions of some of them, some things they do or say, etc.

6. Write a first draft of your news story below. This is just a draft, so don't be concerned with spelling or grammar. (Write a headline at the top.) Use the back of this worksheet if you need more room.

_____

Name _____ Date _____

News Flash
Revising and Writing a Final Copy

DIRECTIONS:

1. Edit and revise your news story about the opening of the Brooklyn Bridge on May 24, 1883, as follows:

---

a. Does your lead answer the questions: WHO? WHAT? WHEN? WHERE?

b. Does your lead begin in a way that will get the reader's attention? Would it be more exciting with a quotation, a question, or a vivid word picture?

c. Did you describe the details in order of importance, with the most important details right after the lead?

d. Can you make your writing more exciting with the use of strong, active verbs, such as *shouted* instead of *said*, or *rushed* instead of *went*, or *hurtled* instead of *fell*?

e. Is your headline good enough, or can you think of a more exciting one?

f. Are your sentences complete? Do subjects and verbs agree?

g. Check spelling with a dictionary.

---

2. Write the final copy of your news story below. Put the headline at the top. Indent at the beginning of paragraphs. (Use the back of this worksheet if you need more room.)

_____

_____

_____

_____

_____

_____

_____

_____

_____

Name _____ **Date** _____

WAR AND PEACE 1

On May 7, 1945, Germany surrendered, ending World War II in Europe.

The following sentences can be rearranged and combined into a paragraph about World War II. Put these sentences into the correct order and write the paragraph on the lines below.

1. England fought on alone.
2. Germany surrendered on May 7, 1945, ending World War II in Europe.
3. They were called the Allies.
4. They fought against the Axis powers, consisting of Germany, Italy, and Japan.
5. At first, the war went badly for the Allies.
6. England and France came to Poland's defense.
7. This war began in 1939 when German armies invaded Poland.
8. The United States entered the war on December 7, 1941, the date of Japan's sneak attack on Pearl Harbor in Hawaii.
9. After many battles, the tide began to turn until the surrender of Germany in 1945.
10. France surrendered and the Germans occupied Paris.

_____

_____

_____

_____

_____

_____

_____

_____

_____

_____

_____

Name _____ Date _____

WAR AND PEACE 2

Here are more sentences about World War II. Rearrange these sentences into a paragraph. Write the paragraph on the lines below.

1. They were taken from their homes and sent to concentration camps, where they were tortured and murdered.
2. This was the killing of ten million innocent men, women, and children by the Nazis who ruled Germany.
3. Historians are still trying to understand this horrible event in the hope of avoiding future holocausts.
4. One of the most horrifying events of World War II in Europe was the Holocaust.
5. After the war, the Germans tried to hide these atrocities.
6. Among them were six million Jews.
7. These were people whom the Germans had decided should be destroyed.
8. Gradually, the world learned what had happened.

_____

_____

_____

_____

_____

_____

_____

_____

_____

_____

_____

_____

Name _____ **Date** _____

MUSIC, MAESTRO!
PREWRITING

Almost everyone is familiar with *The Nutcracker*. This ballet is performed all over the world, in big cities and small towns. Did you know that the music was written by Peter Ilyich Tchaikovsky?

Tchaikovsky was born on May 7, 1840 in Russia. He was a shy person who expressed his feelings with music. Although he became famous, he did not have a happy life. However, he produced some of the most beautiful and popular music ever written, including ballets, symphonies, and concertos. Even people who are not fans of classical music love many of his compositions.

What kind of music do you enjoy? Why do you like it? In this activity, you will prepare a brainstorming list that will help you get ready to write an essay about the music you like.

BRAINSTORMING LIST

1. On the lines below, list your favorite kind (or kinds) of music. (If you enjoy more than one kind of music, list them all.)

_____

_____

2. On the lines below, list some examples of the songs or compositions you like best. (List at least three examples.)

_____

_____

_____

3. List at least two performers, composers, or songwriters you like.

_____

_____

4. List at least three reasons why you like this music. (You don't need complete sentences—words and phrases are enough.)

_____

_____

_____

Name _____   **Date** _____

MUSIC, MAESTRO!
FIRST DRAFT

DIRECTIONS: Write a first draft of an essay about the music you like best. Here are some suggestions for organizing this essay.

1. Keep your brainstorming list in front of you.
2. Introduce the topic in the first paragraph in an interesting way, as in this example: "All my friends think I'm crazy, but I don't care. The music I like best is old. It is called Big Band Music, and was popular in the 1940s."
3. In the second paragraph, list your reasons for liking this music.
4. In the third paragraph, give examples of favorite songs and performers or composers.
5. The fourth paragraph should restate and sum up the topic.

Write your essay below. This is just a first draft, so don't be concerned about spelling or grammar—concentrate on organizing your thoughts and getting them down. (Use the back of this worksheet if you need more room.)

_____

_____

_____

_____

_____

_____

_____

_____

_____

_____

_____

Name _____ **Date** _____

MUSIC, MAESTRO!
REVISING AND WRITING A FINAL COPY

DIRECTIONS:

1. Edit and revise the first draft of your essay about music, as follows:

---

a. Does your first paragraph introduce the topic in an interesting way? Can you make it more interesting with a question or a startling statement?

b. Does your second paragraph state your reasons for liking this music? Can you add anything that would make this more convincing, such as a description of how the music makes you feel?

c. Does your third paragraph give examples of the music, performers, or composers?

d. Does the last paragraph restate and sum up the topic?

e. Can you make your writing more convincing and alive with vivid language, such as sensory words or similes?

f. Are your sentences complete? Do subjects and verbs agree?

g. Check spelling with the dictionary.

---

2. Write the final copy of your essay below. Indent at the beginning of each paragraph. (Use the back of this worksheet if you need more room.)

_____

_____

_____

_____

_____

_____

_____

_____

_____

JUNE

JUNE

"What is so rare as a day in June?
Then, if ever, come perfect days" —*James Russell Lowell*

JUNO'S MONTH ... SUMMER BEGINS ... ROSES AND BERRIES AND JUNE BEETLES ... GRADUATIONS AND WEDDINGS ... FATHER'S DAY ... FLAG DAY (JUNE 14) ... MIDSUMMER EVE ... PARTIES AND BARBECUES ... END OF SCHOOL YEAR

JUNE EVENTS

June 2, 1953: Coronation of Queen Elizabeth II in London

June 3, 1948: World's largest telescope dedicated at Mount Palomar Observatory, California

June 6, 1944: D-Day, when Allied troops landed on Normandy Beach in France

June 8, 1869: Ives W. McGaffey of Chicago patented first vacuum cleaner

June 14, 1777: The Continental Congress designated the "Stars and Stripes" as the national flag of the U.S.

June 15, 1215: England's King John signed the Magna Carta at Runnymede

June 16, 1963: Russia's Valentina Tereshkova became the first woman space traveler

June 18, 1815: Napoleon was defeated at Waterloo by the Duke of Wellington

June 19, 1846: The first baseball game between organized teams took place at Elysian Field in Hoboken, New Jersey

June 19, 1964: Congress passed the Civil Rights bill

June 23, 1868: Christopher Latham Sholes of Wisconsin received a patent for his "type-writer"

June 24, 1947: The first "flying saucers" were reported by Kenneth Arnold of Boise, Idaho

June 25, 1876: "Custer's Last Stand" at Little Big Horn, Montana

June 26, 1870: The first boardwalk in the world was completed in Atlantic City, New Jersey

June 30, 1936: *Gone With the Wind* by Margaret Mitchell was published

JUNE BIRTHDAYS

June 3, 1808: Jefferson Davis, President of the Confederacy

June 14, 1811: Harriet Beecher Stowe, author of *Uncle Tom's Cabin*

June 27, 1880: Helen Keller, blind and deaf author and lecturer

WRITING ACTIVITIES FOR JUNE

Name _____ **Date** _____

RARE JUNE
SIMILES

> "And what is so rare as a day in June?
> Then, if ever, come perfect days" —James Russell Lowell

"*As rare as* a day in June": In this line, the poet uses a *simile* to describe the word *rare*. He compares it to *a day in June*.

> A *simile* is a comparison that usually uses *as* or *like*, as in, "eyes as blue as the sky" or "muscled legs like an Olympic runner."

DIRECTIONS: The sentences below are all abut the month of June. Complete each one with a *SIMILE*, using *as* or *like*.

1. A June morning is _____
   _____

2. My neighbor's garden is _____
   _____

3. I saw a rose that was _____
   _____

4. The first day of summer is _____
   _____

5. The last day of school is _____
   _____

6. A picnic in June is _____
   _____

7. Sometimes, the June sun can be _____
   _____

8. Final exams are _____
   _____

9. When my Dad sees his Father's Day gift, he'll be _____
   _____

10. A graduation ceremony is _____
    _____

Name _____ **Date**_____

RARE JUNE
METAPHORS

> "When June is come, then all the day
> I'll sit with my love in the scented hay;
> And watch the sunshot palaces high,
> That the white clouds build in the breezy sky."
> —Robert Bridges

In these lines, the poet compares cloud formations to *sunshot palaces*. This is a *metaphor*.

This comparison would have been a *simile* if the writer had said that the clouds were *like* palaces. But he doesn't! He actually calls them *sunshot palaces*. A metaphor describes something by identifying it as *something else*. Unlike a simile, a metaphor does not use the words *as* or *like*.

Here are some more examples of metaphors:

> "That baby is an *angel*."
> "He *struck out* on the job interview."
> "She was a quiet little *mouse*."

DIRECTIONS: Here are more phrases about June. Write a sentence about each one, using a metaphor. (The first one is done for you.)

1. a severe sunburn

   My skin was on fire. _____

2. birds singing in a tree

   _____

   _____

3. the last day of school

   _____

   _____

4. a pool on a hot day

   _____

   _____

5. getting a poor report card

   _____

   _____

6. ants at a picnic

   _____

   _____

Name _____ **Date** _____

WHERE IN THE WORLD?
PREWRITING

Lots of people take trips during the summer. If you could travel anywhere in the world, where would you go?

Would you visit your grandparents in another state? Would you choose an ocean resort or a cruise to a far-away island? How about a mountain-climbing expedition, or an archaeological dig in Africa? The whole world is yours from which to select.

Before writing about your choice, it will help to complete the brainstorming list below.

BRAINSTORMING LIST

1. In the box below, write the name of the spot you have chosen. Then list as many words and phrases you can think of that describe this place.

2. In the box below, list *at least* two reasons why you want to go to this place. (You don't need sentences here—words and phrases are enough.)

3. The beginning of an essay should state the topic in an interesting and exciting way. Using a quotation or a question can accomplish this, as in these examples:

"How would you like to be a real-life Indiana Jones? It is possible to have this kind of adventure on an archaeological dig. That's what I would like to do if I could go anywhere in the world."

" 'Venice looks like a storybook illustration of a magical, fantastic kingdom.' That's how my Uncle Jack described his visit to Italy last year, and that is where I would like to go more than anywhere else on Earth."

Write a beginning sentence (or sentences) for your essay below:

_____

_____

© 1997 by The Center for Applied Research in Education

Name _____ Date_____

WHERE IN THE WORLD?
FIRST DRAFT

DIRECTIONS: Write a first draft of a 4-paragraph essay about where in the world you would most like to go. You have already done most of the work by preparing a brainstorming list. Keep this list in front of you while writing your essay, and follow these suggestions:

1. The first paragraph should introduce the topic in an interesting way. You have already begun the first paragraph on your brainstorming list. Copy it, and add whatever more is needed to complete the introduction. Write your first paragraph (2–4 sentences) here:

_____

_____

2. The second paragraph should describe the place you want to visit. Use the notes on your brainstorming list, and include as much detail as you can. Write your second paragraph (3–5 sentences) here:

_____

_____

_____

3. The third paragraph will list your reasons for wanting to go to this place. Use the notes on your brainstorming list, and write your third paragraph (3–5 sentences) here:

_____

_____

_____

4. The last paragraph will restate and sum up the topic, as in this example. "Venice seems to me like the most beautiful and mysterious city on Earth. It would be a dream come true to be able to travel to this exciting place." Write your last paragraph (2–4 sentences) here:

_____

_____

Name _____ **Date** _____

WHERE IN THE WORLD?
REVISING AND WRITING A FINAL COPY

DIRECTIONS:

1. Edit and revise the first draft of your essay, as follows:

a. Does the first paragraph introduce the topic in an interesting way? Can you make it more exciting with the use of a quotation, a question, or a startling statement?

b. Does the second paragraph describe the place? Can you make the description more vivid with sensory language, a simile, or a metaphor?

c. Does the third paragraph list your reasons for wanting to visit this place? Can you make these reasons more believable and convincing?

d. Does the last paragraph re-state and sum up the topic?

e. Are your sentences complete? Do subjects and verbs agree?

f. Check spelling with a dictionary.

2. Write the final copy of your essay below. Put a title on the top line. (You can use the title, "Where in the World?," or make up one of your own.)

    Indent at the beginning of paragraphs. Use the back of this worksheet if you need more room.

_____

_____

_____

_____

_____

_____

_____

_____

_____

Name _____ **Date** _____

JUNE MOON
PREWRITING

June is a favorite month for poets and songwriters. Perhaps that is because the climate is so pleasant at this time of year in many areas. Maybe it is simply because *June* is easy to rhyme, as with *moon*, *soon*, *tune*, and *croon*. Here is a verse by Samuel Taylor Coleridge:

> "A noise like of a hidden brook
> In the leafy month of June,
> That to the sleeping woods all night
> Sings a quiet tune."

Only two of these four lines rhyme. Can you see which ones they are? If you said lines 2 and 4 (*June* and *tune*), you are right! This rhyme scheme is called ABCB—the first three lines don't rhyme, so they are identified with three different letters, as A, B, and C. The fourth line rhymes with the second, so it is B.

Here is a June verse with a different rhyme scheme:

> "The robin sings a happy tune
> Perched upon a branch in June;
> As oak leaves flutter in the breeze
> That blows so gently through the trees."

This rhyme scheme is called AABB—the first two lines rhyme with each other (A, A), and the last two lines rhyme (B, B). Two lines together that rhyme are called a *couplet*, so this verse consists of two couplets.

Poems don't always rhyme, but rhyming is fun to do. Before you write your own poem in rhyme, here are some rhyming games that will give you practice rhyming.

1. Add as many rhymes as you can to each of the words below. The first two are begun for you. (Rhyming words need not have the same number of syllables—they only have to end with the same sound.)

trees:	tease, symphonies, _____
rose:	rows, bellows, _____
sun:	_____
beach:	_____
pool:	_____

2. Add a rhyming line to each of the lines below, making it into a couplet.

Last week I ran along the sand,	The garden had just one red rose,
_____	_____

351

Name _____ **Date** _____

JUNE MOON
FIRST DRAFT

DIRECTIONS:

1. Here are some examples of rhyme schemes that are fun to use:

Afternoons in June are great	**A**
For standing fast next to home plate,	**A**
Then swing a bat with all your might	**B**
And send the ball upon its flight.	**B**

(This verse consists of two couplets, so the rhyme scheme is AABB.)

The sand is hot beneath the sun,	**A**
The waves are high and foamy white,	**B**
The children shout and play and run	**A**
Upon the beach, in June's warm light.	**B**

(This rhyme scheme is ABAB—line 1 rhymes with line 3; line 2 rhymes with line 4.)

2. Write a first draft of a poem about June, using one of the rhyme schemes above. You can write about one of the subjects below, or any other you choose:

—a beach
—a park
—a classroom
—a ball game
—a city street
—a garden
—a pool

Write your poem below. It should have *at least* four lines, but you can make it much longer if you wish. Remember, this is a first draft!

_____

_____

_____

_____

_____

_____

Name _____ **Date**_____

JUNE MOON
REVISING AND WRITING A FINAL COPY

DIRECTIONS:

1. Edit and revise your rhyming poem about June as follows:

> a. Write your rhyme scheme here (example: AABB): _____
>
> b. Is the rhyme scheme accurate? Do the lines rhyme according to your plan? If not, correct it.
>
> c. Read the poem aloud. Does the beat and rhythm sound right? If not, fix it.
>
> d. Would the poem be better if you used more vivid language? Can you put in any sensory words or similes? Can you change passive verbs, such as *touch*, to active ones, like *smash*?
>
> e. Since a poem is usually short, each word is important. Is every word you have used the best one for that spot? If you can think of a better one, change it.

2. When your poem is as perfect as you can make it, write the final copy on the lines below. If you wish, you can illustrate your poem in the side and bottom margins.

_____

_____

_____

_____

_____

_____

_____

_____

Name _____ **Date** _____

Space Travelers
Prewriting

Do you know what the letters UFO mean? They stand for "Unidentified Flying Object." These are often called "flying saucers."

The term "flying saucer" was first used by a businessman from Boise, Idaho, named Kenneth Arnold. On June 24, 1947, Arnold saw nine objects flying over a mountain in Washington state. This was the first report of a UFO in the U.S. Arnold said they looked like "saucers skipping across water." After that, it was popular to call UFO's "flying saucers."

Have you ever seen a UFO? Lots of people claim to have spotted them. Sightings of UFOs go back as far as ancient civilizations thousands of years ago. In more modern times, the first sighting that was well-documented was in Nuremberg, Germany. People there claimed to have observed red, blue, and black plate- or tube-shaped objects battling in the sky over the city.

In recent years, UFO reportings have become more and more numerous. Some of these claims have proven to be phony, or have been objects like weather balloons or aircraft lights. But many cannot be explained.

Many people, including some scientists, believe that these "flying saucers" have come from other planets or galaxies. A lot of stories and movies have been written about aliens visiting the Earth.

In this activity, you are going to write a story about a UFO landing on Earth. First, organize your ideas by completing the brainstorming list below.

BRAINSTORMING LIST

1. On the line below, write a name and description of the main character in your story.

_____

2. Write names and short descriptions of two or three other characters.

_____

3. Write a list of words and phrases that describe the UFO.

_____

4. Describe the place where the UFO lands.

_____

5. Write a list of words and phrases to describe who or what comes out of the UFO.

_____

Name _____ Date_____

SPACE TRAVELERS
FIRST DRAFT

DIRECTIONS: Your brainstorming list will help you get started with a first draft of your story about a UFO. Here are some suggestions:

1. Make the beginning exciting. You might begin by describing the UFO landing as it appears to someone who is watching. Or you could start with a conversation between two kids who stumble upon the UFO while playing ball. Or you could begin with a startling statement such as, *This was the beginning of the end for our civilization.*

2. Use a lot of sensory language (words that appeal to the five senses: touch, sight, hearing, taste, and smell).

3. Use occasional similes (*as blue as the sky*) and metaphors (*in the blink of an eye*) to make your descriptions vivid.

4. Use the information you compiled for the brainstorming list to develop the story.

5. Put a title for your story on the first line. You can use "Space Travelers" or any other title of your choice.

6. This is just a first draft, so don't be concerned about spelling or grammar—concentrate on getting the story down on paper. Indent at the beginning of paragraphs and whenever someone begins to speak. (Use the back of this worksheet if you need more room.)

_____

_____

_____

_____

_____

_____

_____

_____

Name _____ **Date** _____

SPACE TRAVELERS
REVISING AND WRITING A FINAL COPY

DIRECTIONS:

1. Edit and revise the first draft of your story about a UFO, as follows:

> a. Is the beginning exciting? Can you make it more interesting with a startling statement, dialogue, or thrilling action?
>
> b. Can you make your writing more vivid by adding sensory language, similes, and metaphors?
>
> c. Can you add more dialogue to show how your characters think and feel?
>
> d. Are your sentences complete? Do subjects and verbs agree?
>
> e. Check spelling with a dictionary.

2. Write the final copy of your story below. Indent at the beginning of paragraphs and whenever someone begins to speak. (Use the back of this worksheet if you need more room.)

_____

_____

_____

_____

_____

_____

_____

_____

_____

_____

_____

_____

Name _____ **Date** _____

STARS AND STRIPES FOREVER
PREWRITING

THE STARS AND STRIPES
OLD GLORY
THE RED, WHITE, AND BLUE

These are names people have given to the flag of the United States. On June 14, we celebrate Flag Day. At that time, we honor this flag and what it represents.

> On June 14, 1777, the Continental Congress adopted the "Stars and Stripes" as the official flag of the new nation. There is a legend that Betsy Ross made a flag according to this new design. The first Flag Day was observed on June 14, 1877, the 100th anniversary of its adoption. But it wasn't until 1949 that President Harry Truman approved a resolution designating June 14 as a national Flag Day.

Flag Day is not a legal holiday, but special observances are held every June 14. Flags are displayed in homes as well as public buildings and businesses. Parades are held in many towns and cities.

> The flag is a symbol of the United States. It stands for freedom and opportunity, as well as honoring those who died defending it. Many people have expressed their love of the flag in music and words. The flag that flew over Fort McHenry in 1814 inspired Francis Scott Key to write "The Star-Spangled Banner," which is now the national anthem. John Philip Sousa wrote several marches about the flag, the most famous being the rousing "Stars and Stripes Forever." Popular songwriter, George M. Cohan, wrote "You're a Grand Old Flag," part of which goes, "You're the emblem of the land I love, the home of the free and the brave."

In this activity, you are going to write an essay about the flag. First, complete the brainstorming list below:

BRAINSTORMING LIST

1. In the space below, write as many words and phrases as you can think of that can be used to *describe* the U.S. flag.

> [ ]

2. In the space below, write as many words and phrases as you can think of that describe your *feelings* about the U.S. flag.

> [ ]

3. In the space below, write as many words and phrases as you can think of that can be used to describe the *meaning* of the U.S. flag.

> [ ]

Name _____ Date _____

STARS AND STRIPES FOREVER
FIRST DRAFT

DIRECTIONS: Write a first draft of a 4-paragraph essay about the United States flag. Use your brainstorming list and the following suggestions: This is just a first draft, so don't be concerned about spelling or grammar—concentrate on getting your ideas down on paper.

1. The first paragraph should introduce the topic in an interesting way, as in this example: "Does our flag have a deep meaning for you? It does for me. Whenever I see Old Glory waving in the breeze on Flag Day, I get a tremendous feeling of pride." Write your first paragraph (2–4 sentences) here:

_____

_____

_____

2. The second paragraph should develop the topic by describing the flag and your feelings about it. Write your second paragraph (3–5 sentences) here:

_____

_____

_____

3. The third paragraph should develop the topic further by expressing your ideas about what the flag means. Write your third paragraph (3–5 sentences) here:

_____

_____

_____

4. The last paragraph should restate and sum up the topic, as in this example: "The United States flag is not just a piece of cloth with a design of stars and stripes. It is a symbol of our country, and I honor its message of freedom and opportunity." Write your last paragraph (2–4 sentences) here:

_____

_____

_____

Name _____ **Date** _____

STARS AND STRIPES FOREVER
REVISING AND WRITING A FINAL COPY

DIRECTIONS:

1. Edit and revise the first draft of your essay about the flag, as follows:

> a. Does the first paragraph introduce the topic in an interesting way? Can you make it more exciting by beginning with a question, a quotation, or a startling statement?
>
> b. Does the second paragraph develop the topic by describing the flag and your feelings about it? Did you use all the descriptive words on your brainstorming list? Can you add any vivid description?
>
> c. Does the third paragraph develop the topic further by explaining the meaning of the flag? Did you leave out anything important?
>
> d. Does the last paragraph restate and sum up the topic as stated at the beginning of the essay? Can you express your thoughts more clearly?
>
> e. Are your sentences complete? Does each sentence express a complete thought? Do subjects and verbs agree?
>
> f. Are there any run-on sentences? If so, correct these.
>
> g. Check spelling with a dictionary.

2. Write the final copy of your essay below. Indent at the beginning of each paragraph. (If you need more room, use the back of this worksheet.) Decide upon a title for this essay and put it on the first line.

_____

_____

_____

_____

_____

_____

_____

Name _____ **Date** _____

FATHER'S DAY 1

DIRECTIONS: The sentence *beginnings* below all have something to do with Father's Day. Complete each sentence. (Don't forget a period at the end of each sentence!)

1. Father's Day is _____

   _____

2. On Father's Day, I am going to _____

   _____

3. Father's Day comes _____

   _____

4. Sometimes, fathers _____

   _____

5. Fathers usually _____

   _____

6. Father's Day presents are _____

   _____

7. I think Father's Day _____

   _____

8. June is a good month for Father's Day because _____

   _____

9. Some fathers know _____

   _____

10. This Father's Day will be _____

   _____

© 1997 by The Center for Applied Research in Education

Name _____ **Date** _____

FATHER'S DAY 2

DIRECTIONS: The sentence *endings* below all have something to do with Father's Day. Write a beginning for each sentence.

---

1. _____ Father's Day cards.

2. _____ make good Father's Day presents.

3. _____ on Father's Day.

4. _____ my best friend's father.

5. _____ for grandfathers.

6. _____ with my grandfather.

7. _____ Father's Day this year.

8. _____ would make Father's Day better.

9. _____ hard to be a father.

10. _____ make fathers happy.

Name _____ Date _____

Dear Dad
Prewriting

Sometimes, it is hard to express our feelings to people we really care about. It can be easier to say "thanks" in a letter.

Wouldn't Father's Day be the perfect time to send your dad a letter, telling him how much you appreciate him and all he does for you? He would probably like that even more than the most expensive gift! If you prefer, you could write to your grandfather, or a favorite uncle, or even a neighbor to whom you feel close.

Choose one of these people. Before writing your letter, organize your thoughts by completing the brainstorming list below.

BRAINSTORMING LIST

1. In the box below, make a list of words and phrases that describe the appearance and personality of your dad (or the person to whom you are sending a letter).

2. On the lines below, list *at least three* things that you admire about your dad (or the person to whom you are writing).

3. On the lines below, list *at least three* things that your dad (or the person to whom you are writing) does for you. (You don't need sentences here—words and phrases are enough.)

© 1997 by The Center for Applied Research in Education

Name _____ **Date**_____

DEAR DAD
FIRST DRAFT

DIRECTIONS:

1. Write a first draft of a letter to your dad or to someone else you admire, such as a grandfather, uncle, or neighbor.

2. Use the brainstorming list you prepared in Activity 7A to organize your thoughts clearly. Here is one possible arrangement:

    In the first paragraph, tell why you are writing this letter.

    In the second paragraph, write a description of the appearance and personality of your dad (or the person to whom you are writing), and tell why you admire him.

    In the third paragraph, describe things your dad (or the person to whom you are writing) has done for you that you appreciate.

    In the fourth paragraph, sum up your feelings and the reason for this letter.

    (This is just one possible plan. You can use all or part of it in your letter.)

3. Use correct letter form by following the guide below.

_____
(Write your street address above)

_____
(Write your city, state and ZIP here)

_____
(Write today's date above)

_____ (Name of person to whom you are writing)
_____ (Street address of that person)
_____ (City, state and ZIP)

Dear _____, (This is called the *greeting*)

_____

_____

_____

_____

_____

_____

_____

_____

_____

_____

(*Closing*, such as *Love*, *Your son*, here)   _____

(Sign your name here)   _____

Name _____ **Date** _____

DEAR DAD
REVISING AND WRITING A FINAL COPY

DIRECTIONS:

1. Edit and revise the first draft of your letter, as follows:

a. Do you begin by telling why you are writing this letter?

b. Are your thoughts arranged in a clear, logical order, as in the example?

c. Is there anything important that you wish to add?

d. Are your sentences complete? Do subjects and verbs agree?

e. Check spelling with a dictionary.

f. Did you indent at the beginning of each paragraph?

2. Write the final copy of your letter below. Follow correct letter form as set out on your first draft. If you wish to send your letter, you can detach it on the dotted line.

Name _____ **Date** _____

JUNE PARTYTIME

DIRECTIONS: The six sentences below tell about special celebrations in June. Can you rearrange them in the proper order for a clearly-written paragraph?

    Write the paragraph on the lines at the bottom of the page.

1. School proms usually take place in June, too.
2. It is also a time for graduation and graduation parties.
3. June is a popular month for special celebrations.
4. There is no doubt, therefore, that June is a fun month.
5. Lots of people have weekend barbecues and pool parties.
6. There are more weddings in June than in any other month.

    Write the paragraph on the lines below. If you wish, you can illustrate it in the space at the bottom of the page.

_____

_____

_____

_____

_____

_____

_____

_____

_____

_____

Name _____ **Date** _____

A DAY TO REMEMBER

DIRECTIONS: The six sentences below tell about an important anniversary in June. Can you rearrange these sentences in the proper order for a clearly-written paragraph?

Write the paragraph on the lines at the bottom of the page.

1. Many Allied troops were killed or wounded in that invasion.
2. They landed on the beaches of Normandy in France.
3. On that day, Allied troops crossed the English Channel.
4. June 6 is an important date in world history.
5. But D-Day marked the turning point of the war.
6. It is called "D-Day" and occurred in 1944 during World War II.

Name _____ Date _____

JUST ONE STORY
PREWRITING

Margaret Mitchell was one of the most successful and famous American authors who ever lived.

Would you believe that she only wrote *one* book? But this book was one of the best-selling novels of all time. It won a Pulitzer Prize, and was made into a movie that broke all attendance records.

Have you guessed the name of this book? It is *Gone With the Wind*, published on June 30, 1936. In it, Mitchell tells the story of a southern family before, during, and after the Civil War.

When Margaret Mitchell was growing up in Georgia, she heard many stories about the Civil War from older relatives and family friends. These tales inspired her to write *Gone With the Wind*. Its success made her world-renowned and wealthy, but she never wrote another book. It was as though she had needed to tell one story, and this was it!

Are there interesting tales you have heard from your parents, grandparents, or other relations? The story you write doesn't have to be a true retelling of events, just inspired by them.

Think about family stories you have heard, and choose one of them to be the basis of a story all your own. Before you begin, it will help to complete the brainstorming list below.

BRAINSTORMING LIST

1. Write a *short* summary of the story (no longer than 5 sentences).

_____

_____

_____

_____

2. Write the names of the three most important characters below. Next to each name, write words and phrases to describe this person (appearance, personality, relationship to the others, etc.). You can use the real names of the people involved, or make up fictional names.)

_____ : _____

_____ : _____

_____ : _____

3. Write the name of the place where this story occurs. Next to that, make a list of words and phrases describing this place.

_____ : _____

_____

Name _____   Date _____

JUST ONE STORY
FIRST DRAFT

DIRECTIONS: Write a first draft of a story based on an occurrence you have heard about from relatives or other people. Here are some suggestions:

1. The beginning should be interesting enough to make the reader want to continue. It's good to start with an exciting scene, or a conversation that introduces some of the main characters. (For example, *Gone With the Wind* begins by showing the main character, Scarlett O'Hara, in a conversation with two other people. This scene tells the reader a great deal about Scarlett's appearance and character.)

2. Nothing takes place in the middle of *nowhere*, so tell something about the setting where these things are happening. You don't need a lot of details. Just tell where it is and give a brief description.

3. *Show* what the characters are like by what they *say* and *do*.

Write your story below. this is just a first draft, so don't be too concerned about spelling or grammar—just concentrate on getting your story down on paper. (Use the back of this worksheet if you need more room.)

_____

_____

_____

_____

_____

_____

_____

_____

_____

_____

_____

_____

Name _____ **Date** _____

JUST ONE STORY
REVISING AND WRITING A FINAL COPY

DIRECTIONS:

1. Edit and revise your story as follows:

> a. Do you describe each character and show what that person is like by his or her actions, words, and thoughts? Can you add anything that would bring that character more to life?
>
> b. Is the dialogue (conversation) the way these people would really talk? Change any dialogue that seems forced or phony, or where it is not clear who is speaking.
>
> c. Do you show the setting where the action takes place? Would a bit more description make it more real?
>
> d. Can you make your language more vivid by using sensory words, similes, or metaphors?
>
> e. Are the sentences complete? Do subjects and verbs agree?
>
> f. Check spelling with a dictionary.

2. Write the final copy of your story below. Put a title on the first line. Indent at the beginning of paragraphs and whenever someone begins to speak. (Use the back of this worksheet if you need more room.)

_____

_____

_____

_____

_____

_____

_____

_____

_____

_____

Name _____ **Date** _____

A GARDEN OF WORDS

Gardens are often at their best in June. This is the time when flower buds burst into blooms of all colors and shapes.

The garden on this page is a "garden of words." You are going to be the gardener who helps these words "grow" into sentences.

DIRECTIONS: Each of the following "flowers" contains a group of words. Arrange each group of words into a sentence and write the sentences on the lines at the bottom of the page.

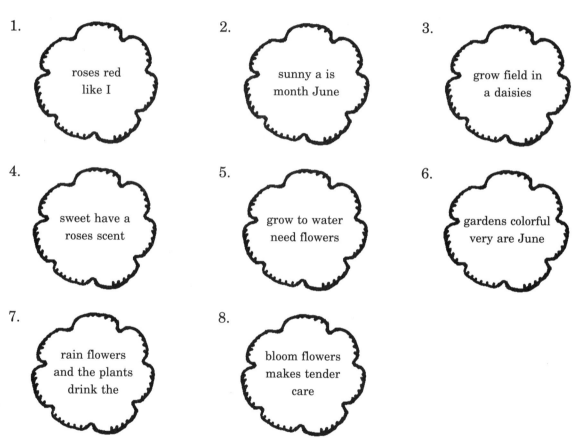

1.

roses red
like I

2.

sunny a is
month June

3.

grow field in
a daisies

4.

sweet have a
roses scent

5.

grow to water
need flowers

6.

gardens colorful
very are June

7.

rain flowers
and the plants
drink the

8.

bloom flowers
makes tender
care

Write the sentences below. Don't forget to put a period at the end of each sentence.

1. _____
2. _____
3. _____
4. _____
5. _____
6. _____
7. _____
8. _____

Name _____ **Date**_____

PLAY BALL!
PREWRITING

June 19 is an important anniversary for baseball fans. It was on that date in 1846 that the first baseball game between organized teams was played. It happened in Hoboken, New Jersey at a place called Elysian Field.

It didn't take long for baseball to become so popular that it soon became known as America's national game.

Baseball has remained one of the country's most popular sports. But is it still the "national game"? Many people say that it has been replaced by football. What do you think? Is baseball still America's national game, or should some other sport hold that title?

It will be easy to write an opinion essay on this topic if you first complete the brainstorming list.

BRAINSTORMING LIST

1. Put a check (✓) in the box next to the topic you have chosen:

   ❏ Baseball is still America's national game.
   ❏ Baseball is no longer America's national game.

2. List three things you like about baseball. (You don't need sentences here—words and phrases will do.)

   _____

   _____

   _____

3. List three things you don't like about baseball (words or phrases).

   _____

   _____

   _____

4. Write the name of another popular sport here: _____.
   Then, list two or three things you like about it below.

   _____

   _____

   _____

5. List any ways you can think of that baseball is better than the other sport.

   _____

   _____

6. List the ways, if any, that the other sport is better than baseball.

   _____

   _____

Name _____ **Date** _____

PLAY BALL!
FIRST DRAFT

DIRECTIONS: Write a first draft for a 3-paragraph essay. Check the theme you have chosen:

❑ Baseball is still America's national game.
❑ Baseball is no longer America's national game.

This is just a first draft, so don't be concerned about spelling or grammar. Concentrate on organizing your thoughts and getting them down on paper in a logical and convincing order. Use your brainstorming list and the suggestions below.

---

1. Your first paragraph should introduce the topic in an interesting way, as in this example: "Who says that baseball is America's national game? Maybe that was true at one time, but no longer. Football is now much more popular, especially among younger people."

    Write your first paragraph (2–4 sentences) here:

    _____

    _____

    _____

2. In the second paragraph, you should try to *prove* the statements you made in the introduction. Give *convincing details and examples* why baseball or some other sport should be considered the "national game."

    Write your second paragraph (3–5 sentences) here:

    _____

    _____

    _____

    _____

3. The last paragraph should restate and sum up the topic, as in this example: "It should be obvious to anyone that baseball's glory days are in the past. Football is now the sport of preference for most people. It is America's new 'national game.'"

    Write your last paragraph (2–4 sentences) here:

    _____

    _____

    _____

Name _____ **Date**_____

PLAY BALL!
REVISING AND WRITING A FINAL COPY

DIRECTIONS:

1. Edit and revise the first draft of your essay about America's "national game," as follows:

a. Does the first paragraph introduce the topic in an interesting way? Can you make it more exciting by opening with a question or a startling statement?

b. Does the second paragraph develop and prove your opening statements? Is there anything you can add to make it more convincing?

c. Does the last paragraph restate and sum up the topic?

d. Can you use vivid language such as active verbs (*slide, smash, trounce, crack*) or similes (*an arm like steel*) to make your writing more effective?

e. Are your sentences complete? Do subjects and verbs agree?

f. Check spelling with a dictionary.

2. Write the final copy of your essay below. Indent at the beginning of each paragraph. (Use the back of this worksheet if you need more room.)

_____

_____

_____

_____

_____

_____

_____

_____

_____

_____

_____

_____

_____

Name _____ Date _____

Summer Sentences 1

People have always watched the sun for signs of the season. In the Northern Hemisphere the noon sun is highest in the sky on or about June 22. This is called the summer solstice. It is the day of the year having the longest period of sunlight. At that time, the Earth's axis is tilted slightly toward the sun. The sun's rays are more direct and intense than at other times, and the Earth absorbs a great deal of heat. Most people look forward to summer. For many, it is their favorite time of the year.

DIRECTIONS: Below are the *beginnings* of 15 sentences about summer. Can you complete them and write an *ending* for each sentence? (Don't forget to put a period at the end of each sentence.)

1. Summer starts _____

2. Summer is _____

3. Summer weather _____

4. On summer mornings _____

5. On summer evenings _____

6. Some summers _____

7. July is _____

8. A holiday in July _____

9. In August _____

10. On weekends in the summer _____

11. Summer vacations _____

12. My favorite summer _____

13. Last summer, my family _____

14. This summer, I _____

15. I wish that summer _____

Name _____ **Date**_____

SUMMER SENTENCES 2

> *DIRECTIONS*:: Below are the *endings* of 15 sentences. Can you complete each sentence by writing a *beginning* for it?

1. _____ in summer.

2. _____ on Sundays in summer.

3. _____ on vacation last summer.

4. _____ the first day of vacation.

5. _____ on the 4th of July.

6. _____ on hot summer afternoons.

7. _____ is my favorite summer sport.

8. _____ is the best thing about summer.

9. _____ at the end of August.

10. _____ is the best place for a summer vacation.

11. _____ with my friends in summer.

12. _____ with my family in summer.

13. _____ to a beach.

14. _____ on a summer picnic.

15. _____ is my summer wish.

Name _____ **Date** _____

HAPPY BIRTHDAY, AMERICA!
PREWRITING

On July 4, 1776, the Continental Congress met in Philadelphia. They had already voted to declare the colonies "free and independent states." Now, they were ready to announce to the world their freedom from Great Britain. Thomas Jefferson had prepared a document for this meeting—the Declaration of Independence. It is one of the greatest messages of all time. Its stirring words about freedom and individual rights have inspired people all over the world, even up to the present time. On that Fourth of July in 1776, the Continental Congress overwhelmingly approved the adoption of the Declaration of Independence. A new nation was born.

The people of the United States celebrate their country's birth every year on this date. In 1873, Pennsylvania was the first state to declare this a legal holiday. Its lead was soon followed by every other state.

Many towns observe the Fourth of July with parades and fireworks and rousing marching bands. Families have picnics and barbecues. But Independence Day means more than spectacular fireworks and John Philip Sousa marches.

In this activity, you are going to write about what Independence Day means to you. First, prepare a brainstorming list.

 BRAINSTORMING LIST

1. In the box below, write as many words and phrases as you can think of that can be used to describe Fourth of July celebrations. (The list is begun for you.)

> red, white and blue; floats; baton twirlers;

2. In the box below, write as many words and phrases as you can think of that can be used to describe the true meaning of July 4. (The list is begun for you.)

> freedom, Revolutionary War, democracy

3. Write a sentence that states the real meaning of July 4 to you.

_____

_____

Name _____ Date _____

Happy Birthday, America!
First Draft

DIRECTIONS: Write a first draft of an essay about the true meaning of the Fourth of July holiday. Use your brainstorming list, and follow the suggestions below. (This is just a first draft, so don't be concerned about spelling or grammar—concentrate on getting your thoughts down on paper.)

---

1. The first paragraph should introduce the topic in an interesting way, as in this example: "What could be more fun than parades and fireworks? These are great ways to celebrate July 4, but we should never forget the real meaning of this holiday. It marks the birth of a nation dedicated to democracy and freedom."

   Write your first paragraph (2–4 sentences) here. (The statement you wrote at the bottom of your brainstorming list can be used as the first or last sentence of this paragraph.

   _____

   _____

   _____

2. The second paragraph can describe the ways in which this holiday is celebrated. Write your second paragraph (3–5 sentences) here:

   _____

   _____

   _____

3. The third paragraph should describe the true meaning of July 4, such as the Declaration of Independence, the Revolutionary War, democracy, etc. Write your third paragraph (3–5 sentences) here:

   _____

   _____

   _____

4. The last paragraph should restate and sum up the topic, as in this example: "I love the parades and fireworks that mark the Fourth of July. Even more important, I love what this holiday stands for—freedom, democracy, and individual rights." Write your last paragraph (2–4 sentences) here:

   _____

   _____

   _____

Name _____ **Date** _____

HAPPY BIRTHDAY, AMERICA!
REVISING AND WRITING A FINAL COPY

DIRECTIONS:

1. Edit and revise the first draft of your essay about the Fourth of July, as follows:

> a. Does your first paragraph introduce the topic in an interesting way? Can you make it more exciting by beginning with a question or a startling statement?
>
> b. Does the second paragraph describe how this holiday is celebrated? Do you use lots of detail to bring these activities to life?
>
> c. Does the third paragraph discuss the true meaning of this holiday? Can you make your argument more convincing by including historical details?
>
> d. Does the last paragraph restate and sum up the topic?
>
> e. Can you add vivid language such as similes or active verbs?
>
> f. Are your sentences complete? Do subjects and verbs agree?
>
> g. Check spelling with a dictionary.

2. Write the final copy of your essay below. Indent at the beginning of each paragraph. (Use the back of this worksheet if you need more room.)

_____

_____

_____

_____

_____

_____

_____

_____

_____

_____

_____

_____

© 1997 by The Center for Applied Research in Education

3607